The Art
of
Navigation

D1496209

The Art of Navigation

Travels
with
Carlos
Castaneda
and
Beyond

Felix Wolf

COUNCIL
OAK BOOKS

SAN FRANCISCO & TULSA

www.counciloakbooks.com
www.TheArtofNavigation.com

Cover and interior design by Carl Brune

CATALOGING-IN-PUBLICATION DATA

Wolf, Felix.
    Navigation : travels with Carlos Castaneda and beyond / Felix
Wolf. -- 1st ed.
        p. cm.
    ISBN 978-0-9822900-1-9 (pbk. : alk. paper}
    1. Castenada, Carlos, 1931-1998--Critism and interpretation.
2. Yaqui Indians--Religion. 3. Shamanism. 4. Nagualism. I. Title.
F1221.Y3C3737 2010
306.092--DC22

                                                        2010002261

ISBN 978-0-9822900-1-9

To the Nagual, a masterful teacher and guide,
whose impeccable spirit held open the door;
and to Carmela, my luminous fellow navigator,
who is a source of happiness and a silent force
behind every page.

CONTENTS

Introduction

The conscious intent of this book is to guide the reader into experiencing the beauty, magic, and simplicity of navigating life. Navigating life requires a different relationship with the world than we normally entertain. This can be illustrated by comparing the following two sets of questions.

We might ask: "What do I want to do with my life, and how can I get the most out of it?"

Or alternatively: "What does life want me to do, and how can I find out?"

In the answer to the last question lies the art of navigation.

To find out what to do with our life and how to get the most out of it, we think, analyze, speculate, and proceed strategically.

To find out what life wants us to do, we are receptive, fluid, alert, attentive, and present.

The two sets of questions and the resulting approaches to life are distinct. I have found, however, that it is exactly by asking and being guided by the second set of questions that we get the most out of life; so much so that we can become one with it entirely.

On a practical level, the experience of navigating life very much resembles the experience of being engaged in a treasure hunt—an all encompassing, multi-faceted, exhilarating, real-life treasure hunt.

I received my initiation into the art of navigation from Carlos Castaneda, a well-known author, anthropologist, and shaman, with whom I was associated for many years, including a three-year apprenticeship, until his death in 1998. Castaneda practiced a sophisticated form of shamanism, or sorcery, that had less to do with the use of supernatural powers than with the intricacies of perception and the mastery of awareness. The ultimate purpose of his shamanic pursuits was to attain a state he called *total freedom.*

Central to Castaneda's worldview was the concept of *intent:* a willful, creative intelligence that is both personal and universal. Castaneda believed that the path to total freedom for an individual was through his or her connecting link with universal intent. The clearer this connecting link and the better the individual and universal intent were aligned, the higher the degree of freedom. In his book, *The Power of Silence*, Castaneda stated that "every act performed by sorcerers was either performed as a way to strengthen their link with intent or as a response triggered by the link itself. Sorcerers had to be actively and permanently on the lookout for manifestations of the spirit. Such manifestations were called gestures of the spirit or, more simply, indications or omens."

From the moment I was touched by Castaneda's world, I was intrigued by this interactive way of living, and the process of "dusting my link with intent," as he called it, became one of the main concerns of my life. After many years of practice, and especially during my personal interactions with Castaneda, I was able to observe how magically and powerfully life unfolded as it was informed by a working link with intent. The discipline that is involved in clearing and strengthening this link and in perceiving and acting on the manifestations of the spirit, I came to know as the art of navigation.

The impulse for writing this book arose from working with troubled teenagers and young adults in a specialty boarding school where my wife, Carmela, and I conducted an innovative therapy program based on Oriental Medicine from 2003 to 2007. In over one thousand group sessions and eight thousand individual treatments, we administered acupuncture and herbal medicine, taught yoga, qigong, and life skills.

Feeling much respected by our young clientèle, we wanted to affect their lives in the best possible way. Initially just in random conversations and answers to questions, we shared what we knew about life, especially how to experience happiness and peace, instead of pain and problems. Over the years, this part of our sessions grew into the core element of our program, which all the other modalities supported.

Seeing so much emotional pain, anger, frustration, depression, and confusion, we naturally intended to go beyond symptomatic relief to find the root of all this pain. Of the many life skills we discussed, the topic of re-introducing magic into life with the art of navigation always elicited the most interest and curiosity in our students. It was through this realization that we began to see their predicament.

Between the ages of fourteen and twenty-four, as our students were growing through adolescence into adulthood, they had to learn a whole new description of life. But this new description did not only bring new and additional elements into their lives, it also took something away they did not even know they had, until they began to feel the cold reality of its loss.

During childhood we live in a rather magical dimension. Existential issues are of little concern, and we are barely even aware of the questions. Life is much more immediate and present. The balance between being in the moment and being pulled out of it by the adult world is still in our favor. Not much thought is spent with what we want to do with our life. Life still seems to be very much in charge.

But as we increasingly pattern ourselves after the adult world, we lose this magical connection with life. Our emerging sexuality amplifies self-observing and self-defining impulses, and gradually, self-realization, self-reflection, and self-consciousness, together with the intent of our social environment, turn our attention inward, separating us from the living world at large. Instead of experiencing life every moment in its entirety, we try to do something with it, or get something out of it, as if it were a definable object.

As we are dazzled out of childhood by our hormones, we are also tricked out of the magic and connectedness we had taken for granted so long. As a result, many young people in this transition grow frustrated and confused—a state of mind that unfortunately tends to persist to varying degrees throughout our lives.

In our work we became aware that much of the anger and self-destructive behavior of our students had its roots in the realization of this loss. Being pulled out of the immediacy of life left them with a growing void, which they desperately tried to fill with intensity, from drugs, self-mutilation, or other extreme behavior.

Offering an alternative way of relating to the world that had a magical dimension and re-connecting our young clients to their surroundings and life at large became our main objective. As solicited by their own interest and demand, we shared more and more of what we knew about the art of navigation. While entertaining the students with some of our own navigational stories, we began to isolate the skills and behavioral adjustments that are necessary to turn navigation into a bona fide way of life. Almost everybody has encountered occasional synchronicities and peak experiences, or episodes of flow, of being in a groove, or in the "zone." All these are elements of the navigational experience. But usually they are perceived as too arbitrary, too few and far between, to serve as a basis for our way of life.

In order to navigate and to turn life into a magical treasure hunt; in order to tune into the music of the universe and to lose ourselves in the dance of life, certain skills and attitude changes are required. Most skills have to do with raising our level of awareness, and we compiled what we knew into a handout for our students. This handout sprouted into the idea of a book, and the book took on the shape of a story.

The story is the true account of how life went through the trouble of teaching a self-indulgent and cynical young man to dance. It is about how it resorted to using the powers of a real sorcerer to get into the deaf young man's head and to make him hear the music. And it is about the painfully slow process it took to get this self-indulgent and cynical young man to move to the music with some consistency.

But then it is also about the joy of dancing, the bliss of abandon, the audacity of surrender, and the incredible lightness of being.

Part I

BEGINNINGS

... But now that I have spoken of that great sea,
the ocean of longing shifts through me
the blessed inner star of navigation
moves in the dark sky above
and I am ready like the young salmon to leave his river,
blessed with hunger for a great journey on the drawing tide.

DAVID WHYTE
Song for the Salmon

A Cognitive Dissonance

t was shortly before seven o'clock on a Thursday evening in July 1998 as I left the freeway and turned onto Venice Boulevard in Los Angeles.

"Great, I am going to be on time!" I thought, smiling to myself.

I had come to town to meet with David, a friend of mine and fellow apprentice of Carlos Castaneda. I was curious to see what he had done with my old apartment after taking it over a few months ago. It had been a most magical place for me—and it still was, as I was about to discover.

The building at the end of Bagley Avenue stood out in the otherwise inconspicuous neighborhood, tucked in between Venice Boulevard and the Santa Monica Freeway. It exuded an air of lightness and happiness, despite the proximity to this enormous interstate with its ceaseless stream of cars. The apartment itself had drawn me in with surprising force during a house hunting mission a few years earlier when I moved from Tucson to Los Angeles to be closer to the Nagual.

"The Nagual" [nah'wahl] was how we referred to Carlos Castaneda, the fabled anthropologist, author, and shaman who had been the main guiding force in my life for more than eighteen years. On a practical level, however, the Nagual and Carlos Castaneda appeared to be two different entities. My interaction was predominantly with the Nagual. He was an impersonal and enigmatic teacher and guide who transformed my life into a breathtaking journey of awareness. Carlos Castaneda was his alter ego, his personal manifestation, the anthropologist and author whom I had rarely met.

▿　▿　▿

Prior to my move I had been flying from Tucson to Los Angeles every weekend for the better part of a year to attend meetings with the Nagual. But with every meeting, the pull had become stronger, and eventually I needed to relocate. I had been looking forward very much to the house hunting mission. Scouting for places, playing with instinct and intuition, and navigating the energy of new environments had always been one of my passions.

For this particular scouting mission I had a natural starting point: the Nagual's favorite restaurant, the Versailles, on Venice Boulevard, serving what was arguably the best Cuban food in town. So I headed to the Versailles straight from the airport to have some *lechon*, the famous slow cooked pork, marinated in garlic and onions, with black beans and fried bananas, my favorite dish at the time.

The plan was to meander leisurely through the surrounding neighborhoods with my rental car to get a general feeling for the area and narrow down my search. My body seemed happy with the *lechon* and was eager to go to work.

In the interest of integrity I feel compelled to mention that I most likely had a double "espressito," the infamously irresistible Cuban coffee they serve at the Versailles, to speed up the transformation of *lechon* into navigational energy. Incidentally, I suspect that this same coffee, in its manifestation of "cappucinito," would later speed up the departure of Carlos Castaneda from this world.

Upon leaving the restaurant I cruised through a few streets in the immediate environment. Several of the small houses and apartment buildings displayed "For Rent" signs, and I was getting excited. Within ten or fifteen minutes, while driving along Bagley Avenue, a big "For Rent" banner on the side of a building caught my eye. It was a relatively new, modern, and cubistic structure, three stories high, with a clean white facade and bright pink window frames. A happy building—completely oblivious to the massive and overpowering freeway right next to it. There was a parking space directly in front of the entrance, so I pulled over and turned off the engine. I looked up at the banner again and felt an instant jolt in my midsection when I became aware of the phone number: 396-4444.

There was something compelling about that moment. The jolt came from deep inside where I already knew that I had found my new home. Mixed into this realization of inevitability was a sensation of alarm that had to do with the proximity of the freeway. In Tucson I lived in a beautiful and serene house in a lush high desert area, and the prospect of living right next to the busiest freeway in the nation seemed bizarre, to say the least.

But something inescapable was taking hold of me, and before I knew it, I had already dialed the phone number. At the time I was fascinated by numbers. They are such easy navigational pointers, ubiquitous and magical in their simplicity. Four was definitely my favorite number, and it had been most of my life.

$$\vee \quad \vee \quad \vee$$

In the mid 1980's when I still lived in Germany, my then wife Victoria and I traveled every other weekend about two hundred miles from Munich to Baden-Baden to play roulette in a fabulous casino. It was a treasured ritual. Over the course of more than six months we always kept the same routine. We arrived in Baden-Baden, a decidedly noble two-thousand-year-old spa town, checked into our hotel at the thermal springs, spent a few hours in the famous and powerful thermal waters that steam up from the depth of the earth, had a delicious dinner at a great little Czech restaurant, dressed up, and then went to the casino.

At the casino we always followed the same routine as well. The idea was to translate the energy of the thermal water into hunches and intuition. The casino is spectacular, on a level with Monte Carlo, no machines, just tables, card games, and well-dressed, soft-spoken people. So we walked around, indulged in people-watching and tried to be as aware and present as possible, always "listening" for the nearly imperceptible tug of a hunch that prompted me to walk unhurriedly to roulette table four to bet ten Deutschmarks on the number four. That was all I ever did. Sometimes I stayed a while longer at the table and repeated the same bet a few times if it felt right.

The stunning and nearly unbelievable result was that every single time we went to Baden-Baden, we won, usually between four and eight hundred Deutschmarks. It always was more than enough to pay for the expenses of the weekend, and we were quite happy with this. Once, early on, I was overcome by a wave of greed and started to double the bet, but the emotion interfered with my hunches and it did not work. So we stayed with the original intent and were rewarded every time.

As a rule I always played the last game of the night, and once, while I put my ten Deutschmarks on number four and the ball started rolling, I perceived a tug in my back. I turned around and felt compelled to put another ten Marks on the number twelve at table three behind me. Maybe it was the result of a quick multiplication of four times three equals twelve, or whatever else it might have been, but there was no hesitation, and no thoughts interfered.

The balls hit nearly simultaneously, the four in front of me, and as I turned around I already knew, the twelve behind me. It was an incredible feeling of connectedness and gratitude that brought tears to my eyes, and well, yes, over seven hundred Deutsche Marks into my pocket.

❧ ❧ ❧

So when I dialed 396-4444, I had a definite feeling of excited anticipation. A friendly female voice answered the phone and I was buzzed in. The woman who met me at the elevator was exceptionally warm and welcoming and took me to the second floor to show a relatively small apartment that was facing the street. I was puzzled. The place was not bad, but I could not see myself living there at all, and my whole navigational excitement began to fizzle. I walked around, stared out the window, but whatever I tried, I could not hook into anything. I asked her if she knew of any other vacancy in the building. She hesitated at first, but then she said: "Well, actually, just today the young couple in 306 told me that they'll be leaving next month. It is a loft apartment, much bigger and more expensive though . . . They might actually be home right now. If you like, we could just go and check. They are nice people."

Number 306 was a two-story loft corner unit with floor-to-ceiling windows in two directions. It was stunning. The young couple was helpful and accommodating and told me to "hang out" as long as I wanted, an offer I gladly accepted. The manager left me alone as well, and we agreed that I call her as soon as I had come to a decision.

The apartment was flooded with light and optimism, but also, as became immediately obvious, with all the exciting sounds and sights of America's busiest freeway, right at the level of the window, at most five hundred feet away. I needed to sit down, and I found a comfortable office chair at the friendly young couple's desk on the upper level. I was mesmerized. With my chin in both hands, I couldn't help staring at the freeway, and all I thought was: "too bad, too bad, damn it . . . too bad."

Cars buzzing east, cars buzzing west, buzzing east, west, right, left, buzzing, buzzing, buzzing . . .

A strong ocean breeze was blowing through the open windows, prompting me to lean back and take a deep breath.

"And light, so much light."

"Wow, what a place. Too bad," I still thought, "too bad. How is this possible?"

The open parking space, the phone number, the smoothness and timing, the friendly welcoming people, my navigational instincts, the jolt of recognition, all seemed to combine to an enormous beacon, forceful and compelling.

But at the time I was obsessed with serenity, quietude, silence, stillness. How did this all fit together? And so I sat, glued to the chair.

The couple left on an errand and encouraged me to stay as long as I needed.

"Just close the door behind you when you leave," they said on their way out.

After a while I got up to close the windows. I thought about soundproofing, curtains, earplugs. . . . I thought about our house in the Tucson Mountains, the rustling sounds of desert creatures, birdcalls, distant coyotes. . . .

Back on the chair my thoughts gradually quieted down, and quite automatically, my attention settled on my breathing. I don't remember how it happened or if anything actually triggered it, but suddenly there was a change in my awareness, something had shifted.

On a more basic level of perception, I sensed that a tremendous amount of energy was passing through this place. When I simply allowed my sense perceptions to happen, without relating them to anything at all, the picture changed completely. What I *saw* now were different layers of vibration, woven together into a powerful stream of energy, flooding the apartment, flowing in on one side and out on the other. There was no place to hide. It was incredible. It felt like sitting in the middle of a river.

What an opportunity.

What if I manage to go along with it? I thought, allow it to flow right through me, 24 hours a day, 7 days a week, 365 days a year, whenever I am home?

Of course! I realized. What a gift!

It suddenly seemed so obvious that all that was needed was to allow all this energy to pass right through, through the apartment, through my life, my body, my mind, and allow it to carry away anything that was no longer needed.

Even then, while gazing at the cars as they were simultaneously flying in opposite directions, I already began to sense a stillness that had no precedent in my life, a stillness far deeper than the silence of the high desert.

Moved to the core by this realization I called the manager and told her that I would happily take the apartment.

∨ ∨ ∨

Now it was more than two years later, and again I was slowly cruising down Bagley Avenue, savoring the last rays of the sun. It was one of those soft, milky late afternoons in Southern California that feel as if time has been suspended. I assumed that it was the cool vapor of the nearby Pacific that filtered the sunlight into this mellow amber glow that was one of my favorite things about living here.

I had recently moved about an hour further south and had come back to Los Angeles just to see David.

"I have a lot of interesting information I would like to share with you," he had said over the phone.

Only a few months had passed since Carlos Castaneda's death, and the enigma already began to unravel. His death had turned out to be a momentous event for us. The Nagual had been at the center of my world for most of my adult life. My involvement with him had been as total as my personality permitted. I had read every one of his books at least ten times—literally. Besides having served as a road map for my life's journeys, they had become the blueprint for my understanding and adaptation of the English language. Additionally, during recent years I had had the privilege of simultaneously translating many of the Nagual's talks into German during his international workshops. I had become so familiar with his syntax, his way of thinking, that I often found myself falling into complete synchrony with his words, knowing what he would say next. As a result I heard myself speaking the German translation the same moment his English words came through my headphones. It was outright eerie. The sustained and total concentration that is necessary during simultaneous translations allows for a unique and quite intimate connection between two minds.

I had originally moved to the United States in an attempt to be closer to this fabulous living myth that Castaneda had created. There had been no real hope to actually meet him at the time. Nobody knew his whereabouts, even though *Time* magazine had run a cover story on Castaneda in 1973, declaring him the "Godfather of the New Age Movement." He was so elusive that the magazine had been unable to find a photograph of him to accompany the article. All they came up with was a pencil sketch by a former fellow student of Castaneda. Many questioned his authenticity and some his existence.

I spent nearly two years in Mexico, exploring remote regions, meeting countless *brujos*, *curanderos*, and other mysterious people, secretly hoping to encounter a "man of knowledge" like Castaneda's teacher don Juan and to be initiated into another world—a separate reality.

And then, my unbending intent and my navigational persistence finally paid off, and I actually found him and his eclectic crew of cohorts. As a result, a whole new level of intensity ensued. All this time he had been hiding successfully in the middle of Los Angeles, in West LA to be precise, in a humble little house, behind tall hedges, on a quiet street, aptly named Pandora Avenue.

In the mid 1990's the Nagual had made himself more accessible and was working with a group of associates and apprentices. The group of people he had regular and personal contact with consisted of approximately thirty to forty members. As mandated by the Nagual's perception of "energetic necessities" the group was structured by a definite though fluid hierarchy. Different members had vastly different access and exposure to the Nagual and his teachings. David and I had been somewhere in the middle most of the time, but towards the end we met him nearly every day, several times even in his house, which was a rare privilege.

Carlos Castaneda did not die entirely unexpectedly. But when it actually happened, the effect on most of us was utterly life-changing.

▼ ▼ ▼

"Hey Dave," I exclaimed, hugging him like a long lost brother. David had come down with the elevator to greet me. I studied his face. He looked unchanged, always the clever, competent, slightly mischievous attorney, with a hint of deceptive vulnerability. A bit softer around the waist perhaps, but then, he also liked the Cuban food at the Versailles.

"Good to see you," he said. "How is Carmela?"

"Oh, she is fine, she sends her love." I answered.

Carmela and I had met the previous year. She had come out of nowhere, unwittingly scooping me up out of this tremendous vortex created by the Nagual's disintegration. For most of us, Carlos Castaneda's death was a definitive implosion, creating a vortex of energy that spun our individual fates in unimaginable ways. Some of his closest cohorts simply vanished, never to be seen again. One took her life. Her body was found a few years later in Death Valley. A small group of apprentices continued to disseminate his teachings through workshops that are still being offered worldwide to this day. Quite a few scrambled to restore their previous interpretations of reality, their lives before meeting the Nagual. Others found themselves at new points of departure.

As far as I am concerned, I found myself in intergalactic space. That is still the best analogy I can find, even in retrospect, ten years later. The Nagual clearly was the sun I had been orbiting for over eighteen years. My wife Victoria had shared my orbit for most of that time until the nature of this particular solar system required us to enter into separate orbits. Double planets were not a possibility. Social order relationships were not supported. So, in an often extremely painful process, Victoria and I finally managed to re-invent our relationship to fit into the Nagual's world. We moved apart, though still in love, establishing individual orbits. But, unbeknownst to us, the gravitational forces created irreversible realities, and as a consequence, we were doomed to love each other from afar.

▼ ▼ ▼

Carmela had been a friend and fellow student at the College of Oriental Medicine where I studied at the time. She had caught my attention because of her striking similarity with three female members of our group.

The core art of the Nagual and, from my perspective, the practical essence of his teachings was the art of navigation. He often referred to us as "Navigators on the Sea of Awareness." Navigation is an alternate way of moving through life and relating to reality. Whereas the vast majority of people move through life primarily guided by their thoughts, a "navigator" moves through life as a result of his or her direct link with life, the universe, infinity, spirit, or Intent, as the Nagual preferred to call the universal consciousness that pervades all existence. Since the art of navigation is the subject of this book, I will leave it at this first attempt of a definition and trust that it will become clearer as we move along.

The similarity that had struck me when I met Carmela was not simply a superficial resemblance. Termed "cyclicity" by the Nagual, it was of a more intrinsic nature, a likeness that can be felt intuitively rather than seen. Cyclic beings may unexplainably remind us of their respective counterparts, or we might even mistake one for the other. They often have similar fates, mannerisms, tastes, or even professions. Perceived energetically, cyclicity stands out like clothes from the same designer, or cars of the same brand. The Nagual likened cyclic beings to beads on a curtain, strung together by Intent, and whenever he encountered cyclicity, particularly among his apprentices, it was of special significance to him and informed his navigational maneuvers.

Energetic perception is nothing particularly fancy. It is simply perception prior to thought. It is the first and direct impression we have of something or someone before we label, compare, judge, or categorize. Because of our inherent obsession and preoccupation with thought, most of us forgot how to perceive energetically.

A navigator, if on the sea of awareness or on a regular ocean, uses cues for guidance. Cues that help to navigate an ocean may be lighthouses, beacons, buoys, currents, the position of stars, the direction of the wind, or the presence of seagulls. On the sea of awareness, in the navigation of life itself, a navigator's cues are elements of perception that stand out in ways that are transcending thought, reason, and causality. Such cues are independent from the world of thoughts. As a matter of fact, the less thought, the clearer the cues. Cyclicities can be such cues. Other and much more commonly used cues are synchronicities, which are two or more events that occur in a meaningful manner without being causally related. We often look at synchronicities as unexplainable, baffling, or practically impossible coincidences.

Whereas the average navigator might be much more familiar with synchronicities, hunches, omens, intuition, and other forms of silent knowledge, the Nagual, as a guide and leader of a group of people, was also intrigued by cyclicities.

Carmela was clearly and unmistakably cyclic to three structurally important female members of our group. The three women were Carol Tiggs, the female counterpart of the Nagual, a.k.a. the Nagual Woman, Renata Murez, a long term member, and Victoria, my wife. The latter two had been paired by the Nagual due to their cyclicity for the purpose of mutual support.

The Nagual was continuously manipulating our group's structure by pairing and grouping members in an attempt to create different levels and dynamics of collective awareness. He was intrigued with the idea of generating a critical energetic mass that would help us achieve internal silence together. He speculated that, once we could sustain internal silence as a group, we would then be able to shift into collective conscious dreams of unparalleled solidity and realness.

Carmela's cyclicity was so obvious that when I had a mental image of Renata, Carmela's face was often superimposed, or vice versa. During workshops, practitioners sometimes approached Carmela and asked her questions that were meant for Renata, even though the two did not look much alike in the classical sense. Naturally I was intrigued and wanted to bring this to the Nagual's attention. However, at this point there was no more energy to add new members or to act in any other way on this discovery. Unbeknownst to me at the time, his health had deteriorated beyond the point of recovery.

In the gravitational events that ensued, Carmela and I, initially unaware, moved closer and closer together. And when the whole mythical solar system finally imploded and I found myself in intergalactic space, I was not alone. Otherwise completely disconnected, disoriented, and deeply aware of an unspeakable loss, I was floating comfortably in a little escape capsule with one of the sweetest beings I had ever met.

∨   ∨   ∨

"You are so lucky to have her," David said.

"I know Dave, believe me, I know," I agreed.

We took the elevator up, looking at each other in this forced closeness. I was silently wondering how David had been affected by all these events.

"You are looking good," I broke the silence.

"So do you." David smiled back at me.

David and I had been paired by the Nagual in a similar way as Victoria and Renata, except that we were anything but cyclical. The Nagual never elaborated, but from what I could *see*, there was no overlap in our personalities at all. It appeared as if we were the two different ends of a spectrum, two halves of an energetic possibility. Where David ended, I began, and vice versa. Our differences were so profound that we did not even bother to argue. David was soft-spoken and controlled; I was rather boisterous and compulsive. David was structured, strategic, reasonable, and prepared. He wrote everything down. I was and did none of these things. David is gay and I am straight. He is a Virgo, I am a Sagittarius, and the list went on.

It is quite clear to me, however, that our configuration was not just arbitrarily dissimilar. There was something precise in our lack of overlap. Beings with such a polar complementariness can make productive and balanced working teams. When operating as a unit, they produce a strong and compelling completeness and are able to confront others without being perceived as confrontational.

Cyclic beings follow another dynamic. They are different manifestations of the same energetic blueprint. As such they are great mirrors for each other. If we have a lot of problems with ourselves, we will also have a lot of problems with somebody who is cyclic with us. For this reason we usually do not cultivate cyclic relationships. Also, because of the substantial overlap, cyclic relationships are generally not productive. Creativity thrives on differences, and similarity can breed complacency. With all this in mind, however, cyclicity should be recognized as a potentially significant source of navigational information, much like a checkpoint in a treasure hunt.

▿ ▿ ▿

Many years ago, I took part in a car-rally treasure hunt on the island of Malta, in the Mediterranean. We were given a map and initial directions in form of a riddle. Solving the riddle would guide us to a landmark or checkpoint where we would receive the next hint or riddle and so on. We spent nearly all day crisscrossing the island, discovering and exploring fascinating places, solving puzzle after puzzle. We were constantly in unexpected situations, having many beautiful encounters with local people who sometimes were part of the game and sometimes not. I remember getting into a lively conversation with the owner of a bakery where I stopped to ask for directions. After he learned that my grandfather had been a baker, he insisted on sharing his "secret" recipe for Maltese Almond Cakes with me, and I reciprocated with a special Streusselkuchen (German crumble cake) recipe that I happened to know.

In some cases a new hint was an inscription on a building, in others a cryptic message from a shoe cleaner, sitting on a street corner. Somehow we all made it to the "finish line," which, in this case, was a fabulous restaurant where we all shared our tales of navigation and celebrated one of the most exciting and magical days of our lives.

▿ ▿ ▿

The Nagual was engaged in a more complex navigational maneuver, a treasure hunt of mythical proportions. He not only navigated his own life, but he was also the chief navigator of a large group of sailors on the sea of awareness. David and I were two of these sailors, and due to our complementariness he had grouped us together. We were always invited together to the various gatherings, and we were given the common task to call and invite other apprentices to regular weekly meetings. There was no default membership in the Nagual's world. Every single meeting was by invitation only, and you never knew if something was going on to which you were not invited. Or worse still, chances were that you could just drop through the cracks and find yourself permanently uninvited.

The dynamic of the interaction between the Nagual and his apprentices was intense. Due to his exceptional charisma we were magnetically drawn to his presence, and everybody was seeking to spend as much time with him as possible. Most of us were terrified by the prospect of being expelled. There were no rules, however, that we could follow to insure our membership. The Nagual's navigational maneuvers were generally neither obvious nor transparent to his apprentices.

Besides rare chance encounters, meetings with the Nagual were usually lunch invitations, gatherings at his house, or much more commonly, group sessions that took place in various yoga studios throughout West Los Angeles. During these group sessions he entertained us with his magical stories, and we practiced "Tensegrity," a set of movements resembling Qigong and different forms of martial arts. Besides generating health and wellbeing, the main purpose of these movements, which he also referred to as "Magical Passes," was to facilitate internal silence in the practitioner. Internal silence or the ability to stop our compulsive internal dialogue was the steppingstone to anything worthwhile in the world of the Nagual.

▽   ▽   ▽

I followed David into what was now his apartment and felt an instant sense of ease and pleasant familiarity. Even though he had furnished the place differently, the overall feeling had not changed at all. Where my magnificent twelve-foot "Bird of Paradise" plant had stood, there was now a bookshelf, and in the place of my hammock were a few filing cabinets. But the character and energy of the apartment was still dominated by transparency and openness, by the high ceiling, and by the immense amount of light flooding in through the huge windows. I could not help but taking a deep breath.

"Oh my God, the sunlight is gorgeous," I exclaimed. It was just before sunset, and the last rays were streaming in, bathing everything in soft amber light.

"Are the parrots still around?" I asked when my eyes fell on the big leafy tree outside the east window.

"Oh yes," David answered, "the flock seems to be getting bigger all the time."

I had loved those parrots. Apparently they were the descendants of domestic birds that had escaped or were set free over time, and now about ten different varieties from macaws to parakeets were thriving and multiplying in the mild climate and diverse vegetation of Southern California. For as long as I had lived there, a good-sized flock of red masked parrots had regularly been roosting in the large tree next to the house. They had given me so much joy with their boisterous nature and the exotic jungle soundtrack they provided.

"Do you remember that parrot joke the Nagual told us once in Mexico City?" I asked.

"Oh yes," David chuckled, "that silly joke about cognitive dissonance."

The Nagual was a fabulous storyteller, but he rarely told jokes. On that particular day he had given a talk about using a state of mind he called "cognitive dissonance" to stop our internal dialogue. A cognitive dissonance results from having two conflicting and irreconcilable thoughts at the same time. It is the perception of incompatibility between two elements of knowledge. Generally it creates an uncomfortable tension and the desire to reconcile the conflict, to eliminate the dissonance. If this seems impossible, our thought processes can "freeze" temporarily, much like a computer would freeze when given two conflicting commands. "We don't know what to think anymore," and with some luck we might indeed stop thinking.

For example, one day we may learn that our mother had a secret lover during our entire childhood. Yet all this time she appeared to have had a happy and harmonious marriage, caring lovingly and impeccably for her family. Such a revelation would certainly be shocking and leave us with two strongly conflicting ideas of our mother. This is an untenable situation for our mind. Normally we would go through every conceivable mental operation to resolve the conflict and to restore a sense of certainty. But in a case this fundamental and compelling, we might just realize the futility of such a resolution and let it be. Letting it be, suspending judgment and allowing uncertainty, creates a precious opening, and it can lead to a profound experience of internal silence.

The Nagual's joke was less straightforward and much less fundamental. Nevertheless, when I first heard it, it produced a short cognitive dissonance, a moment of silence, an oscillation of thoughts, a suspension of judgment—and laughter:

A man is walking down the street and after turning a couple of corners he notices that a large parrot seems to be following him. The man speeds up and turns another corner but the parrot is still behind him. Puzzled and slightly annoyed the man stops and confronts the parrot. "Why do you keep following me?" he asks.

"Because I am a parrot," the bird answers.

⌄   ⌄   ⌄

I ventured upstairs and stepped out onto the roof patio and through a small gate onto the roof itself. All the upstairs apartments had a small enclosed patio with roof access. Hardly anyone ever made use of it though.

The sun had now set and all ten lanes of the Santa Monica freeway, just below us, slowly illuminated into a vast band of light stretching all the way to the hazy horizon. David had quietly followed and was now standing beside me, also watching the river of cars. It was still rush hour but the cars were moving at a fairly steady pace in both directions.

There was an interesting effect I always experienced while gazing at the opposing streams of cars. All I had to do was to keep my eyes out of focus and my attention on the cars as they were leaving my field of vision on both sides. Keeping the awareness on both sides simultaneously prevented my eyes and my mind from focusing. This generated a state of alert internal silence that became more and more profound, the longer I held this gaze.

Gazing in such a manner created refreshing breaks in my stream of consciousness, which I would use to inform a creative process or to change a mood that had become obsessive. Such breaks also allowed me to catch a glimpse of the way my mind worked, particularly if they were sustained. If I was lucky and stayed alert, I would catch the first thought that sneaked back into my mind after the pause—and maybe the second and the third. Catching and observing my thoughts as they arose I found to be an exciting and empowering practice. Anyone who has watched a cat staring at a mouse hole will have a pretty good idea of the general dynamics of thought watching. The cat never breaks her gaze.

When my thoughts re-appeared after a moment of no thought, I had a natural tendency, either of getting absorbed by the thoughts, or of judging or labeling them instantly. This I tried to avoid at all cost. Instead I aimed to simply stay alert and allow the thoughts to pass through my awareness without any interaction whatsoever. Judging and labeling my thoughts while they arose meant that I was thinking about my thoughts instead of just watching them, and so nothing was gained, and I would lose this fascinating vantage point of the silent observer.

I understood that this silent observer, or non-discriminating awareness, is the awakened mind, our essential self that most of us forgot. These precious breaks in the stream of thinking, these moments of alertness without mental activity allow us to remember our true self, even if only for a moment.

Of course we are not remembering anything in the conventional sense. There is no content to what we remember. There are no words that could describe it. Perhaps the experience can be likened to a short moment of awakening during a dream at night. A brief flash of awareness that tells us that we are dreaming, too short to remember who we are outside the dream, too short to even interrupt the dream.

The Nagual had gone out of his way to emphasize the importance of these episodes of internal silence and alert observation. He maintained that these breaks get longer with practice, and even if they are short, they accrue over time to develop a critical mass, in a manner of speaking.

Moment for precious moment, the experiences of the silent observer are creating a foothold. Moment for precious moment, the certainty of our thought based world softens and dissolves—until we remember and wake up.

v v v

I pulled my attention out of the stream of cars and allowed my eyes to focus on David. I wondered if he ever had discovered the magical side of the freeway.

I never quite understood how he related to this living myth around the Nagual. Unlike most of us, he had not been drawn in by the Nagual's writings. He had not picked up the scent of magic by being handed a copy of *The Teachings of Don Juan* or any of the other books many years ago by a friend under some kind of meaningful circumstances. As a matter of fact, he had not read a single one of the about eight million copies of Carlos

Castaneda's books that had been sold worldwide at the time he became an apprentice. A friend of his, who had been a Castaneda fan for many years, had taken him to one of the few public appearances of the Nagual. Interestingly, however, while his friend felt himself rejected, David was hooked instantly and subsequently drawn in deeper and deeper. What had taken me fifteen years of single-minded tracking and navigating had happened to David basically overnight, without any effort on his part.

Now, looking at him after this moment of inner silence that the freeway had so generously provided, it occurred to me for the first time that David and I actually might have been guided by two different Naguals.

As far as our world was concerned the term nagual had a personal and an impersonal meaning. On the personal level a Nagual was a guide and a leader. On the impersonal level the term nagual referred to the formless aspect of the universe, the infinity of universal consciousness, reality undefined by space and time, the unmanifested, the spirit, Intent.

The manifested and concrete world of form, our everyday world defined by time and space, was called the tonal, and so was a person's worldly form and manifestation.

A Nagual, then, can be seen as a bridge between the concrete and the abstract, a guide who, by facilitating a transformation of consciousness, leads people from the manifested to the unmanifested, from the experience of space and time to the experience of infinity and timelessness, from the world of thought to the experience of spirit.

Living in the experience of spirit is the mastery of the art of navigation. It entails living the life of life itself.

In order to accomplish this feat, Naguals have to represent both ends of the bridge, so to speak. They have to have regular, clearly defined worldly personalities, and they have to be undefined conduits, windows, and facilitators of infinity.

A Nagual does not lead by volition. Personal ambition is out of the question. It would probably be more correct to say that the unmanifested utilizes a Nagual's peculiar energetic makeup to inform the manifested. The only variable available to a Nagual is his or her degree of impeccability.

Carlos Castaneda, besides being an anthropologist and an author, was also a Nagual, as was his teacher, a Yaqui Indian shaman he had called don Juan Matus.

For most of the years that I had been exposed to Carlos Castaneda's work it had radiated an unbroken and consistent mood and intent. There was a relentless emphasis on impeccability and freedom, but also on abstractness and transcendence. It had engaged my spirit with unparalleled force and changed my life irrevocably. In essence, his work dealt with the evolution and mastery of awareness, and it was permeated with the scent of total and transcendental freedom. It was this scent that had fueled my navigation all these years. These were the teachings of don Juan. For more than twenty years Castaneda had funneled these teachings through his writings and perpetuated the intent of his teacher.

With the publication of *The Art of Dreaming* in 1993 the mood had changed, and throughout my personal affiliation with the Nagual, the prevailing mood and intent had always felt significantly less abstract than before. It is my understanding that this was a result of the different predilections and energetic makeup of the two Naguals. As far as I could tell, Castaneda had finally disengaged from the intent of his teacher and allowed his own predilection to surface.

Don Juan had illustrated these different predilections with an analogy. He said that a warrior, who had attained a certain mastery of awareness, finds himself in a huge haunted house with many mysterious rooms. Utilizing his mastery of awareness, he can now explore one room after another, or he can leave the house altogether. Don Juan's predilection, which I shared, had been to leave the haunted house with all its possible explorations of the human mind and to walk out the front door into infinity.

Castaneda, however, seemed to have been fascinated with these explorations. He clearly intended for us to enter lucid dream states as a group and to move collectively from room to room, or from this plane of existence into parallel worlds. He believed our world of everyday reality to be a collective dream. He felt that if a sufficient number of practitioners could enter consciously into the same dream, a reality as solid and real as our everyday world would be created. Some of us were prolific lucid dreamers, and such a proposition did not seem particularly far-fetched. I have no problem believing in the possibility of such an endeavor. Strangely though, I was never really interested. I passionately loved the idea of intending to leave the haunted house altogether, the haunted house of human concerns, however exotic they may be.

David, like many other apprentices, had clearly connected to these more concrete aspects of the Nagual's intent. To be a member of a group of dream travelers was a magical proposition. My own fascination with the prospect of simply merging with infinity must seem rather boring in comparison. Sensing my intent, the Nagual occasionally teased me by calling me a Buddhist. Or rather, looking at me with a most mischievous smile, he whispered with faked concern, pretending he did not want anybody to overhear:

"Felix, you are not a Buddhist by any chance, or are you?"

Even though there was this significant difference in mood and intent of the Nagual's earlier and later work, he always had embodied both aspects, concrete and transcendental. In any case, for us his predilection was ultimately secondary. First of all he was a conduit, facilitating a link with infinity, the spirit, universal consciousness. In Castaneda's own words: "The Nagual is a Nagual because he can reflect the abstract, the spirit, better than others. But that's all. Our link is with the spirit itself and only incidentally with the man who brings us the message."

This link with the spirit is the basis of the art of navigation. As navigators, every act we perform should either strengthen this link or be a direct response triggered by the link itself.

▼   ▼   ▼

David pointed at the gigantic disc of a magnificent full moon that had just begun to rise from behind the San Bernardino Mountains. This was truly spectacular. The moon was red and so big that it looked like the sun rising behind a layer of fog. We were slowly crossing the roof, walking back towards the apartment. What a nice omen. I took it as an indication for being at the right place at the right time.

Little did I know at this point that the events of this evening would culminate into the unexpected conclusion of my apprenticeship, nearly three months after the Nagual's death.

▼   ▼   ▼

We sat down at a small table, which was exactly at the same place where my table used to be, so I ended up sitting in my favorite spot. I made myself comfortable, turning the chair with the back to the wall. This way I could lean my head against the wall and let the moon shine right into my eyes as it slowly rose through the center of the tall east window. There was no need to turn on the light. The moon, the freeway, and the city provided enough illumination for our meeting. David offered some tea, which I happily accepted. It was fun watching him being the caring host. He was so gentle and warm, fully allowing his feminine side.

He was always soft spoken, but he also had the hard and unyielding edge of his profession. In any social or professional setting he was a forceful authority, always backed up by facts and logic. Watching him making and serving us tea and seeing his energy softening, triggered the memory of a trip we once took together to the Mexican town of Tula.

▽ ▽ ▽

We had just completed one of those incredible workshops in Mexico City. Starting in 1993, the Magical Passes, or Tensegrity, were taught in workshops, initially in North America and later all over the world. During some of those workshops the Nagual was present, but mostly they were conducted by some of his closer associates. The ones in Mexico City I always perceived to be exceptionally powerful. The high elevation and the energy of the city itself, which was as close to the birthplace of the myth of the Nagual as it gets, would have been enough to provide a powerful setting. But the passion of over twelve hundred mostly Mexican participants usually created indescribable levels of energy. Twelve hundred determined "warriors" practicing martial-arts-like movements in unison from morning to evening for three to four days is an event to behold.

The energy level was so high that I usually could not sleep more than two or three hours a night—or not at all. The few hours of sleep were filled with lucid dreams and unexplainable perceptions. This particular event had taken place in a convention center right at the Paseo de la Reforma, the heart and aorta of Mexico City. It was close to midnight and I had just stepped out onto the median of this vast boulevard. As I was standing there I could have sworn that I felt the heart of this magical city beating right under my feet. There was no thought of sleeping that night.

The next day David and I left for Tula, which was the mystical epicenter of the Nagual's world. The ancient part of Tula had been a major power center and ceremonial site of the Toltecs, whom the Nagual saw as the originators of his lineage. The Toltecs, according to Castaneda, were "men of knowledge" and masters of awareness from the ancient Mesoamerican past. Tula also had been the site of some of the most intriguing events Castaneda had described in his writings.

We were charged to the brim with the energy of the workshop and silently speculated that Tula might facilitate a shift in awareness or otherwise inform our journey in significant ways. It was the first time David and I had embarked on an adventure together, and I was curious how our synergy would play out.

It was only a two or three hour drive from Mexico City to Tula, which we definitely passed in a state of heightened awareness. There was an unusual brilliance in colors and definition to everything, a pronounced sense of timelessness, and a deep feeling of contentment, none of which was tied to anything in particular. It was amusing how we fell into the role-play of a married couple. David had packed some food and drink and tried to make me as comfortable as possible. I was driving and he was sitting next to me, reading the map, cutting apples, and turning more and more female by the minute. It was quite eerie and without a precedent. We were comfortable with each other and there was no ambiguity, but this strange transformation during the drive to Tula created a cognitive dissonance all by itself. In retrospect it seems as if he had changed into a dress, grown breasts and long hair by the time we reached our destination.

The power that this place held for us mesmerized us immediately. The two days we spent there grew more and more dreamlike as time went on. With as little internal dialogue as possible we just absorbed and allowed ourselves to be absorbed.

We spent eternities wandering alone and together through ancient ceremonial sites and gazing at the awe-inspiring statues of the four mysterious Toltec warriors that held so much meaning for us. Synchronicities abounded to the point of creating goose bumps, and time dissolved into an infinity of perceptions beyond interpretation.

27

We did not shape-shift into crows, nor did David turn into a woman, but on our return to Mexico City we were saturated with a precious sense of uncertainty and boundless magic, and our perception of reality and particularly of time had definitely been shaken up.

∀ ∀ ∀

"So what's new, Dave? Tell me everything! I've been completely out of the loop." I said, after we both had settled in comfortably.

"Well . . . " he smiled, briefly savoring his role as the "man of knowledge" as it were. "There is still no trace of Florinda, Taisha, Talia, Kylie, and Nury", he began.

David had always made it his special job to be informed about all matters having to do with the Nagual and Castaneda's inner circle. His memory was brilliant, and he had taken copious notes throughout his affiliation with the Nagual. He had managed to win and maintain the trust of former and present close associates and members of the inner circle, and whatever he could not find out any other way, he dug out from public records.

He was the scholar. Knowledge and gossip were his commodities. This was his predilection, and the prevalent level of secrecy and cultivated uncertainty that was the hallmark of our living myth had driven him to the extreme.

I always thought that the secrecy with which the Nagual had surrounded himself was entirely pragmatic. His maneuvers were subtle and esoteric. Given his level of notoriety, he could not have withstood the voracious dynamics of the media. Society at large is a living entity and behaves like an organism. Any attempt to unsubscribe from the common description of reality is met with suspicion, paranoia, and ultimately prosecution.

The Nagual had opened our eyes to the mechanisms that shape our view of the world and our experience of reality. He had made us aware of how our compulsive internal dialogue perpetuates and solidifies the description of the world that is fed to us from birth; and he was intent on helping us to stop this process, so we could indeed unsubscribe from the common description of reality and regain our magical nature.

To that end we needed to disengage from our thought processes, to pull out of our mental constructs, so we could command our thoughts, rather than being enslaved by them. Our mental constructs, of course, also contain our sense of identity. So, in order to facilitate this rather radical maneuver of dis-engaging and dis-identifying from our thought processes, the Nagual encouraged us to dream and intend new and different identities for ourselves, more in sync with our heart and the universe at large. And when he felt we were ready, he gave us a new name, not for us to get lost in a new identity, but to live with the understanding that any identity is a mental construct that can be chosen deliberately. Instead of living from the point of view of a factual identity, the Nagual guided us to cultivate our link with the spirit and live by the dictum of this link.

Facts, certainty, definites, certificates, personal histories and the like were counterproductive to this process. But David nevertheless felt compelled to maintain the records, to secure the facts. He had researched mercilessly and had even begun to collect all his findings on a website, "devoted to exploring and evaluating the legacy of Carlos Castaneda."

"I heard they found Nury's car abandoned somewhere in Death Valley," I said.

"Yes," he answered, "no sign of her though. I drove out there as soon as I found out. It was terrifying. I spent all day walking around the desert, just trying to understand what had happened."

I kept shaking my head in disbelief. My mind refused to speculate.

The innermost circle around the Nagual had consisted of six women who had been his closest associates. Three of these women we referred to as "The Witches." They were Florinda Donner, Taisha Abelar, and Carol Tiggs. They had been with the Nagual the longest and were powerful and remarkable beings in their own right, involved in different aspects of upholding the myth and in teaching its core precepts.

The other three women were long-term associates with fundamental and structural roles pertaining to the organization of the apprentices and the workshops. Kylie Lundahl was the "chief warrior" so to speak. Fierce, loyal, and impeccable, she was the archetype of the Tensegrity practitioner. Talia Bey was the chief organizer and CEO of the worldly aspects of our mythological enterprise. Nury Alexander had a special role. The Nagual referred to her as the "Blue Scout." She was something of a "special ops navigator." Her lucidity, speed, and high vibrational energy predisposed her to "run ahead" and supply the Nagual with navigational input.

All six of these women had been close to the Nagual, and the day after his death all of them, with the exception of Carol, disappeared. Only Nury was ever found, her skeleton that is, bleached by the merciless sun of Death Valley.

"I have no idea where they all went" I said, "but I don't believe for a second Florinda would kill herself."

Florinda was one of the most delightful creatures I ever met. She had the energy of a hummingbird and was the most talented lucid dreamer of all. Everybody loved her and I was no exception. Even though born in Venezuela, she was of German descent, and I had felt a strong connection with her. Quite a few times I had had the privilege of meeting with her for lunch, dinner, or a movie, which was always a special treat. I missed her deeply.

We were quiet for a moment. The full moon just fueled my longing and did little to soothe my heart.

Then David continued. In the preceding months he had spent countless hours meeting with scores of people that were related in one way or another to Carlos Castaneda, the witches, or other core members of the group. He had researched any available legal document, including Castaneda's will. He had attended public hearings that were initiated by various legal claims following Castaneda's death. He had met with people who had been secretly filming Castaneda's house for many months prior to his death and who had diligently examined his trash all this time. He had researched real life biographies of core members and was still working on completing them.

In short, David had left no stone unturned.

I was in awe. I was in awe by what he had uncovered, but I was even more in awe by the level of his fervor, by the peerless dedication and impeccability with which he had pursued this task.

His total devotion to the deconstruction of this myth had itself taken on mythical proportions.

Encouraged by my interest, David was on a roll. He talked and talked

30

and talked, never showing much emotion, unraveling and deconstructing until the moon had long left my face in the dark.

The picture that emerged from a strictly conventional point of view had to be utterly disconcerting. Carlos Castaneda, the person, could be portrayed as a consummate and ruthless trickster, and his world, to a large extent, as a world of fabrications and deceptions. Judged by traditional ethics and fact based standards of authenticity, his personality and, by extension, all his teachings could be depicted as deeply flawed.

Every once in a while, David paused and curiously examined my face to gauge my reaction. But my face did not show any reaction. I was totally absorbed in a most peculiar state of mind.

I knew without a doubt that everything David was saying was thoroughly researched. He did not even attempt to make a point. He just reported the facts. Not once did I feel like contradicting, while, brick by brick, he took apart the house in which I had lived for eighteen years.

What intrigued me even more than David's relentless dedication was that every inconsistency he uncovered, every potentially reprehensible act he exposed, every brick he dislodged, triggered visceral memories of all the power, beauty, magic, and wisdom that the Nagual had brought into my life.

It was a stunning experience, and as a result, as I realized in retrospect, my habitual mental operations ceased. My thoughts were turned off as if someone had flipped a switch. Mesmerized by the moon, all I could do was witness the simultaneous emergence of two mutually incompatible realities that were both as factual and relevant to me as life and death.

This was to be my ultimate cognitive dissonance.

Paradise Lost

My journey into the mythological and magical world of the Nagual began in Bandarawela, Sri Lanka, in January 1980. It was preceded by a series of powerful and mysterious events and completely transformed my life from the start.

Already in the summer of 1977 I had started to read Castaneda's first book, *The Teachings of Don Juan: A Yaqui Way of Knowledge*. It contains lengthy descriptions of altered states induced by psychotropic plants, and it failed entirely to capture my attention. As a matter of fact, after forcing my way half way through the book, I surprised myself by angrily throwing it across the room in a fit of frustration. I never had done this before with any other book. I remember mumbling something like:

"I am so sick of this drug glorifying shit! Enough Timothy Leary already!"

My reaction was way out of proportion and actually quite surprising. Having grown up during the 1960s, I had abundantly experimented with hallucinogenic and psychotropic substances and was thoroughly convinced that some of these mind-altering experiences have great potential for psychological and spiritual development.

Maybe it was just that I had read one too many books on this subject, or I had spent one too many nights philosophizing "under the influence," that I had reached my limit. Later I realized that Castaneda never glorified the use of psychotropic substances at all. The detailed descriptions of plant induced altered states in his early books that many still associate with his name, came out of his anthropological field studies, in which he examined the use of hallucinogenic plants among the Native Americans of the Southwest. His research, which earned him a PhD, had always been quite scientific. He eventually summarized that *"the purpose of entering states of non-ordinary reality is only to draw from them what we need in order to see the miraculous character of ordinary reality."*

Perhaps I was not only frustrated because I felt saturated with the subject of mind-altering substances, but also because it is ultimately futile trying to describe these experiences.

Be it as it may, the magic evaded me, and the book ended up lying in the corner of my room for days, drawing my scornful eye now and then.

I was living on Formentera at the time, a small island next to Ibiza in the Spanish Mediterranean, spending my time reading and working part time as a travel agent. Somebody had given me *The Teachings of Don Juan* as a "must read," just like the other cult books of the time such as Tolkien's *The Lord of the Rings* and Frank Herbert's *Dune*.

Eventually I must have picked it up from the floor and gleefully thrown into the wastebasket. In any case, it disappeared from my consciousness.

❧   ❧   ❧

Two years later, at the age of twenty-five, I was married to Mona and we were living in Sri Lanka. Mona, who was ten years older than me, had been burned out from a career in advertising and wanted to paint; and I had read so many cult books that I had boldly decided to write one myself. Sri Lanka seemed the perfect place to realize our dreams. We did not have much money, Mona couldn't really paint, and I had never written anything substantial. All we had, it seems, was plenty of unexplainable confidence.

We did not move to Bandarawela right away. This move was triggered by a fateful event in late spring of 1979 that nearly ended my journey before it began.

After exploring the island for several weeks, we found a perfect house near the town of Weligama on Sri Lanka's south shore. We had already been sweating for hours in our little black rental car when our guide and driver turned onto a dirt road that paralleled the main highway west of Weligama. A short way up a hill, past a small fishing village, we saw a house that caught our interest and asked the driver to stop.

The colonial style building had clearly seen better days but it was fairly big and spectacularly situated on about five acres of a small peninsula with its own white sandy beach and a coral reef to protect it. The grounds were covered with high coconut palms that were gently swaying in a cool breeze. It was serenely beautiful, and we were speechless.

The owner of the house came out to greet us. He was quite an eccentric looking individual with a huge flamboyant Dali moustache, slightly bulging eyes, and a colorful sarong tied around his sizable belly. He was friendly and spoke fluent English. He introduced himself as Kiri Eya, which curiously translates into "Milk Brother," and after a lengthy negotiation he agreed to let us rent his house for four hundred Rupees a month. This was the equivalent of a teacher's salary and about four times the going rate in the area, but still only about twenty-five dollars for us.

We signed a two-year lease and moved in right away, but it took some coaxing and patience until Kiri Eya and his wife Anulla actually moved out. After a few weeks they found a smaller place further inland for which they only had to pay fifty rupees a month. Anulla was not happy though. While she had to contend with the smaller house, Kiri Eya kept the profit from the rent for himself and converted it into coconut rum on a daily basis.

In the beginning our learning curve was monumental. We were the only resident foreigners at least thirty miles around, and the cultural adjustments we went through are a story by themselves. But we were happy and renovated our new home extensively for over a month, inside and out, creating our dream. Once everything was finished, on a moonlit night, we took a walk around the property and sat down under a palm tree to take it all in.

It was quite overwhelming. The moon and the night breeze had turned the leaves of the coconut palms into a glittering canopy under which our now bright white house with its deep blue shutters and doors literally seemed to float in space. The whole mirage was framed all the way to the horizon by the vast and glistening Indian Ocean as it broke on the reef in ever-changing bursts of white. My eyes filled with tears. It was such a magical moment, and I could not believe our good fortune.

We were indeed happy then. Over the next few months we proudly hosted many of our friends who came to visit from Germany. And when nobody was visiting, Mona painted and I worked on my book, a science fiction novel. We had been advised to hire a servant; otherwise we would not be respected. After some trials and errors we found Ariyawatti, a young woman half my height, who turned out to be a real gem. In the beginning she was so shy that she used both hands to cover her face whenever she talked to us. As a matter of fact, she did not speak a word of English, so we communicated with sign language and gestures. We arranged for daily English classes and paid her a teacher's salary, when normally servants just earned room and board. Our guests showered her with gifts and doted on her "cuteness," and as a result of all this, her behavior and attitude changed quickly, and she was soon envied and shunned by all her former friends and neighbors. In no time our "good intentions" had turned this poor young woman into an outcast in her own world.

We did many stupid things. We lost respect in town because we did not want to haggle over everything and ended up paying a premium for our groceries. We put up private property signs because we could not get accustomed to everybody just walking into the house at any given time. We started giving a few rupees to the children that brought us flowers, so they came about five times a day. We bought a baby monkey whose mother had been shot, and as a result everybody was out hunting for baby monkeys, hoping we would buy a few more. The same happened with a parrot we bought from the children, and the list went on.

Eventually we learned, adjusted, and adapted; we even studied some Singhalese, the local language. Despite these occasional incidences of cultural friction, we lived in paradise most of the time. If my life had been indulgent up to then, it was even more indulgent now. It was a local custom to tenderize the meat with cannabis, or ganja as it was called there, and we had big bags of it in the kitchen. Children kept bringing them to the door for pennies a pound. Following and expanding this custom, I cooked, baked, and smoked the plant extensively. The local coconut rum, or arrack, was equally cheap, plentiful, and delectable. And, quite unnecessarily, I was smoking at least a pack of cigarettes every day.

My philosophy at the time was Hedonism with a capital H. After reading everything I could get my hands on from early adolescence, all the German heavyweights, Nietzsche, Schopenhauer, Hegel, Kant, Marx, Engels, Freud, Adler, Jung, etc., all the standard works on philosophy and psychology, I had come to a frustrating yet also liberating conclusion:

In order to understand my mind and the world it perceives, I would have to be smarter than my mind. Since this is not possible, I can never truly understand anything. Consequently, the best I can do is to pack as much fun into life as possible—no holds barred. Every other purpose is based on idle speculation.

It seemed logical at the time, and I was determined to turn my idea of hedonism into an art form. Fortunately, Mona was more mature, and her sobering influence slowed the pace of my self-destruction.

Life was good. We generously overlooked minor disturbances and decided we had found paradise. Following my philosophy we spent more and more time frolicking, indulging, and partying, rather than writing and painting. Ariyawatti enjoyed taking care of the household and made sure we did not do any chores.

So, month after month passed while we drifted deeper and deeper into a void of debauchery, and gradually, we got lost in our idea of paradise.

⌄ ⌄ ⌄

Until one day, all of a sudden, everything changed.

We had been in Weligama for nearly a year when we finally succeeded in talking my mother into visiting us from Germany. It was to be her first flight ever and her first time outside of Europe. She had never seen palm trees or indigenous people living in straw huts.

We picked her up at the airport after a sixteen-hour flight, and her mouth never closed on the drive to Weligama with all the exotic sights. She was in an altered state, and we were happy for her experience.

The next morning at about four o'clock she stood at our bed with a panic attack and wanted to go back home. Everything was too alien, and her jet lag did not help. We managed to calm her down and within a few days she slowly settled in and started to enjoy herself.

One morning, about a week later, while my mother had fallen asleep sunbathing in a hammock, I saw two fishermen standing next to her. On second look I was horrified to see that they actually both had their sarongs lifted and were exposing themselves.

When I ran out they took off immediately. With the little Singhalese I knew, I angrily yelled after them to get lost and stay off the property.

Then I went to talk to my mother who fortunately took it with a sense of humor and did not seem threatened. I explained that the fishermen are out on the boats all night, drinking plenty of liquor while fishing, and as a result, some of them end up quite drunk during the day and, unless they pass out, they are usually up to no good.

A short while later I grabbed my spear gun to go snorkeling and spear fishing as I did nearly every morning. While walking down to the beach, I saw the two fishermen from earlier still standing there. I had no intentions to communicate with them but they must have thought that I had come after them with the spear gun. It was a powerful pneumatic gun that looked quite threatening. So when the two of them caught sight of me they yelled some obscenities and ran away.

I ignored them and went for my dive. While snorkeling around the reef I noticed that they had stayed at the beach, and whenever I had my head up and looked in their direction, they threw up their fists and yelled something into my direction. I did not catch a fish that morning, and when I came out of the water, the fishermen ran away towards the village.

I went up to the house, rinsed my gear, dried off, and put on my sarong.

Hardly ten minutes later I noticed a strange rhythmic chanting and the clacking sound of metal, and we all listened up.

I could not see anything yet, but this did not sound good at all. Immediately I started to close and barricade all window shutters and the back and side doors. We had had a few minor confrontations with some of the inebriated fishermen before and had made sure we were able to barricade the house securely. There was no telephone, no neighbor, and nobody to help.

The chanting came closer and suddenly, through the cracks in the window shutters, we could see a mob of about thirty fishermen approaching the property. They were armed with machetes and the iron bars they use to break the corals in order to sell them. Some of them looked definitely drunk and wild. Meanwhile Ariyawatti had started screaming and crying and, between sobs, she was translating what they were chanting:

"Come out, Mahatja, come out, we will cut off your legs; we will kill the women and burn the house." Again and again.

We moved quickly. I brought a small table to the front door, which was still open. There we collected everything that could be used for defense. All we had were a few machetes, knives, tear gas, and three spear guns, on which I cut the strings to get more range. Then we made our stand.

Mona and I stood in the front door with the weapons between us. Ariyawatti was on the floor tugging on my sarong, sobbing hysterically. "They want to cut your legs, Mahatja. They want to kill everybody and burn the house, Mahatja, Mahatja, Mahatja . . . " My mother stood behind me, frozen.

There was a low stone wall, a roped gate at the end of the driveway, and a hedge of hibiscus separating our property from the surrounding grounds, no real barriers; and yet, so far, the mob had stayed outside. They kept moving along the outside perimeters, chanting and yelling, getting more and more agitated. Eventually (it was impossible to gauge time in this situation) they smashed the private property sign at the main gate and started to move towards the house. Whenever Mona and I stepped outside with our spear guns in hand, they ran back, just to regroup a moment later.

I could see them clearly now. There were about three or four truly fearsome-looking guys with red bloodshot eyes who were leading the charge every time. It was obvious that they wanted to see blood.

The build-up continued. With every new charge they ventured closer to the house, more and more aware that we were limited in our response. A few of the men began to pick up rocks and hurled them in our direction, forcing us to step aside. Rocks started to hit the walls, the shutters, and crashed inside. It was getting really serious now. They were barely sixty feet away and closing in.

It was a most amazing experience. Something was absolutely imminent and yet, I cannot recall a trace of fear. There was just movement, stepping out, dispersing, ducking back in, throwing rocks back, stepping out, aiming the spear gun, dispersing, ducking rocks again. . . . There was only pure action, no thoughts, just instinct, presence, extreme awareness, a clear sense of imminence, and then . . .

All of a sudden and totally unexpected, my mother pushed me aside and thrust herself into the middle of this war zone. I saw bloodshot eyes wielding an iron bar, aiming for her head, two, three hands reaching out to grab and prevent the blow, more bloodshot eyes, rage, puzzlement, and then suddenly the film stopped.

The scene was bizarre. My mother, towering over everybody, screaming, crying, shouting, her arms swinging wildly over her head, had stopped the world. More than two dozen wild men turned from rage to bewilderment, staring at this unexpected phenomenon. The ones with the bloodshot eyes were still kept in check by the remnants of sanity in the others.

I found myself racing back to the storeroom, grabbing two big bottles of beer. Holding them out in front of me I shouted all the good words in Singhalese I knew: "Yalua, yalua, friendship, friendship, hondai, hondai, good, good . . . " The scene was still frozen, blank faces, angry faces, bloodshot eyes. And then, all the way from the back, a fairly well dressed tall young man slowly walked towards us. All eyes were on him. He took his time, savoring the attention. When he finally stood beside me, he spoke—in English:

"They say you don't want them to break the corals and sell them. They say you don't allow them to walk through the property. They say you don't like them."

"This is not true at all," I quickly answered, "I love this country, I am writing a book about how beautiful everything is here and how friendly the people are. I never said anything about the corals. Everybody is always welcome here. Who said all these things?"

He translated every word to the fishermen, who commented loudly: "Ah, hmm, oh," shaking their heads from side to side, some started to smile.

"Kiri Eya said so," he answered my question.

Kiri Eya told them, my god. Kiri Eya, this son of a bitch. Damn him!

It all became clear in an instant. He was spending his days drinking with the fishermen.

"Kiri Eya?" I said, "You know why he is spreading all these lies? Because he wants you to get rid of us so he can move back into the house after we spent all this time and money renovating it."

"Ah, oh, hmm . . .," big smiles, major headshaking. Oh yes, they understood. Kiri Eya wasn't really popular with them at all, and it seemed easy for most of them to swing around. Bloodshot eyes still had death written all over them, but the others pulled them away, waving, laughing, some even gently touching my mother while they moved away.

We basically just stared at each other. I hugged my mother a long time.

Then the young man came back, returning the beer.

"We are sorry," he said, "please take back the beer."

"Oh my god, no," I answered, "keep the bottles, by all means, we are sorry, we had no idea about Kiri Eya and all this . . ."

Then he walked off, waving and smiling.

That night we had police protection. My mother took two Valium. The next day we went on a weeklong trip around the island before we dropped her off at the airport.

Paradise was lost.

A Separate Reality

t had been a radical awakening. Our dream of paradise was shattered, and we decided to move to the hill country where people were more used to foreigners after centuries of colonization and tea cultivation. With much luck we found a former tea estate bungalow outside the small town of Bandarawela with still about ten acres of tea, coffee, and tropical fruits. We were able to rent it for the same amount, four hundred rupees a month. Actually, the owner was so thrilled with us living there and taking care of the property that he did not want any rent at all. We insisted, however, to pay at least as much as we had paid before.

He was a fine gentleman in his eighties, an Oxford-educated horticulturist and a cousin of the former Prime Minister Sirimavo Bandaranaike, the world's first female head of state. All he wanted from us was to send him an occasional package with coffee and fruits from his estate, which his caretakers had consistently neglected to do. We gladly obliged, and he happily received at least two parcels a month at his Colombo address.

Ariyawatti the gem and Felix the parrot moved with us to the hill country. Our baby monkey unfortunately had died of pneumonia after he got away one evening and spent all night on the roof in the rain.

So finally, sometime in late spring of 1979, we arrived at the beginning of my magical journey, the Hill Crest Estate, Bandarawela, Sri Lanka.

ⱴ   ⱴ   ⱴ

Felix the parrot? Well yes, that was the name we had come up with. When the children brought him, his name had simply been "Petapu," which means parrot in Singhalese. All dogs are named "Dog," all cats

"Cat" and all parrots "Parrot." Pet names were not the custom in Sri Lanka. Felix seemed a good name for a parrot; even so he never got quite used to it and always referred to himself as "Fewix."

Of course, we did not give him my name. At the time my name was still Paul and I was Paul until just a few months before the Nagual's death, when he gave me my new name, Felix. But that is another story, and I am not there yet.

Hill Crest was a gift from the spirit. It was a wholly different place, way up high on top of a hill, sometimes floating above the low white clouds that filled the valleys around us after a morning rain. The view to the south, where the rim dropped down into the lowland jungles about ten miles in the distance, was breathtaking.

The house was surrounded by an old rose garden, beautifully designed by our gracious landlord, bordered by a hedge of jasmine, filled with passion fruit vines. In the backyard, around the servants' quarters, grew papaya, pomegranate, cherimoya, bananas, and a whole grove of coffee trees. The slopes of the hill were planted with tea, which was harvested commercially.

Life was different in Bandarawela. At about 3600 feet above sea level the climate was milder and the mood was more refined. We were careful not to alienate anybody. The memory of our battle in Weligama stayed with us for good. This was unfortunately ensured by some dramatic news that reached us a few months later through Ariyawatti's family. Kiri Eya had moved back into his house, and one day while his brother was visiting, he had gotten into his own argument with a group of fishermen. In the ensuing fight, his brother was killed, and Kiri Eya ended up in the hospital with multiple skull fractures. Those fishermen obviously weren't kidding.

But Weligama was far away now, over a hundred miles beyond the distant blue rim. Now we were sitting in our small garden pavilion between hybrid roses and bougainvilleas, sipping tea and watching birds. It was superbly beautiful again, but worlds apart from the satiety of beach life. There was a restlessness in the clear mountain air, and gazing across the valleys into the distance awakened a profound longing in me.

We became acquainted with a few neighboring plantation owners and were introduced to the intricacies of tea. I also learned to harvest, process, and roast our own coffee and spent a great deal of time tending the grounds.

While my writing project had stalled long ago, Mona's painting really took off. The serenity of our new environment suited her well, she disappeared more and more into her own world, and every month she finished a large oil painting. Her themes were feminine, esoteric, and surrealistic.

We rarely had visitors and spent our days above the clouds, sometimes literally so. When I had run out of things to do in the garden, I played with water colors, trying to ease my increasing longing for something indefinable. The serenity of Hill Crest was slowly stripping down my hedonism, transforming it into something more like the void of nihilism.

There were great moments, though. I will never forget the day the rains started, after the dry season had parched the land for many months. On our walks through the grounds we had found tiny little Barberton daisies everywhere and replanted them into our garden. There were many hundreds of them now, covering every free area we could find. We had just barely kept them alive during the drought, but it looked like most of them had taken root.

And then, one day, the monsoon started and the sky opened up. It was indescribable and breathtaking. We had never experienced anything like it. The rains poured down for days and everything exploded into life. Our Barberton daisies literally shot out of the ground. A few mornings in a row we could see about two inches of fresh brown earth sticking to their stalks.

Their big brightly colored blossoms opened all at the same time, the first day the sun came out. It was magnificent. They all looked at us with big red, yellow, and orange smiles the moment we stepped out the door. Steam was still oozing out of the dark cool earth everywhere, dissolving in the morning sun. Dazzling!

But soon nihilism was back with a vengeance. In Weligama, the ganja, the alcohol, the partying, the beach, and the palm trees had created the mirage of paradise and a meaning in hedonism. Here, the indulgences and tropical island clichés were mostly gone. What we had mistaken for paradise was lost, and the lack of meaning became painfully apparent. Eventually we would have to earn money again, and I had no plan for our life that was even remotely motivating.

45

So, even with all the flowers smiling at me, with all the stunning and serene beauty around me, I was lonely, deeply unfulfilled, and sometimes even suicidal.

In a magical universe, it would have been my desperation and my intense longing that attracted the mysterious events that followed. But in my world at the time, which was still void of magic, they all seemed to happen simply by chance.

But even then I could not help noticing the dreamlike elements that characterized these events. Each one of them was amplified or exaggerated in a strange way, not entirely unexplainable, but quite improbable. In retrospect they all followed the same dynamic, as if they had been scripted. One event seemed to feed into the other, gradually forming a vortex that pulled me inescapably into a different reality by the day we left Bandarawela.

v v v

It all started the morning Ariyawatti came running into the living room, her eyes wide with terror:

"Sir, Madam, come quickly, big cobra in kitchen," she burst out.

We followed her immediately.

The cobra was indeed huge, about seven or eight feet long and, at the moment, rolled up in a corner, her head up in the classic pose, ready to strike.

This was a big problem. Though we were in awe and loved snakes, particularly cobras, we had to get rid of her. There was no anti-venom available in Bandarawela, and a bite by such a large snake would mean certain death.

I closed the kitchen door and went to the shed to get the forked pole I had prepared to pin down snakes. It was about fifteen feet in length to allow for a safe distance. I had to customize it a little bit because this cobra was much bigger than anything we had had to deal with so far. A loose wire was attached to both tips of the fork, tight enough to pin the snake against the wall or the floor. Armed with this pole and a large machete we went back to the kitchen. I had no idea how to capture and remove the cobra alive without endangering our lives, so the only option I saw was to kill her, once I had safely pinned her down.

I cracked the kitchen door open and carefully looked inside. The cobra was still in the same corner, looking bigger than ever—a beautiful creature. Her hood markings were spectacular, even from the front. Her tongue was anxiously testing the air. With a slight hesitation I slid the pole through the small opening. While the tip of the pole was approaching her, the snake struck a few times through the air. I kept advancing the fork towards her body slowly. When it was about one foot away I forcefully pushed forward and managed to pin her down with the first attempt.

The cobra was furious now, her huge fangs exposed, hissing, and striking in our direction. She was pinned tight about two feet below her head, and I made sure that there was no way she could free herself. When I was confident that it was safe to approach her, I asked Ariyawatti to take the machete and try to cut off the snake's head.

Ari was a brave soul. The cobra was sacred in her culture, and it was considered bad fortune to kill one. But the idea of having a huge poisonous snake moving around the grounds and her kitchen was even more terrifying to her than killing it. And not for anything would she have allowed Mona to do it. So, without hesitation, Ari moved in, and with a few desperate blows she chopped off the cobra's head.

It was a horrendous moment. As much as we were relieved, we were also in shock about having killed this magnificent creature.

The hood had not been destroyed during the decapitation, and I carefully cut it away from the body, removed all tissue from the skin and stretched it out on a piece of wood to dry. I kept it for many years as a talisman and a powerful reminder of this encounter.

The rest of the body—and it measured indeed over seven feet—I took down to the highway where we kept a large refuse container. As I arrived at the gate there was a man standing by the side of the road. This was quite unusual. There were neither direct neighbors nor a bus stop anywhere close. He was simply standing there as if he had just materialized, and he seemed equally surprised to see me. As a matter of fact, it must have been quite puzzling for him to see this 6'4" tall foreigner coming down the hill, carrying a huge dead snake. He smiled, his eyes wide open in curious anticipation.

"Hi," I greeted him. "How are you doing?"

I could not place him at all. He seemed youthful and energetic, though not necessarily young. He wore bright white tennis shoes and had a light, feline gait as he walked towards me. He wasn't Caucasian but he did not look indigenous either. His English was flawless without any discernible accent.

"Hi there. I am well, thank you. Is this a cobra over your shoulder?" he said in one breath.

"Yes," I replied, my face getting serious, feeling somehow guilty and caught. "She was in our kitchen and we had to kill her, unfortunately."

"Most extraordinary," he exclaimed, kneeling down and running his hands over the snake that I had just unloaded onto the ground.

I told him in detail what had happened; glad to get some of the tension off my chest. He listened attentively, nodding frequently, even padding my back once in a gesture of support.

I liked this man immensely. He had such an otherworldly air, which I only came to appreciate fully once we had parted. He was totally non-judgmental, supportive, and genuinely warm. I don't think I had ever met anybody quite like him.

"Are you interested in astrology?" he asked out of the blue after a moment's silence.

I must have just shrugged my shoulders.

"I know an excellent astrologer," he continued. "If you are interested, I could bring him to your house some time."

"Oh yes," I replied, becoming actually quite curious now. "Come anytime, we are usually home."

He seemed satisfied and got ready to leave.

"A great pleasure to meet you," he smiled, reaching out to shake my hand.

"My pleasure entirely," I said, holding his firm handshake for a moment.

Then he moved away swiftly, waving, and smiling, disappearing around the bend towards town, gliding along softly on his white tennis shoes, seemingly oblivious to gravity. I did not even know his name.

I could not forget this strange and dreamlike encounter. I could not make any sense of it, and I caught myself waiting impatiently for my new friend to come back with his astrologer, hoping this would somehow restore my familiarity with the world.

Barely a week later I saw them coming up the driveway while I was working in the garden. I was excited, told Ari to get Mona from her studio, and serve us all some tea in the living room.

The astrologer was a fierce looking man with a dark complexion. He seemed extremely old, and I was surprised that he did not show the slightest sign of exertion from walking up the hill. He did not smile at all and greeted me formally. My friend seemed even lighter and more insubstantial beside the old man than I remembered him. His name was Samuel, as he introduced himself now, and he served as the interpreter. The astrologer who did not volunteer his name did not speak English. But they did not speak Singhalese either. When I asked, Samuel said that the astrologer was from India and they were speaking a Hindu dialect. I would not have known.

We sat down and exchanged a few polite formalities and the old man wanted to know what we were doing in Bandarawela. We answered his question as well as we could, and then I steered the conversation towards astrology. With slight apprehension, I inquired about his fee for a horoscope. He answered through Samuel that a horoscope would not be necessary. He would just read my hand and tell me what I needed to know, and any amount I wanted to give him would be fine.

I was surprised. His eyes softened and he smiled while he gestured for me to show him the palm of my right hand. I obliged and he took my hand and looked at it for a long time. When he seemed to have seen enough he talked to Samuel in a low voice.

Samuel translated: "Your father died before you were born. Is that right?"

I was stunned. "Yes," I said, "one month before I was born, in a motorcycle accident." How on earth had he known that?

"You have problems with your right knee and your right elbow," he continued.

That was correct too. I had torn my right meniscus, playing soccer as a child. My right elbow had been dislocated and broken while wrestling with a friend when I was about twelve years old. I was mesmerized.

Then the old man talked to Samuel again who translated a detailed account of events that were to happen the next two years. Mona wrote

49

everything down. Then he took Mona's hand and added a few details pertaining to her.

When we were finished writing, the old man looked at me fiercely and added a few words which Samuel translated again:

"Your whole life will be dedicated to the military and medicine."

When Samuel saw my puzzled face he talked with the old man and then corrected himself, saying:

"The next twenty years you will lead the life of a warrior or military man and the rest of your life will be dedicated to medicine and healing."

I had no comment. It sounded intriguing, but it didn't mean anything at the time.

Seemingly that was all the old man was intending to say and after a few polite exchanges, we gave him twenty dollars, which he gladly accepted, and then they left. Samuel kept waving until they were out of sight.

We were still mesmerized from the initial statements, but none the wiser as far as the predictions were concerned. As it turned out, the detailed predictions for the following two years came true . . . partly. His long-term predictions are another story though. Sadly, we never saw either one of them again.

Around the same time when we met Samuel and the astrologer, Lucy appeared in Bandarawela. She was a mysterious and ethereal looking lady in her late sixties. Originally she claimed to be French, but when I asked about her unusual accent, she said that she actually grew up in Belgium and had lived all over the world, working in diplomatic service. We had no reason to doubt her story at the time. She was tall and slim, her face still quite beautiful and her white hair usually pulled back in a short ponytail. With her delightful French accent and her elegant features she would have fit perfectly at a table in one of the street cafes at the Boulevard Montparnasse in Paris. And yet, to our amazement, she apparently had decided to retire to this remote little mountain town in Sri Lanka, all by herself, making her the only white person, besides us.

Shortly after the astrologer's visit she had simply knocked at our door and introduced herself. We invited her in for tea and she reciprocated by having us over at her house for homemade ice cream and a game of Scrabble a few days later. Her house was quite nice and just across the valley from us, at the edge of town. Lucy never spoke much about herself and remained enigmatic and puzzling. One of the more intriguing secrets she shared with us was her custom of eating a teaspoon of dirt every day. She claimed this had kept her healthy all her life. She was serious. We actually saw her once, teaspoon in hand, walking around her garden looking for a suitable sample of healthy looking soil. She just rinsed it down with a glass of water.

While sitting over Scrabble and ice cream in her large kitchen, she mentioned that the kitchen bench we were sitting on was actually filled with books.

"I don't know if you are interested in any of them," she said, "but feel free to look through them and take whatever you like."

Mona wasn't much of a reader, but I was curious and opened the bench. It was a corner bench with two large compartments filled to the top with books, at least thirty or forty of them. I always had loved books and just the smell of them made me excited. I had not read a book since we arrived in Sri Lanka.

I took them all out, one by one. Beside a few local travel books and some horticultural magazines, there were only romance novels, a whole series of medical romance novels with the silliest titles imaginable. There was absolutely nothing else, except one other book that is. I had seen it immediately, it had been lying right on top, but I did not consider it as an option at first. I had read a book by the same author once, a few years prior, and I had hated it so much that I had thrown it all the way across the room in dismay, after reading barely half of it.

Here in Lucy's kitchen bench, floating on a sea of literary sap, I found Carlos Castaneda's second book: *A Separate Reality*, and I was disappointed. But with there being absolutely nothing else even remotely intriguing, I decided to take it with me to give it another try. If there had been a single piece of "real literature," or even a spy or crime novel, I would not have even considered it.

Lucy just shrugged her shoulders, smiling: "I don't know whose books these are. You can keep whatever you take."

Back at home I put the book on the desk in my studio, where it stared at me for a few days before I finally picked it up. The studio was actually an enclosed porch with large windows along the front and the sides, making it look more like a winter garden. There were two of these enclosed porches, one on each side of the house. They were both framed with climbing roses and looking out over the garden and the estate to the south. High trees were filtering the direct sunlight so that it never got too hot, but there was still enough light for painting until late in the afternoon. It was perfect for Mona's artwork and had even inspired me to take up watercolor painting.

My studio also served as Felix' playpen, I had built him a little jungle gym in the corner where he couldn't cause too much mischief and could practice his language skills without driving Mona crazy.

A few days later I started reading.

After flipping listlessly through the pages at first, I read an excerpt on the back cover that caught my attention. It was a quote from don Juan:

"A man of knowledge is free . . . he has no honor, no dignity, no family, no home, no country, but only life to be lived."

I liked it. This struck a cord in me and I was hooked. The introduction pulled me in deeper, and soon all resistance was gone. As it turned out, I could not put the book down until I had turned the last page.

Something unexplainable was going on. It was as if the book had come alive in my hands. A deep and powerful intent had reached out and connected me on a visceral level with a different aspect of reality. I felt deeply affected and changed in a fundamental way after only one reading. Actually, it was not just a different aspect of reality. It felt more like a door had been pushed open, revealing a reality of infinite possibilities that was transcending all my philosophical constraints. The intent between the lines was tangible and alive, connecting me to a source that was independent from the book itself.

I could not believe what was happening. On a deep and intuitive level it felt as if all my existential questions had been answered, without me having the slightest clue what these answers were.

But the strangest part of all was definitely that this whole experience seemed to have nothing to do with the content of the book. Even though the stories and experiences that Castaneda relates are interesting and extraordinary in their own right, they could be read entirely from an anthropological point of view, and by themselves they have no transcendental significance at all.

As it was, and as far as I am concerned by an act of grace, this humble little book served as a conduit, connecting me with something unfathomable and exhilarating, and suddenly my life began to acquire meaning and purpose.

❦ ❦ ❦

With all this happening within a few short weeks, the energy had shifted and we felt strongly that our time in Sri Lanka was drawing to a close. We decided to leave for India at the end of February, which still gave us one more month of enjoying the abundant beauty of our little Shangri La.

Then, in our final few weeks, the last of the mysterious events began to unfold.

Lucy had barely settled in when she surprised us with her sudden decision to move from her near perfect home to a humble little house about five miles out of town. When she showed it to us we were speechless. It was situated on top of a windswept hill with no garden and hardly any vegetation around. It seemed outright insane, but we had to hold back our opinion because she told us that everything had been arranged already. She had agreed to leave her present house to a Peruvian doctor who presumably worked for the United Nations and who had been in the area for a few weeks. Seemingly she had been in touch with him for a while.

It was totally incomprehensible. Lucy had loved her place. She had tirelessly worked in her garden and planted a myriad of things. It had been so important to her to be able to walk to the market. What on earth had happened? Her only explanation was that the new house was much cheaper and cooler. There was no point in arguing with her.

We were curious about this persuasive Peruvian doctor and asked Lucy to bring him over for tea. Apparently he was eager to make our acquaintance as well. Besides our curiosity we had an ulterior motive to meet him. We were determined to talk him into hiring Ari once we were gone.

As soon as Ari had learned that we were planning to leave, she went crazy. She threw fits, locked herself in her room for whole days, cried, pleaded, threatened suicide, and became entirely unmanageable. We seriously considered taking her with us back to Germany, but the implications in terms of immigration, cultural differences, and our lack of financial resources made it impossible.

Since she belonged to the lowest caste in Sri Lanka, her only option within her own culture was to work as an unpaid domestic servant without any freedom, and understandably, she would not even consider it any more. Lucy already had a servant girl who she was happy with, so the possibility of Ari finding employment with this Peruvian doctor seemed like a gift from heaven. She did not want to hear any of it, of course, but we knew that she would eventually warm up to it, considering her alternatives. So, all we needed to do was to convince the Peruvian doctor that he needed Ariyawatti.

Dr. Miguel Pereira, as he introduced himself, seemed like a nice and well-educated South American gentleman. He said he had come here to do a research project at a United Nations agricultural station near Bandarawela. He looked slightly overdressed in his sports blazer and his shiny black shoes, but since my main interest was to gauge his integrity, I was delighted about his impeccable appearance. Ari had been like a daughter to us, and we were quite anxious about whom to leave her with.

We got along fine with Miguel. He was funny and sharp, and we spent an entertaining afternoon together. When we finally steered the conversation toward our main concern, he seemed taken aback at first by our suggestion of hiring Ari. He appeared nearly alarmed. He said that he did not need anybody; he would eat out a lot and travel a great deal. But we made a compelling case and eventually talked him into considering it, if only on a trial basis.

Finally Miguel gave in and agreed to have Ari work for him, at least for a few weeks, and then re-evaluate. This was good enough for us. We were convinced that Ari would soon make herself indispensable and find new happiness in spoiling and doting on "Miguel Mahatja."

Miguel was curious about what had brought us to Sri Lanka and he seemed genuinely impressed by our adventures. He did not volunteer any information about himself. The only detail we could get out of him was that he was from Lima, Peru, where he apparently taught at a university.

I immediately pulled out my address book and asked him if we could visit him if we ever came to Peru. I always had been intrigued by Peru and was sure that our travels would lead us there sooner or later. My address book was full of names of friends and acquaintances from all over the world whom I had met on my travels, and nobody had ever refused to offer me an address or contact information. So I started to write: Dr. Miguel Pereira, Lima, Peru, and then I looked at him and asked if he had an address or a phone number.

He just smiled at me, paused for a moment, and with a sparkle in his deep, black eyes, he simply said:

"You will find me."

Startled, I closed my address book. "Hm, well, I guess, I can look you up in the phone book once we are there," I mumbled, slightly confused about his unusual answer.

He just kept smiling at me mischievously.

We did not see Miguel again until the day of our departure. However, in the nights following our encounter, he kept appearing in my dreams. When I wanted to tell Mona about it, I blanked every time. My memory of the dreams seemed vivid, but I could not put them into words, not even into coherent thoughts. Lucy was in some of the dreams and so was Samuel and other people whom I had never seen before. Upon awakening I was always left with a feeling of urgency and significance, but however hard I tried I could not remember what it had been all about. What I did remember, was that I had felt awkward in most of these dreams, unprepared and challenged. The only recurrent image that stayed with me was Miguel's mischievous smile, and his mocking words kept echoing in my head: "You will find me."

❦ ❦ ❦

Ari had made peace with the situation, but to be on the safe side we had sent for her mother to come up for a few days during the transition. She had brought along one of Ari's sisters, and with all of us cheering her up on our last day together, Ari was doing actually quite well.

At this point we were not much better off than her. It was a painful good bye. We loved her dearly. We loved Hill Crest, Bandarawela, Lucy, and Felix. Our heart was bleeding when we waved our rose garden good bye, closed the gate behind us and drove Ari, her mother and sister, and her few belongings over to what was now Miguel's house.

We unloaded everything onto Miguel's porch. Felix was agitated now, jumping and fluttering around in his cage. At the top of his little lungs he recited his whole vocabulary. "Petapu, Petapu, Fewix, Feewix Feeewix, hello, good morning,", and a whole plethora of Singhalese words and animal sounds. Oh, how I would miss this little critter. He had been with us nearly from day one. How much joy and laughter he had provided us. Now we were abandoning him too.

I could not see clearly anymore. My eyes were filled with tears. Ari was in Mona's arms, shaking and crying loudly.

We had to move fast. This was unbearable. I hugged and kissed Ari good bye, tears streaming down my cheeks, hugging Lucy, thanking Miguel, Ari's mom, sister, again Ari, one last time. "Yes, we will write. I promise."

We got into the car and motioned the driver to leave. Then there was only waving, blowing kisses, more waving, and in a blink of my tear-filled eyes they were all gone.

▿ ▿ ▿

The only one I would ever see again was Miguel. I did find him indeed, just as he had predicted, over fifteen years later, not in Lima but in Los Angeles. For now we would forget about him completely. There were so many other things on our mind. I briefly recalled his mysterious smile a few weeks later when I noticed that the page with his name in my address book was missing. Mona had no idea how this had happened, so we just shrugged it off. Strange, though.

The second time we remembered him was when we learned through a letter from Ari's family that he had left Bandarawela not long after our departure. Now without a job, Ari had signed up with an agency that recruited Sri Lankans for domestic employment in the Middle East. She had left soon after. That explained why she never answered any of our letters. Tragically, neither we nor her family ever heard from her again. I did not want to think about our fateful encounter with the cobra and the bad luck that was associated with it. We were devastated and felt responsible.

The third time Miguel popped into my awareness was ten years later in the summer of 1990. I just had come out of a ten-day silent meditation retreat at a Buddhist monastery in Surat Thani, Thailand—my first such experience. It entailed spending ten days in complete silence, meditating between eight and ten hours a day. The only distractions were two vegetarian meals a day, half an hour of yoga in the morning, and an instructional talk by a resident monk or nun in the afternoon. It had been the most powerful experience of my life, and the resulting degree of internal silence was profound. About a week later I was back in Germany by myself in the house of a friend who was out of town. I was sitting on a meditation cushion, surrounded by a few books, which I read during meditation breaks. I wanted to extend the clarity and peace of inner silence as long as possible, so I continued meditation practice in small increments during the day in between other activities. One of the books right in front of me was Carlos Castaneda's most recent title at the time: "The Power of Silence." The book was open, laying face down. Next to it was a copy of a detailed pencil sketch of Castaneda by one of his former fellow students. It was the only available image of him, and I used it as a bookmark.

As I came out of an extended and deep meditation, my eyes opened onto the pencil sketch and I instantly recognized Miguel. How could I not have seen this earlier? There was no doubt; Miguel Pereira and Carlos Castaneda were one and the same person. I gasped, but my mental silence was quite resilient, and I integrated this realization with surprising calm.

Later I did some research and found that nobody with the name of Dr. Miguel Pereira had ever been on the faculty of one of Lima's universities, and there was no United Nations agricultural station anywhere near Bandarawela.

Even in the pencil sketch his eyes had a mischievous glint, and I could clearly hear his heavily accented voice:

"You will find me."

57

Facing Oncoming Time

We took the train to Colombo. The railway through Sri Lanka's hill country was built in the late 1800s to transport coffee and tea to the capital, and it is one of the most scenic routes in the world. We had booked two seats in the observation salon, the last carriage, which had comfortable recliners and oversized windows, affording spectacular views. After stowing away our extensive luggage we took our seats in front of the convex glass panel that formed the end of the train, and a moment later we started moving.

Gently but irresistibly we were pulled backwards while our eyes and our hearts tried to hold on to the familiar vistas of Bandarawela. For a while we could clearly see Hill Crest Bungalow sitting on top of its hill, and we searched across the valley for Miguel's house, but soon everything receded into the haze.

The effect of being pulled backwards out of our Sri Lankan dream was quite magical and meaningful. As it happened, our memories of what we were leaving behind were soon overtaken by the breathtaking scenery that swept over us and layered itself over the past.

At a most leisurely pace our little train climbed, circled, and zigzagged up the mountains, unveiling a visual symphony of tea gardens, rice paddies, waterfalls, river gorges, tunnels, and cloud forests in front of us, all receding again and turning into the past before our eyes.

We were filled to the brim with this experience, with the receding memories and with the anticipation of traveling through India and Nepal for the next three months. At the time we could not have been aware of the metaphorical power and significance of our magical train ride.

My departure from Bandarawela had marked the beginning of a new life for me. It was the beginning of an open-ended journey based on the art of navigation. My encounter with the nagual while reading *A Separate Reality* had awakened me to a new mode of operation, a new and different way of living life. I was hardly aware of this yet while being pulled backwards through the cloud forests of Horton Plains, but something was slowly awakening and beginning to affect my way of thinking.

The events of the past few weeks had introduced me to Intent, to the spirit, to the awareness of the universe. I was still largely shielded from the full realization, and it would take a lifetime to develop this relationship, but there was no going back. The cynical, nihilistic, and self-centered ways of an entirely thought-based life were slowly beginning to yield to the more organic and interactive relationship with the world that is the essence of navigation.

In retrospect, starting this journey in the observation salon traveling backwards seems like a beautifully humorous gesture of Intent.

The Nagual always maintained that the average man traveled through life in the caboose, always looking back, always keenly aware of his personal history, his experiences, and his identity as an accumulation of the past. It was one of his favorite analogies. A warrior who wants to become a man of knowledge, however, has to turn around and face life as it unfolds in front of him. Instead of facing receding time he has to face oncoming time, as he put it. Life in the caboose versus life in the engine.

I love this analogy. It seems incredibly intuitive, and it is easy to feel the difference. The caboose may be comfortable and familiar or even entertaining, but the action is in the engine. It is in the engine where the wind of life blows through our hair, where perception is fresh and exhilarating. Navigation can only happen while facing oncoming time where nothing is familiar. Even looking back for just one moment might prevent us from perceiving an important gesture of the spirit.

∨　∨　∨

Once in Colombo, we wanted to end our Sri Lanka adventure on a dramatic note and checked into the Galle Face Hotel, a magnificent and powerful colonial monument where we had tea many times before but never actually stayed. The marble and pillar structure felt solid and grounding and we absorbed as a much of its reassuring energy as we could to gather strength for our journey through India.

We just needed two days to see a few friends, say good-bye and to ship personal belongings and Mona's paintings to Germany, so we could travel lightly.

What had been foremost on my mind for weeks, however, was the opportunity to find the sequels to *A Separate Reality*. I did not know how many books Castaneda had written at this time, but I knew that there were more than two. I called some of the larger bookstores but nobody had even heard of his name.

On our last day, while walking near the central railway station we passed a man who caught my attention. There was something in the way he had smiled at us that prompted me to stop and ask him if he knew a bookstore with a good selection of English books. Without a moment's hesitation he pointed to a traveler's hotel near the railway station, just a few hundred yards away, and said that they had the most extensive used book collection in town.

We went there right away. He had been correct, and I was thrilled to find a copy each of *A Journey to Ixtlan* and *Tales of Power*, Castaneda's third and fourth books. These were the only two Castaneda books in the store.

Mona was happy about my newfound purpose and enthusiasm. She had been genuinely excited when I found these books.

"This is amazing!" she exclaimed. "You are always so lucky. I didn't think we would find anything here. This will be really good for the long train rides that are ahead of us. You will have plenty of time to read."

"Too bad they didn't have any German copies," I replied.

"That's ok, this way I can keep practicing my English some more," Mona said, her eyes widening with frustration.

She had not enjoyed reading *A Separate Reality*. There were too many words she needed to look up in the dictionary or ask me for their meaning. This had made reading into a chore. She also did not get hooked into the underlying intent of the book and consequently was not very intrigued.

As far as I could see, Mona lived already in a separate reality most of the time. She was perfectly practical and functional, and she had been successful in her advertising career, but her soul lived in a world of her own. Her twin sister had died at birth, and sometimes I thought that this had provided Mona with her own personal link to another dimension.

She was born in Lithuania and grew up in the countryside where she had spent her childhood wandering through the fields all by herself, making friends with fairies and other ethereal creatures. These were her happiest memories, and I knew without a doubt while looking into her big, wide-set blue eyes when she told me about those beings that they had been more real to her than anybody else. Her parents had shown no understanding of her sensitivity, so she left home at the earliest possibility and never looked back.

I met her in France on a bicycle tour through the Loire Valley. I was the tour guide and she was a guest. We were bicycling twenty to forty miles a day along the Loire River in a small group of about fifteen people, visiting castles. At night we stayed in exquisite little hotels and dined for hours. I had taken on this job after graduating from college to have some time to figure out what to do with my life.

Mona had been a difficult guest. She couldn't stand to ride in the group, so she always let herself fall behind to be alone. As a result I had to ride back and forth all day long to make sure that she did not get lost and that whoever was at the front knew where to go. It kept me fit, and I spent a lot of time riding beside Mona, trying to speed her up.

We fell in love, and at the end of the season I caught up with her in Hamburg, Germany where she lived at the time. We were an unlikely pair, not only because of the age difference, but our personalities were as different as it gets. But we were both dreamers, and we dreamed together for nearly ten years.

Our dream of Sri Lanka was slowly fading away as our train pulled out of Colombo's central station. This time it was an ordinary train. We neither traveled in the caboose, nor in the engine. We just sat in a regular crowded compartment. Mona read a travel book to prepare for our journey to India while I dove headlong into *A Journey to Ixtlan.*

There was indeed plenty of time to read. The train from Colombo to Talaimannar, the ferry terminal for Rameswaram in India, took about eight hours. The ferry across the Palk Strait which is only thirty miles wide, another four, and the train ride from Rameswaram to Madras about eighteen hours. So by the time we arrived in Madras, I had long finished reading both of my precious new books and integrated their contents into my DNA.

Train travel on the Indian subcontinent is not necessarily a comfortable affair, but I did not care. I have had a love affair with trains as long as I can remember. My grandfather, who must have shared my passion, regularly took me to the railway station just for our entertainment. I can still smell the peculiar scent of the old steam engines and railroad ties, hear the whistle of the station attendant, the huffing of steam, the grinding of metal, and the announcements of faraway places. This must have been the birthplace of my longing, the beginning of my quest for freedom, which for so long had been synonymous with movement and travel.

To put no unnecessary strain on my love of trains, we had bought a first class India Rail Pass, valid for ninety days and unlimited travel. Unlimited indeed. By the time we were done "loving" we had clocked over twelve thousand miles on India's endless rail system and my train-craving had been seriously diminished for a long time.

Now we were in Madras, and everything was still ahead of us. Internalizing the contents of the new books had supercharged me with the mood of the warrior, and I was mesmerized again. It felt as if the pages had been laced with magical chemicals, affecting my perception of reality. Processing Castaneda's writings was not an intellectual affair. It penetrated into every aspect of my life.

A Journey to Ixtlan turned out to be a roadmap, a manual for "stopping the world." Stopping the world means to stop our compulsive and ceaseless stream of thoughts that upholds our interpretation of reality. Stopping the world means to allow our thoughts to fall away while our mind stays completely alert and aware.

Perception in such a state of stillness or silent awareness is pure and direct. There is no knowledge about what we perceive other than a direct, wordless, intuitive knowing. Knowing in such a way is experienced as a whole body perception, rather than the perception that is differentiated by our regular senses. It is a bodily awakening from the dream of thoughts.

The content of the book consists of a variety of techniques that don Juan had taught Castaneda. Techniques such as paying attention to signs and omens, erasing one's personal history, losing self-importance, disrupting one's routines, becoming a hunter, and using death as an adviser. The sum of these techniques are called the warrior's way, because they are designed to create and hone the attitude and mindset of a warrior in battle, such as alertness, courage, readiness, impeccability, precision, and abandon. Following and practicing these techniques moves the practitioner out of the world of thoughts into the present moment and into direct contact with life. A warrior who has gained such a direct relationship with life is called a "man of knowledge."

The path of the warrior and the transformation of a warrior into a "man of knowledge" are the core and essence of all of don Juan's teachings. While *A Journey to Ixtlan* offers a roadmap, *Tales of Power* is a firework of wisdom and magic, fueling and guiding the reader's intent further towards this seemingly impossible somersault out of the dream of thoughts into the unfathomable totality of life.

I was hooked. But no matter how excited I was at the time, stopping the world of thoughts and awakening into a state of pure being completely eluded me. I was still deeply asleep, dreaming instead of magic and power for a long time to come.

A few years later I would travel thousands of miles through Mexico, visiting three different towns named Ixtlan, secretly hoping that something magical would happen once I found the right one. It seems silly now, but the excitement, mystery, and practical wisdom that this extended treasure hunt brought into my life was without a precedent.

The actual Ixtlan that gave the book its name was part of a metaphor. Don Genaro, one of don Juan's cohorts used it to describe the profound shift in awareness that takes place when the warrior finally "stops the world." In the metaphorical story, don Genaro desperately tries to go back "home" to Ixtlan, which in the story is his hometown, but in the metaphor it stands for the world, before he had stopped it, the world that had been his home for all his life. Stopping it was like awakening out of a dream, the dream of thoughts that supplies us with certainty, factuality, familiarity, time, and identity. Even a partial awakening shatters all that, just like waking up from a normal dream unmasks and shatters the reality of that dream. Once don Genaro had awakened and realized the dreamlike quality of his life up to that point, part of him wanted to go back into the coziness of the dream, back to Ixtlan. But upon awakening, Ixtlan and the coziness and familiarity of the world were forever lost.

I thought I understood the metaphor, but seemingly I was in no hurry to wake up. My dream had just begun to gather steam, quite literally, considering all our train travel. My life had just begun to evolve into a treasure hunt and I was excited, feeling like a warrior now, riding an "Iron Horse" through India, hunting for power and magic.

I was keen to play with my newfound knowledge, my new understanding of how we can use cues in the world around us as guideposts on our hunt for power and magic. India seemed to be the perfect playground, buzzing with energy and steeped in mystery. The power I was after, of course, was not of the conventional kind, associated with money and influence. I was intrigued by the power I felt while standing near the ocean during a storm or while sitting quietly under a tree that was thousands of years old. I wanted to tap into the power of ancient sites of worship or just find an arbitrary spot where the energy of the earth was abundant.

I did not really have any idea where this treasure hunt would lead me, nor did I care much, but it seemed clear that the checkpoints were places and events of power, energy, and intensity.

Our itinerary was quite erratic. Whenever prompted, we followed hunches or recommendations of fellow travelers. Sometimes we interrupted a journey on a whim and ended up in completely unpredictable situations, staying with strangers or in places where nobody spoke English. We did not have any particular expectations. It was just fun and exciting to act on the understanding that there was something like an ideal or even magical route that we could discover by being observant and finding the right cues.

Many of our moves were probably quite whimsical, tainted with "mental masturbation" as the Nagual liked to call the fanciful operations of the human mind. But even though our navigational skills were still hit-and-miss, this way of traveling had a dreamlike quality that was addictive—and in the end a powerful and coherent pattern emerged nevertheless:

Following the guidance of the spirit and facing oncoming time, promptly produced a good look at time itself, or, more specifically, a series of encounters with impermanence and death.

65

A Dance with Impermanence

ndia is a universe by itself. It is an unmatched feast for the senses with an intensity I have never encountered anywhere else. Our three months and over twelve thousand miles of travel afforded us an immensity of experiences. Most of them got lost over time in the formless ocean of my memory. A few resisted, however; one series of events stood out, events that I remember with crystal clarity, and that I kept remembering and retelling throughout my life.

In a most gentle and generous way, India and Intent granted us a series of memorable lessons on impermanence and death. In retrospect, it seems so appropriate that any serious attempt at becoming a "man of knowledge" would have to begin with an examination of mortality.

Death had not been an integral part of my life up to this point. The only dead person I had ever seen was my grandfather during a brief open-casket ceremony at his funeral. I did not get a close look, and all I saw was his waxen face. I was quite shaken because I had loved him dearly, but the image soon faded away.

My second encounter with death was different and much more personal and dramatic. I had just gotten my driver's license and my first car, a Volkswagen bug, and I was traveling through the Black Forest region in Germany with Loretta, my high school sweetheart. We were hopelessly in love. Following a romantic impulse I had turned into a narrow road leading up the side of a mountain that was covered with vineyards. I had heard that from the top of the mountain it was currently possible to see the sun setting exactly behind the famous Strasbourg Cathedral on the other side of the river Rhine.

It was getting late and I was driving faster than usual. The road zigzagged through the vineyards steeply up the side of the mountain. I carefully went around the bends and then accelerated, pushing the pedal to the floor. Just before the next bend I hit the brakes and slowly turned again. It worked just fine, accelerating, braking, turning, accelerating, and so on, rapidly climbing up the mountain.

We had nearly reached the top and were just moments away from the lookout when we hit upon a stretch of the road where a recent rain shower had washed some sand onto the pavement right before a curve, and we saw it too late. I slammed on the brakes, but there was absolutely no reaction. Just like on ice, we slid over the edge and sailed into the blue sky.

Now, forty years later, I can still recall every nuance of this experience. The first thing that struck me was how easily the steering wheel turned once we were in the air, and then, clearly and unmistakably, time came to a halt. We were fully airborne when the movie suddenly paused. I sat behind the strangely useless steering wheel and my whole life passed through my mind. It was not a brief flash of compounded memory. It was the most leisurely examination of every aspect of my life that I deemed important. There was not the slightest sensation of urgency. There was no panic, no fear, not even concern. I knew for a fact that I was about to die and that everything was just fine; and I felt strangely blessed that Loretta was with me at this decisive moment. As I finished my life review, I felt happy, and then the lights went out.

I awoke on all fours, kneeling on the inside of the roof. Loretta was lying below me, and my body was careful not to crush her. I looked into her eyes: "You ok?"

She was puzzled for a split second: "Yes, I think so."

Then, without hesitation, I literally dove through the rolled down window, pulled the door open and whisked Loretta out of the car which was upside down. We ran away along the steep slope at full speed, convinced the car would explode any moment. Then we fell into each other's arms sharing an indescribable and exhilarating moment of rebirth, one of the most memorable moments of my life.

The car had leapt over the edge, hit the slope at an angle, toppled, and rolled over sideways four and a half times before it came to a halt on its roof. What had kept it from rolling all the way down the hill were two strands of thick wire that were part of the vineyard. Now the car was hanging precariously but neatly wrapped in wires on the slope that went down at least another thousand feet. Lucky, lucky us. Neither of us had even a bruise.

My old VW did not explode, the radio was still playing, and the engine kept running defiantly; so eventually I dared to go back and turned off the ignition.

While we were still in each others arms trying to comprehend this miracle, the owner of the vineyard came racing up on his tractor, screaming at us, his head nearly exploding in rage:

"You damned idiots, how dare you, you are going to pay for the damage, you are going to pay ... "

He was beside himself and would not stop ranting about the little damage we caused to his vineyard, a few hundred dollars as it turned out, which the insurance would pay promptly. There was not a trace of human concern in him, not an iota of compassion, and no appreciation for the miracle he had just witnessed. Looking at his foaming outburst of madness, we felt like two aliens who had just materialized in a world beyond their comprehension.

▽   ▽   ▽

This event gave me immeasurable insights into the nature of reality, but it was more a story of survival and rebirth than of impermanence and of the finality of death.

Realizing impermanence and using death as an advisor was a cornerstone of don Juan's teachings and Castaneda's work. This is by no means an intellectual or philosophical exercise. Impermanence has to be felt and understood on a cellular level. It has to be tangible and truly present to affect our experience of life. By suppressing the reality and finality of death, we are forcing ourselves into a dream, into a virtual reality where nothing is finite, where we behave as if we will live forever, where words and acts don't have the power of always being potentially our last.

In our modern cultures the deathless virtual reality has become the default situation. Real death is hidden; corpses are made up and painted to look alive or asleep at best. On the other hand, unreal death, virtual death

69

is broadcast and celebrated constantly. Our movie and television screens are filled with death, particularly violent death. In the United States it is estimated that by age eighteen, an average person has seen over eighteen thousand murders and eight hundred suicides on television alone.

If all this is not enough to take the reality and finality out of death, religious speculations about some form of resurrection and a personal life after death are ubiquitous, completely missing the point. Based on a radical misunderstanding of scripture and the spiritual wisdom of the ages, eternal life is taken to mean life after death, instead of the awakening into the timeless quality of life in the now. This misunderstanding happens easily because our conceptualization of eternity is flawed. Most of my life I thought of eternity as an infinitely long time. Unfortunately this gave me the wrong idea. Since I could not conceptualize an infinitely long time, I ended up thinking of eternity as an extremely long time, rather than the absence of time altogether. Consequently, eternity had to be beyond the horizon of our earthly existence. It had to come after life. Once I had realized that eternity has to indeed mean the absence of time, eternal life acquired a whole new meaning as well: life outside of the experience of time, life in the now, life as an experience of presence.

∨   ∨   ∨

Allowing the full reality and finality of death into my life, paradoxically showed me the only way to transcend it: holding on to the now, keeping time out of my perception of life.

Apparently our playful and whimsical navigation through India did produce some magic after all. Without any conscious effort, only solicited by our intent, death generously began to offer its wisdom, in a manner so artful and poetic that sheer coincidence was out of the question.

∨   ∨   ∨

Our first appointment with death took place in Bombay. Upon arrival, we were picked up at the train station by Mona's friends, Karin and Gunther. They were representatives of a large German shipping company and lived in a luxurious high-rise condominium on Malabar Hill, Bombay's most exclusive neighborhood. We knew them quite well because until recently they had been living and working in Colombo, and we usually had stayed with them whenever we were in town.

We were all happy to see each other again, and they had arranged for a welcoming party. It was a nice break from the intensity of the open road, or the open train track as it were. We were planning to stay a few days with them to get some rest and to explore Bombay.

As soon as we had unloaded our luggage in the guest suite, Karin gave us a tour through their huge condominium, which was high up on the thirty-second floor. We were stunned and marveled at the fabulous view from every single window. Karin explained a few sights and then drew our attention to an area with heavy vegetation on top of Malabar Hill.

"This is Doongerwadi, the Parsi Towers of Silence," she said with an ominous voice.

"The Parsi towers?" I had no idea what she meant.

"This is where the Parsi feed their corpses to the birds." Karin grinned mischievously, aware of the effects of her statement.

"They what?" Mona's eyes widened.

"You can't actually see the towers from here, they are hidden behind the trees, but you can always see the birds." Karin went on, handing us a pair of binoculars.

She was right. We could clearly see four big vultures circling over the area, even without the binoculars, and crows were everywhere.

The Parsi, we learned, are a small but influential religious community based in India. They are followers of Zoroaster, or Zarathustra, a Persian prophet and poet who lived at least 3000 years ago. He saw the universe as a cosmic struggle between truth, or true reality, and lie, or false reality. The purpose of mankind, according to Zoroaster, is to move from false reality towards true reality through active participation in life and the exercise of good thoughts, words, and deeds. False reality appears to be synonymous with the virtual reality that is generated by our compulsively thinking mind, and good words, thoughts, and deeds readily translate into impeccability and integrity. All of which shows that our higher purpose and the recipe for liberation hasn't changed much over the ages.

The Parsi rites regarding death are based on the belief that fire, earth, and water are sacred elements that should not be defiled by the dead. Therefore burial and cremation have always been forbidden in Parsi

71

culture. Instead, corpses were placed on top of Dokhmas, or Towers of Silence, where the vultures would remove the flesh from the bones, aiding the release of the spirit. The offering of their bodies to the birds is also seen as a last act of charity by Zoroastrians.

The Towers of Silence on Malabar Hill have a large circular roof that slightly slopes towards the center. It is divided into three sections by three concentric rings. Male corpses are arranged in the outer ring, female corpses in the middle ring, and the innermost ring is for the dead bodies of children. Once the birds have eaten all the flesh, the bones are left to be bleached by the sun. Eventually they are collected in the ossuary pit at the center of the tower. Here the bones gradually disintegrate and the remaining material is washed into the sea by rainwater.

I was completely intrigued. Over the next few days I was drawn to the window again and again, watching the vultures descend onto the hidden towers. The grounds were off-limits to Non-Parsis but our vantage point was close enough for these fascinating funeral rites to leave a lasting impression on my mind.

I could not help but imagine how it would feel to be a Parsi, having to leave the body of someone I loved on top of a tower to be hacked apart and eaten by birds. I had seen the long necks of vultures completely disappearing in decaying animal corpses. In comparison, the swift finality of cremation or the relative if deceptive integrity of a buried casket seemed to be much more bearable.

I allowed my imagination to run free, and while I tried to ponder my own death and disposal, I realized that I would not want this to be my destiny either. There was something disconcerting about the idea to be so utterly exposed and slowly ripped apart, even as a corpse. I suppose, this scenario was incompatible with my sense of vanity at the time, which tragically extended all the way to my imagined corpse.

"Aren't you getting a little bit too morbid with this?" Mona asked while I was watching the vultures again with the binoculars.

"Morbid?" I shook my head, "I am thrilled. I love this."

I did not want to let it go yet. It seemed like such a great gift to find this fascinating window into the intricacies of our mortality. There was no morbidity in my interest. I had learned that to become a man of knowledge I had to use death as an adviser, and this had removed the barrier that I normally would have felt while dwelling on something as unpleasant as death. It even felt liberating. I much liked the idea of using death as an adviser, but in order to do so, I had to establish a relationship first.

∀   ∀   ∀

Bombay was quite forthcoming in this regard. It even had a little farewell present for us in form of a taxi ride to the train station on the day of our departure. We did not know how long it would take, so we asked the driver to hurry. That was a big mistake.

Driving in Bombay traffic was already a surreal experience under normal circumstances. From our point of view everybody was driving on the wrong side of the road to begin with. Traffic lights, lane markings, and any other form of regulation were sporadic and arbitrary at best. Besides cars, buses and motorcycles, there were also countless bicycles, rickshaws, people and animals on the streets. Add one apparently suicidal taxi driver who obviously lived in an entirely different dimension, and we got the roller coaster ride of our life.

The moment he pulled into traffic we were mesmerized. We screamed, held our breath, and laughed hysterically. He was completely oblivious to the laws of physics, passing everything and everybody, left and right. We literally flew through a maze of intersections, where half a dozen or more streets were connected through huge unmarked circular spaces. It was total chaos on fast-forward. He was not a skilled driver in a conventional sense, nor did he seem reckless or pushing his limits. He seemed totally abandoned and relaxed, dreamily navigating this chaos in a way that was utterly unfamiliar to us. We rolled into a ball in terror, sometimes protecting our heads with both arms from certain impact. We flew against the doors, the ceiling, and each other. But his faith and serenity were contagious and gradually we started to relax and accept our fate with growing exhilaration. It was one long, unbroken, breathless experience, and suddenly we were at the station, as if we had popped out of hyperspace.

Clearly, death had noticed my interest and was coming out of the closet with a sense of humor. The taxi ride had been an exciting encore indeed, less poetic perhaps than the vultures above the Towers of Silence,

73

but it had felt more imminent and dramatic, and both of these events had a scripted quality and timing that made me curious how this dance would continue.

▼ ▼ ▼

The state of Goa, which is tucked away on India's central west coast, has anchored itself in my mind with its vast and endless white beaches. Some of them were nearly a quarter mile wide, stretching all the way to the horizon in both directions. It was truly magnificent.

Goa had been a Portuguese colony for 450 years until 1961, and it was unique among all the other parts of India. I remember a visit to a local market in Margao where everybody looked different, as if we had stumbled onto a movie set. Many people had a distinctly Portuguese look and their clothing and ornaments were extravagantly colorful and exotic. Christian churches were everywhere, often right next to Hindu temples or Buddhist stupas. It was a fascinating place, one of those lands at the end of the rainbow, partially outside of time and space.

We stayed in a charming little beach bungalow surrounded by coconut palms, looking out over dazzling white sand onto the deep blue Arabian Sea. Every morning the fishing boats unloaded their catch onto the sand and we bought a basket full of giant prawns and lobsters for next-to-no money. The beach restaurant would prepare them for a nominal fee, and so it happened that we had all-you-can-eat prawns and lobster for lunch and dinner every day. Most of the time they just sautéed a pan full of onions, added curry spices and tossed in the crustaceans at the end. It was delicious every time.

After a little over a week I developed an agonizing itch all over my body, and we took this as a sign that it was time to leave. On the train out of Goa I suddenly came down with high fever and chills. It was unbearably hot, my lungs were burning, my heart was racing, and I could hardly breathe. The further inland we traveled the hotter it became and the more miserable I felt, but there was no way to leave the train. By the time we started climbing up the slopes of the Western Ghats that separate Goa from the interior, I was lying on the luggage rack above our seats, fading in and out of consciousness. I was freezing and burning and hallucinating and finally passed out altogether. Mona didn't know what to do. She just tried to give me water whenever possible.

I don't know if I had an allergic reaction to the immense amount of shellfish or if I had caught a virus, or both. When I started to lose consciousness while the train zigzagged so painfully slow up those mountains I was seriously wondering if I was going to die. I had never felt so ill and faint in all my life.

Once the train finally reached the Deccan Plateau, it was already night, the air was significantly cooler and dryer, and I slowly began to recover. Soon after I regained consciousness I was able to climb down onto my seat, drink water, and eat a few bites of food. Pune, our next destination, was still many hours away, so I made myself as comfortable as possible and kept fading in and out of fever dreams.

Perhaps an hour later, I awoke to some commotion around a passenger who sat across the aisle four rows ahead of us. When I opened my eyes, two men were just lifting him out of his seat and carefully laid him down in the aisle. He was a well-dressed man perhaps in his seventies and he seemed unconscious. I was wondering why nobody had put a pillow under his head when one of the passengers who sat next to him took a scarf and covered his upper body and face.

Suddenly I realized with a jolt that the man was dead.

"Did you see what happened?" I asked Mona.

She shook her head. "No, I had been sleeping. I just opened my eyes when they took him out of the seat. It is amazing . . . nobody seems to care."

"He was probably traveling alone," I suggested.

We were looking around, curious to see the reaction of the other passengers, waiting for something to happen, but all we saw were tired, uninterested faces, settling back, resuming sleep.

I was sitting on the aisle and the body was barely ten feet in front of me, rocking steadily in the rhythm of the train tracks. The thin white scarf that covered him was nearly transparent, and the ceiling fan kept pushing it against his face, animating his features. He had a tremendous presence in his death. I could not take my eyes off him, and even when I closed them, I still saw the body as if it were burned on my retina. The man was dressed all in white, and with the white scarf over his face the neon light seemed to lift him off the dark brown floor and make him float. Nobody bothered him. Occasionally somebody carefully stepped over the body to get in or out of a seat. The conductor ignored him completely. Peacefully and gently rocking, with the scarf and his clothes undulating in the breeze, the dead man stayed with us, sailing through station after station all the way to Pune.

I took him into my fever dreams, having visions of out-of-body experiences, where I was staring at my own corpse. One moment I awoke in tears after dreaming of my mother grieving over my dead body. For long periods I was sitting awake, just staring at the corpse through half-closed eyes, trying to imagine how the old man's life had been. After deliberating on several different versions, I decided that he must have been a retired government employee who had recently lost his wife. Now he was living with the family of one of his sons in Goa and he was on his way to visit his daughter and grandchildren in Pune. He had probably just been dreaming of playing with his grandson when the spirit left his body.

As we arrived in Pune, the train personnel made us all keep our seats until paramedics had carried my dead friend out on a stretcher.

I felt a sense of loss when he was gone. For all I knew, it could have been me.

▽   ▽   ▽

Mumtaz Mahal, the daughter of a Persian nobleman and apparently a woman of legendary beauty and grace lived in Agra from 1593 to 1631. At age nineteen she was married to Prince Khurram who later became the emperor Shah Jahan I. It is said that, even during her lifetime, poets would sing of her incomparable beauty, gracefulness, and compassion. Khurram was completely taken by her, and according to the court chronicler and court historians, the royal couple had the most intensely affectionate and erotic relationship imaginable. Such devotion and loyalty was unheard of in the world of polygamous Muslim royalty. Despite bearing thirteen children, Mumtaz traveled with him everywhere and was his confidante and trusted companion. When she died while giving birth to their fourteenth child, Khurram apparently went into secluded mourning for a whole year and devoted himself to the creation of her tomb, the Taj Mahal, arguably the most magnificent mausoleum in human history.

I had always avoided tourist attractions, and even with the undoubtedly unique and majestic Taj Mahal I could not easily overcome my ambiguity. We picked a time for our visit before the arrival of the tour buses and fortunately the line at the entrance was not too long. As is usual in such places, we had to fend off hordes of beggars and hawkers, and by the time we lined up at the entrance booth we were already hot and irritable. The moment we entered the tomb I gagged. In the small entrance hall everybody had to take off their shoes and the resulting odor was repulsive. Overwhelmed by it, I held my breath, but to no avail. The smell followed us everywhere. There must have been a draft coming through the entrance and through the hall of shoes, assuring that this stench filled the entire Taj Mahal.

We followed a guided tour for a while, intrigued by some of the detail pertaining to the construction of the mausoleum. The entire colossal structure was built with unique translucent white marble, which had to be transported all the way from Rajasthan. Everything was intricately ornamented with inlays, utilizing 28 different precious stones that were brought from places as far away as China and Arabia. It took 20 years, 20,000 workers, 1,000 elephants and countless specialists from all over Asia to complete the Taj Mahal. The facts were as dizzying as the still persistent odor was nauseating. We had to cut the tour short and headed for the exit.

I was disappointed. We meandered through the gardens for a while longer, trying to absorb the splendor from the outside. We were impressed, but no matter how hard we tried, we were not captivated at all by this wonder of the world.

We left Agra a few days later early in the morning, and as we came out of the hotel we nearly ran into a bicycle rickshaw. The driver jumped off in a flash and tried to talk us into hiring him. I never liked human powered rickshaws. It made me uncomfortable to watch the driver sweat and huff while we were sitting comfortably in the back. I realized that this was the way they made a living, but usually we ended up hiring a regular taxi.

The fact that we nearly bumped into each other seemed serendipitous though, and his disarming smile prompted us to make an exception.

"I know a beautiful shortcut," he said happily, when he realized that he had secured the hire.

We loaded our backpacks and climbed in. It was just before sunrise and still pleasantly cool, so we did not feel too bad for the driver. He wound his way through narrow alleys, leaving the old town on a path along the Yamuna River, which was still shrouded in morning fog. It was indeed a beautiful ride. The Red Fort appeared before us out of the haze. It was another magnificent monument to Muslim architecture and had been a palace during the reign of Shah Jahan.

Right when we were about to pass the Red Fort, our driver stopped and pointed to a window in the main facade.

"This is where Shah Jahan was imprisoned for fourteen years until his death, after he was overthrown by his son," our rickshaw driver explained. "From here you have the best view of the Taj Mahal."

We climbed out of the rickshaw and turned around.

What we saw can only be described as an act of grace—a visual poem.

In the very first rays of the sun and shimmering through the early morning fog, the Taj Mahal finally revealed itself to us. The great white tomb slowly emerged as a translucent mirage of perfect proportions, growing more luminous and three-dimensional by the second. It was framed by a changing glow of pink and red, as the sun climbed above the horizon, waking up this sleeping beauty, carving it out of the mist.

As we stood awed, my heart was overwhelmed by the magnitude of the gesture of love and devotion that had prompted this work of genius—and even more so with the mental image of Shah Jahan, being condemned to behold this sight through his window for what must have been an eternity.

For a timeless moment our world came to a halt.

Floating before us in the distance, the Taj Mahal had opened a portal into another dimension—and once the world started turning again and my thoughts returned, I lost myself in the riddle of love and death.

❧   ❧   ❧

Varanasi or Benares, as it was known in colonial times, is a place of power if there ever was one. Located at an auspicious crescent-shaped bend on the sacred river Ganga, it is India's religious capital and one of the oldest cities on earth.

Mark Twain wrote:

"Benares is older than history, older than tradition, older even than legend, and it looks twice as old as all of them put together. "

It became quite obvious what he meant as we made our way through the ancient maze of more than eight hundred temples and shrines that line the narrow winding alleys, leading down to the river. The air was thick with incense and buzzing with the devotional energy of the thousands of pilgrims that are flooding into this town day after day.

The Ganga is worshipped by Hindus and personified as a goddess in Hinduism. Hindus believe that bathing in the river and drinking its water purges sins and helps to attain salvation. Most Hindus make a pilgrimage to the Ganga at least once in their lives. But they not only come to Varanasi to bathe in the Ganga. It is a common sight to see dying pilgrims and muslin-wrapped corpses being carried down to the river on bamboo seats and stretchers. Varanasi is so holy that it is believed that those who are cremated at one of the countless funeral pyres along the Ganga will attain *moksha*, the liberation from the cycle of birth, death, and rebirth.

The transcendental core belief in Hinduism is essentially the same as in all other major religions. Most Hindus believe that the spirit, soul, or true essence of every person, called Atman, is eternal, i.e. outside of time. Atman is ultimately indistinct from Brahman, the universal spirit. According to the Upanishads, one of the principal scriptures of Hinduism, *moksha* or liberation is attained when we realize our timeless nature and our oneness with Brahman. The different methods that the sages have taught to attain this realization are called yogas.

Since our thinking mind can neither understand nor relate to the eternal and infinite reality of Atman and Brahman, religious practices revolve around personal and concrete gods such as Vishnu, Brahma, Shiva, and Shakti, or one of the countless lesser deities like Ganesha and, of course, Ganga. All of these are universal archetypes we can relate to, and ultimately serve as steppingstones into Brahman's unfathomable reality.

Varanasi is also the site of the Deer Park where Gautama Buddha gave his first talk on the principles of his teachings, which makes it one of the most revered places and pilgrimage sites in Buddhism as well. The

Buddha taught a way of life intended to make us realize the true nature of reality. This true reality is described as undifferentiated oneness, and as such, on a transcendental level, it seems to be essentially identical with Brahman in Hinduism. Both belief systems are beautifully tolerant and coexist peacefully. We frequently saw small groups of Buddhist monks in their colorful saffron and crimson robes, providing a touch of serenity as they made their way through the devotional frenzy of Varanasi.

Death was everywhere in Varanasi, especially on or near the Ganga. All day long we could see people on boats dispersing the ashes of their loved ones. Dozens of funeral fires were burning along the banks of the river at all times, and occasionally, if a family could not afford enough firewood to burn the remains to ashes, half-charred bodies ended up floating down the river. Sometimes we would see small groups of women, dressed in white saris and with their heads freshly shaven after their husbands had died. Modern Indian law had spared them from sati, the ancient custom of wives throwing themselves on their husband's funeral pyre.

One evening after dinner we went for a walk along the river and sat down on some rocks next to a family that was just finishing building a pyre. Everybody was involved and seemed to know exactly what they were doing. I realized that it was actually quite difficult to build the pyre just right, so it would not collapse or fall apart or have the corpse roll off in the middle of the ceremony. The family members smiled at us encouragingly and seemed rather honored by our interest, so we did not feel like we were intruding. The corpse of an old woman, wrapped in muslin, lay on a beautifully ornamented sheet and was covered with flowers. When the pyre was about knee high, two of the men lifted the body with the sheet and placed it on top of the wood. They gently folded the cloth around it and then continued to build the pyre until the corpse was completely enclosed.

A priest held a short ceremony and then one of the men, probably the eldest son, delivered a well-spoken eulogy before he lit the pyre with the help of kerosene and a torch. The wood must have been dry because the flames exploded powerfully into the night sky within moments. The pyre was roaring, and we all watched mesmerized as the sheet, the flowers, the muslin, and the woman's hair incinerated nearly instantaneously. In the absence of a breeze, the smoke and the bursts of steam that came out of the corpse were rising straight up, and only occasionally did we catch a whiff of burnt flesh. It was probably a good thing that we could not see too much of the body when the flames first reached it. It was still covered with wood and surrounded by flames.

Once the initial burst was over, the fire settled down into smaller white flames that were getting hotter and hotter. The body was still releasing water in bursts of steam and we could hear the sizzling sound of burning fat. After a while the pyre was compacting into a glowing furnace, and the charred body became clearly visible on top. Occasionally someone would tend to the fire and add a few logs here or there. It was now burning hot and steady, and nothing much happened for a long time. Small yellow flames danced around the corpse emitting tufts of black smoke. We couldn't take our eyes off this little inferno as we once again pondered life and death.

Suddenly something flew into the fire, startling me, and causing a burst of sparks. It happened again, and this time it hit the charred body. I looked around and caught sight of two young boys as they were picking up stones and throwing them at the fire, apparently aiming for their grandmother's head. I was shocked at first, but nobody else seemed to be concerned. As a matter of fact, their father was right next to them and did not interfere.

The boys got increasingly excited and competitive in their endeavor and I cringed every time a stone flew towards the fire. Finally one of the stones hit the head with enough force, and with a dull clacking sound the skull cracked open. A stream of thick pink fluid popped out and exploded in a huge dense white cloud of steam. Either the white cloud seemed unusually cohesive or my stunned mind did not let it dissipate. It just kept rising into the night sky until it eventually disappeared. It was an incredibly powerful display that I would never forget.

One of the older men of the family who was closest to us must have seen our consternation. He came over and explained that it was unusual that the skull had still been intact, and that the boys cracked it open so the soul could leave the body and only bones and ashes would remain.

It was a moonless night and the reflection of the fires on the slow flowing river created an eerie medieval atmosphere. Dogs were barking in the distance. Huffed voices and wailing Indian music seemed to

81

come from everywhere. We took our time walking back to the hotel and stopped several times along the waterside, gazing across the holy river. We could not see the other bank, just a few boats, drifting through the haze. There was hardly a ripple on the surface. Ganga had merged seamlessly with the heavens for the night, and it was peaceful. As I closed my eyes to join the silence, I saw a skull exploding in a pink flash and transforming into a dense white cloud, whispering something I could not understand.

▿ ▿ ▿

We stopped in Calcutta on our way to Kathmandu to get our visa for Nepal. Calcutta was the reverse image of Bombay. Where, with some goodwill, Bombay could be seen as a giant and bustling city with some localized islands of slums, Calcutta was one giant and bustling slum with some localized islands of city.

We were not prepared for what we encountered. It was the Calcutta of Mother Theresa, one of the largest and poorest slums in the world. Just looking out the train window while traveling into and out of Calcutta and a rickshaw ride between two train stations supplied us with more images of pain and suffering and of crippled and starving bodies than we thought existed. Trying to share this experience seems futile. Not even television images can communicate the true extent of such misery. And, in all honesty, we were blocking out the impact even while walking through the midst of it.

We decided to take refuge on one of the "islands," the downtown business district. Now *that* was a different story. There were beautiful designer stores, parks, a golf course, and even a polo club. It was exquisite. We listened to the piano and the sounds of tropical birds, restoring our equilibrium as we were having tea and sandwiches on the terrace of the Grand Oberoi Hotel, "the epitome of luxury and hospitality," as it proclaimed on the menu cover.

Whenever we were overwhelmed with "cultural idiosyncrasies" that threatened our idea of the world, we took refuge in the best hotel in town for a little while until the reality attack was over, and the air conditioning had cooled us down enough to tackle the next round.

Over tea we could have wondered why one of the oldest and most spiritual civilizations in the world hasn't come up with a better system of coexistence.

Or, we might have had more fun blaming the British for this social mess. After all, they supported and rigidified the Indian caste system during the colonial rule. Yes, I think blaming the British would have been a good idea. It would have left us feeling much better, simply by not being British.

Or we could have pondered the fact that we still always felt bothered and annoyed instead of compassionate whenever we saw poverty and suffering.

But probably we just complained about the sandwiches being too expensive.

Or maybe we did blame the British.

We left the Grand Oberoi to take a stroll down one of the shopping streets. It was late afternoon and the sidewalks were packed with busy looking pedestrians, many of them in suits despite the heat. The area was the main business district of a metropolis of twelve million people. We had barely walked a hundred yards when we noticed a small diversion ahead of us in the stream of shoppers. It was a small ripple in the flow, as if there was an obstacle on the sidewalk.

We saw him only at the last moment and veered to the side. Most people, seeing him too late stepped right over him. He was the most wretched looking creature one could imagine: a man, perhaps in his fifties, a mere skeleton of skin and bones, completely naked, his own excrement smeared all over his body. He was lying motionless and face down on the asphalt in the blazing sun. I saw a slight movement in his chest. Thank God, he was not dead . . . only dying.

Nobody did anything about it; certainly we didn't. The stream of busy pedestrians picked us up again and carried us away. I don't remember if I felt bothered or compassionate or just speechless. Our dance with impermanence had hit a low note, and we longed for higher elevations.

ᐁ ᐁ ᐁ

The bus ride up the Himalayas into Nepal had mortality written all over it. When I saw the driver of the overnight express bus to Kathmandu, I felt instantly compelled to look over my left shoulder in all seriousness for the first time. I had learned that a warrior can always consult his death by looking over his left shoulder, and death will advise him.

We had been warned by fellow travelers and travel books about frequent accidents along this route. The buses as well as the roads were generally in bad condition and one single driver often drove the whole sixteen hours with only short breaks, most of it through the night. A long stretch of the road went along river gorges with drops of up to one thousand feet and, of course, there were no guardrails. In some places the river is supposed to be lined with the wreckage of busses.

I never liked bus rides, and all this information seemed more than I wanted to know at the moment. Meanwhile, the wild-eyed driver who had the ego of an airline captain was impatiently revving the engine and sucking on his cigarette as if it supplied oxygen. His body looked ravaged by caffeine or whatever else he took to stay awake behind the wheel. His two male "flight attendants," who felt pretty important themselves, stored the luggage, checked the tickets, and assigned the seats.

I looked over my left shoulder with slight apprehension, but I only saw the weary faces of our fellow passengers. There was no fleeting shadow, no chill running down my spine, no input that would have made me run for the exit.

"What do you think about this driver?" I asked Mona.

"It will be all right," she shrugged. "At least he doesn't look drunk."

"Good point." I laughed and settled back, deciding to accept my fate.

I didn't really know what to think about fate. I only knew that all the locals behind my left shoulder and in the rest of the bus had a different attitude towards fate than we did. This had struck me again and again during the two years that we spent on the Indian subcontinent. The lifelong immersion in the concepts of karma and reincarnation by both, Hindus and Buddhists, produced a significantly different relationship with fate, life, and death. Here most people grew up with the perception of living a continuum, rather than a unique and singular life.

Just the other day, during the eulogy at the cremation of the old woman in Varanasi, this different attitude had been strikingly obvious. The son honored and described his mother's life entirely in karmic terms, related to her previous and future lifetimes. First he recalled all the good and fortunate events in her life as a result of the virtuous aspects of her previous lifetimes. And then he talked in great detail about how all her goodness and religious devotion in this life will guarantee her happiness in the next. Even the instances of hardships she had to endure, he described in terms of resolving the karma of previous lifetimes and earning good karma for the next life.

This was the general understanding we had experienced countless times. All too often it appeared to us that the fatalistic aspects of this perspective caused people not to value an individual life enough, as we saw in the case of the dying man in Calcutta. One could explain and excuse all of life's shortcomings as being the result of karma from previous lives, so that there was little motivation to change things for the better.

On the other hand, there also seems to be a great opportunity in this way of thinking. Upholding the reality of a continuum of lifetimes can prompt us to identify with that aspect of us that is the essential constant throughout all these lifetimes. It can prompt us to identify with our timeless essence, rather than with the temporary manifestation we call our life.

▽ ▽ ▽

With a few roars of the engine and the deafening sound of the horn, the driver signaled our departure. As soon as the last food vendor had jumped off the bus, we started rolling. The first few hours we were driving through lowlands and the roads were still fairly decent. It was quite obvious, though, that our bus driver was from the same tribe as our taxi driver in Bombay. With dreamlike abandon, his head tilted slightly back and to the side, a cigarette hanging from his lower lip, he thundered through the villages, keenly aware of the physics of size and velocity that would give his bus the edge any time, should someone dare to come into his path. With his oversized aviator glasses, which he didn't take off until it was positively dark outside, he seemed as concerned with the world outside as a bored pilot in front of a flight simulator. But he knew his machine, and apart from his antics, his driving was flawless.

Sometime during the night we started our ascent into the Himalayas and the road got curvy and rough. It was pitch black outside and we couldn't see anything, which was probably for the better. I tried to stay awake, so I could at least watch the driver, but to no avail. Normally I was not particularly fearful, but all this contemplation of impermanence and death had left its mark. I found myself in a limbo. After beckoning and intending it for several months now, the reality and unavoidability of my own death had entered my everyday awareness. But rather than giving more depth and definition to the experience of the here and now, it triggered apprehension and confusion. The alchemical process of turning the realization of impermanence into liberation required a somersault that I could not yet conceive.

∨ ∨ ∨

I awoke as the bus came to a screeching halt. I assumed that we were having a bathroom break and I gladly took the opportunity to stretch my legs. But when I got off the bus I realized that the driver had stopped for a different reason. There was no bathroom anywhere. In the first morning light I could see that we had been driving along the edge of a spectacular river gorge for the longest time. The driver had stopped here for some special Nepali sightseeing. From where I stood, I could see eight different wrecks down by the river, six of them buses, and from some of my fellow travelers I learned that one of the wrecks had happened less than a week ago.

Over the next hour or so we stopped two more times for the same reason, and in between the wreck-viewing breaks we always knew by the excited comments of our fellow passengers when we passed another one. I was beyond fear at this time. The general excitement had pulled me into the exhilaration of being part of an adventure. It was altogether unbelievable. In many places the road was partly washed out with the shoulder broken off, and sometimes it was just wide enough for a single vehicle. If this was not enough, it was littered with fallen rock. Malfunctioning brakes or a moment of inattention were not an option, particularly once we had started downhill.

As we finally rolled into the central bus station in Kathmandu a few of the passengers applauded our driver, and we enthusiastically joined in.

Our dance with impermanence was over—for now.

A Place of Power

I t turned out that our surreal journey along the edge to Kathmandu had been strangely fitting. We might as well have come through a wormhole. As far as we could tell, the town and the surrounding valley were trapped in a time warp.

Nepal had been closed to the outside world for more than two hundred years and had only opened its borders in the mid twentieth century. The first international flight landed in 1974. When we arrived six years later the modern world had clearly descended upon this mountain kingdom, but it was still only a thin veneer.

Most visitors in the early years had been mountaineers and young refuge seekers, looking for their idea of a Shangri La. The latter had enjoyed the Kingdom's liberal attitude towards mind-altering substances and freely employed them for their explorations and escapes, particularly the ubiquitous hashish. Rather than jumpstarting Nepal into modern times, this first wave of visitors had served as a buffer and preserved its anachronistic and exotic nature, which made it easy to get lost in the time warp.

As we walked to our hotel from the bus station, the world as we knew it slowly faded into memory. There was even something unique in the scent of this place. I was not able to isolate or identify all the different aromas that we found ourselves immersed in, but, deep inside, they felt familiar and archaic. As soon as we moved away from the main roads where the smell of combustion engines adulterated this effect, we slipped through the veneer into a past life that smelled of cooking fires, animals, manure, straw, earth, old stones, and raw human habitation.

Heavy cobblestones made it difficult to walk. Small, crooked houses with low doors and tiny windows lined the alleys. Heavily loaded mountain people with leathered faces carried their wares to unseen markets. Groups of locals squatted at corners, cooking over open fires, chatting and laughing. Soiled children were playing and waving as we walked by. A little girl came out of an ancient looking stone house and squatted over the open sewage ditch along the side of the alley to defecate. Then she sat down on the cobblestones and rubbed herself clean on a few stubs of grass that grew there before running back into the house.

As we came closer to the legendary Kathmandu Guest House where we hoped to find accommodation, more and more Western faces started to appear. Trekking outfitters, travel offices, and coffee shops popped up, and the scent of fresh baked bread and pies enriched the olfactory landscape. Not surprisingly, a largely cannabis-based traveler culture had produced a most delicious supply of any kind of pie imaginable. We were tempted to put down our heavy backpacks in one of the coffee shops but wanted to secure our accommodation first. As we trekked on, we passed a small travel office that doubled as a used book store, and right in the center of the window, impossible to overlook, I found the last missing sequel of my roadmap, *The Second Ring of Power*, Carlos Castaneda's latest book to date.

This was perfect. Over the past three months since we left Sri Lanka I had read, re-read, and consulted his three previous books countless times, and their mood had penetrated me deeply. They had imbued our journey with magic and purpose, a priceless experience. But more, they had profoundly changed the way I related to the universe and to life itself. What had been a solitary struggle for getting the most out of life, not unlike a parasite tries to get the most out of its host, had gradually turned into a much more organic and integrated relationship with the universe. It was still somewhat haphazard and far from being a harmonious dance for most of the time, but the illusory wall of solitariness was crumbling, and I could hear the music. As a result, life acquired an interactive quality that had been unknown to me before. Occasionally it lost its fragmented nature for a moment, and all that was left was a singular process of infinite complexity where there were no questions, only answers, and a deep sense of gratitude.

Outside of these rare moments, however, it was impossible to resist the self serving mechanisms of my mind as it perpetuated its dream of specialness. Life had undoubtedly acquired a different quality, but my overriding motivation, throughout, had been and still was to become someone special, a man of knowledge and power, whatever I thought this to mean.

We bought the book, and at the Kathmandu Guest House we were fortunate to get a beautiful quiet room with a view of the gardens. We had four more weeks before our return flight to Europe, and as we checked into our room, we already knew that we would spend most of this time in Kathmandu. We were curious how long four weeks would feel while being trapped in a time warp.

The Katmandu Guest House had been a private mansion, owned by one of Nepal's ruling dynasties until it was converted into a hotel in 1967. As the first hotel in the area it became an integral part of Kathmandu's mystique. There was something incredibly benevolent and soothing in its energy. It catered to an eclectic mix of people, and I never met anybody who was not captivated by its charisma. There was nothing fancy about it, and despite the rather humble accommodations, its guest book is filled with names of famous people from around the world and of all walks of life.

For us, the unique energy of the hotel fulfilled a specific purpose. Arriving in Kathmandu on the roller coaster bus and immersing ourselves in the ancient imagery and scents of the town had produced an altered state. We had lost our bearings. This was very exciting and in part we wanted to maintain this openness and uncertainty. But in another part of our hearts we yearned to restore a sense of familiarity. We could have achieved this by staying in a Western style hotel or by subconsciously muting the sensory input that we perceived as alien and anachronistic. But, fortunately, we navigated to the Kathmandu Guest House, which was pleasant and reassuring enough without being too familiar. Here we were suspended in a beautiful limbo of openness, and not surprisingly we spent a good deal of time on its magical grounds.

The most powerful place of the hotel was a lush little courtyard, named Buddha Garden. It was lovingly landscaped and dominated by a life-sized statue of a sitting Buddha. This enchanted oasis allowed just enough of Kathmandu's raw, mysterious energy to waft in to keep us slipping out of the awareness of time and space—again and again.

∀ ∀ ∀

While traveling, it had become obvious that my wellbeing and awareness were strongly related to my physical surroundings. Particularly when choosing hotels and restaurants, I had learned that it is not enough to consider only rational parameters like price, quality, comfort, and convenience. I realized that each place has its own specific energetic quality that is often strong enough to significantly affect our lives.

Initially I found it cumbersome to second-guess every hotel room and every dining table, wondering if it felt right to my body. But over time these perceptions became more and more natural and fluid. The less I was concerned with why a place was right or wrong, the smoother was our navigation. Of course, places don't just feel right or wrong. Sometimes they turn out to be powerful amplifiers of whatever state we are in. Other times places that have a strong natural energy carry a special intent, like the purgatory of Varanasi, for example. In such an instance it would seem prudent to align our own intent with the intent of the place. In the case of Varanasi this would mean to think, breathe, and live the intent of purification while being there.

Navigating places is not a linear affair. It involves all our senses, including reason. But reason plays a much smaller role than we are usually comfortable with. Historically we used the arts of dowsing, geomancy, sacred geometry, and feng shui to optimize our relationship with the environment. Settlements, palaces, churches, temples, and ceremonial sites were never built in arbitrary locations. The longevity and power of cities, dynasties, and even religions are most certainly connected to the power of places and structures.

Many aspects of these particular energies are obvious and accessible to reason. If a place is perceived as extraordinarily beautiful, majestic, or ancient, it is naturally powerful. If millions of people pour their intent and worship into a pilgrimage site or shrine, it becomes increasingly more powerful. But the finer, more subtle and personal aspects of navigating these energies rely on bodily perception, instinct, and silent knowledge.

I was obviously on a spiritual journey, even if I would not have seen it this way at the time. My intent was to become a "man of knowledge," and in this regard Nepal provided auspicious background energy. Located between the highlands of Tibet and the Ganga Valley of Northern India, Nepal is a natural spiritual vortex, blending elements of Buddhism and Hinduism in unique and ancient ways. The kingdom is the birthplace of Gautama Buddha, and Kathmandu houses the largest and most sacred Shiva temple in Hinduism. Countless travelers have passed through this vortex on their journeys of awareness, spending time in ashrams and monasteries or exploring altered states of consciousness and alternative forms of life. Nepal is also home to eight of the ten highest mountains of the world, which afforded a myriad of trekkers and climbers the experience of a lifetime and spiritual epiphanies of a different kind.

The Kathmandu Guest House with its protective and nourishing energy seemed to embody and reflect all these elements without overwhelming us. It had a distinct and noticeable energy field. Everyone working there was uniformly relaxed and literally beamed with friendliness. Our room was perfect. We slept well and woke up refreshed and happy every day. We never got sick while eating in the hotel restaurant or café, which is close to a miracle in Kathmandu. Since the property had been the residence of a ruling dynasty, I am sure it was chosen and built by knowledgeable craftsmen, familiar with feng shui and the energies of the land.

But even within the walls of the compound we found subtle differences in energy. My favorite place was in the Buddha Garden, just across from the statue, in the shady grass under an old tree. I usually found a reclining garden chair, which I positioned so I could see the Buddha when I looked up from my book. That's were I spent most of my days whenever we were not engaged in the occasional time travel through the valley and beyond. The sensation I had while sitting on this specific spot was a sense of contentment, a feeling of peace, and of not wanting to get up. I could read for extended periods of time without getting tired, and my understanding of what I was reading seemed deeper and more profound.

Once my attention was on this direct relationship between places and bodily wellbeing, I could not help but noticing it wherever I went. It seems to be a basic sensation that only needs to be re-awakened and calibrated. I always found it extraordinarily useful throughout my life.

For example, several years later while I was looking to buy a house in Tucson, Arizona, I initially considered many different neighborhoods.

But before I even looked at individual properties, I decided to draw an energetic map of the whole town to narrow down my search. To accomplish this task I spent nearly a full day crisscrossing the town in my car and making marks on the map whenever my body noticed a positive or negative shift in wellbeing. It turned out that there was only a fairly small area where I felt really good, and it was not at all where most people had suggested that we buy a house. It was a conclusive scouting mission. While driving down a major street, even in parts of the town that looked quite uniform, I would suddenly feel a definite change in mood, often after driving over a small hill or across a wash. I did not give it much thought and just kept making marks. At the end of the day about six to eight square miles in the foothills of the Catalina Mountains emerged as the only area where I felt comfortable enough to buy a house and settle down. A few days later we found and bought a beautiful house. It happened to be the only one we looked at, and it proved to be a marvelous, powerful home.

⌄ ⌄ ⌄

Depending on one's predilection, a spiritual journey could be entirely internal and take place in a cave or a monastery, and most of these navigational considerations would be irrelevant. My own journey involved many years of extensive travels and countless different locations, and a correlation between places and awareness became strongly apparent. The confluence of energies and timing that happened for me at the Kathmandu Guest House made it a turning point in my life. While reading on my favorite spot in the Buddha Garden, the cumulative intent of the past few months was soon to catch up with me and transform my life for good in an unexpected way.

⌄ ⌄ ⌄

Meanwhile our surroundings and particularly the outlying areas of the valley kept pulling us into a different time and stretched our perception of reality. The ancient scents and medieval scenes we encountered on many of our excursions awakened a different aspect of myself that was unknown and yet strangely familiar.

One afternoon we were hiking through a rural area that was dotted with small farms and fields. A thin layer of smoke hung in the air, filtering the sunlight into a soft yellowish haze. The scene reminded me of the cover of a fairytale book. The smoke smelled of many different fires, rich scents of hay, earth, and animals. While passing a small farm dwelling that had been built from brown clay and ancient-looking wood, we noticed a large family resting in the shade on a flattened stack of hay. Looking closer we could see that all the members of the family were intently engaged in de-lousing each other's hair and cracking between their teeth whatever they found.

I was mesmerized. The raw simplicity and archaic poetry of the scene connected so strongly with me that it produced a cognitive dissonance and put my mind into state of suspension. Thoughts wanted to come into my head, but somehow they could not find an entrance.

⋎ ⋎ ⋎

A state of suspension characterized much of our stay in Kathmandu. On a basic level there was the uncertainty of our immediate future. After living two years on the Indian subcontinent, we would be flying to Europe, into uncharted territory, in just a few weeks. We did not have a plan other than to continue traveling as soon as possible, which meant that we had to materialize a considerable amount of money. We felt as if we were between lives, and the different quality of time in which we found ourselves immersed just emphasized this transitional feeling.

In this suspended state, all the events of the past few months had a chance to catch up and integrate with our lives. I realized that keeping my attention on death and impermanence had pulled the world much closer to me. There was a new quality of intensity and finality, but also of determination and purpose.

On one of our last days in Kathmandu I was sitting on my chair in the garden as usual. I was smoking a cigarette while reading about the attributes of a warrior. I read that a warrior, above anything else, has to cultivate his willpower.

I paused and put the book into my lap. "Willpower," I thought. "Do I have willpower?" I felt my eyes narrowing and my chin moving slightly forward. "Do I have willpower?" I held the question for while longer, squinting into the blue sky.

"Well," a voice came forward in my head, "this is easy to find out. You just have to stop smoking; then you know that you have willpower."

"No, no, no, no, wait, wait," another voice suddenly appeared. "This is too hard; let me start with something easier. . . ."

"What?" the first voice fell in. "Now you want to talk yourself out of it?"

"I am afraid," the second voice admitted.

The voice continued, "The stakes just went up. Now you have to stop smoking as well as stop drinking to find out if you have willpower."

I closed the book in a wave of panic, but it was too late. I was stuck. Either I had to stop smoking and drinking now, or I had to live with the fact that I had no willpower, and that the path of a warrior and becoming a man of knowledge was merely a daydream.

I was smoking more than a pack of cigarettes a day at the time and had gotten used to drinking beer and wine on a regular basis. Once I thought about it, I realized that there was hardly a day when I did not have at least two glasses of wine or a few beers for dinner, sometimes more. This never had occurred to me as something unusual. Many times I had tried to stop smoking though, and it never lasted longer than a few days.

I oscillated for a few moments. But there was no way out, and the time and place were perfect to make a decision.

I terminated my internal dialogue.

"Of course I have willpower," I decided. "I will stop smoking and drinking—effective immediately."

And then the most magical thing happened. I threw away my remaining cigarettes and I would neither smoke nor drink a drop of alcohol for many years to come. And even after I softened my stance eventually, I never succumbed to an addiction again. What surprised me the most was how easy it had been. I did not even feel so much as a craving, after I had made my decision.

My compulsiveness did not disappear, however, it just changed the way it expressed itself. I became an expert on mineral waters, obsessed with sobriety and with following my new path.

Anything seemed possible now.

Part II

TRIALS AND TRIBULATIONS

*Start close in, don't take the second step or the third,
start with the first thing close in, the step you don't
want to take ...*

DAVID WHYTE
Start Close In

The Hard Part

The world looked strangely unfamiliar as it flew by outside my train window. The trees were too lush and green, the gardens too beautifully manicured, and the houses and streets too new and clean to be real. The train itself appeared to produce neither sound nor vibrations and was traveling at an unbelievable speed. I was by myself and couldn't quite make sense of all this. After arriving in Frankfurt on our flight from Kathmandu, Mona went on to Hamburg to see her family and organize an art show with her paintings. I had taken the Inter City Express to Munich to visit my parents before leaving for France where I planned to work again for the next few months.

My face was glued to the window. I could not remember Germany looking so perfect. Perhaps I was still in a time warp. Or I had come out slightly ahead, and this was the future. I got up and walked around. The neighboring compartments were occupied by schoolchildren on a field trip, and their teacher was standing in the corridor, smoking a cigarette and looking out the window.

"Do you have any idea how beautiful it is here?" I blurted out the moment our eyes met. He looked at me as if I were crazy.

"Hm, yes, I guess so . . . " he mumbled slightly annoyed.

I immediately regretted my outburst and retreated to my compartment, embarrassed. I had never particularly liked Germany, or being German for that matter. As part of the postwar generation I had been thoroughly conditioned to be unpatriotic. Beyond that I had always perceived Germans as too opinionated, serious, materialistic, and obsessed with precision and cleanliness. I admired the Mediterranean way of life, the French laissez faire, the controlled chaos of the Italians, and the Spanish siesta culture.

But at that moment, something had neutralized my own opinionated German self. With my judgment suspended, I enjoyed the precision and cleanliness of this futuristic train ride to my heart's content. After two years of exotic rawness and traveling twelve thousand miles in Indian trains, gliding in soundless comfort through this immaculate landscape felt like heaven.

As I came closer to my hometown, however, heaven started to fade away and made room for a growing apprehension as my internal dialogue intensified.

"How does a warrior deal with his family?"

"Well, impeccably, I suppose, just like with everything else."

But I had no idea what this meant in practice. My apprehension came from the wave of pressure that I was anticipating, a pressure to conform to expectations. After living outside the mold for so long, I felt myself approaching a minefield of expectations.

I had just begun to live in a new paradigm, by a new set of beliefs. It entailed living in a direct relationship with intent, beckoning life for guidance rather than imposing my own ideas. Instead of engaging in strategic planning and establishing a career, my interest and attention were directed toward silent knowledge, intuition, signs, omens, synchronicities and other manifestations of spirit. I had developed a passion for unpredictability, for erasing my personal history, for stalking and gathering energy. There was no way I could share any of this with my family and friends without triggering a wave of resistance.

But, of course, I couldn't help myself; I ended up sharing anyway. As was to be expected, many waves of resistance and emotional battles ensued over the years. It is a delicate problem when you realize that your intent is no longer compatible with the intent of someone close to you.

"So, what are your plans now?" was one of the first questions my stepfather asked while we were still driving home from the train station. "You can't keep working as a tourist guide. These things don't look good on a resume," he continued.

"Leave him alone now!" my mother interceded. "He only just arrived."

"Great!" I thought, but I was too tired to argue at this point.

❧ ❧ ❧

Individual intent is a force that originates from our innermost beliefs. It is the force that creates our reality and shapes our life in a complex interplay with the intent of the people around us, with the collective human intent, and with universal intent. Individual intent is superficially related to wanting, but essentially these two impulses are quite distinct, and sometimes even opposed. For example, if, on a deep level, I am conditioned to believe that money corrupts my soul, I would most likely intend it away. At the same time, on the level of my mind, I might desire material success. This would most definitely result in a problem. In a manner of speaking, intent could be seen as the will of the heart and wanting as the will of the mind. Ideally they should be aligned.

Alignment is a key principle when it comes to the force of intent. Given that there is no conflict between the heart and the mind, the more aligned my intent is with the intent of the culture around me, the more it will manifest. Intuitively we know this, so we want everybody to believe what we believe. This, of course, results in even more problems. Conflicting intents are like opposing energy fields. The wave of resistance that formed in the room while I was sharing some of my new views with my parents was so strong as to be nearly tangible. It was as if the viscosity of the air had changed, creating a pressure on my midsection and throat. Even while my parents were still pretending to be interested in the intricacies of navigation, a battle of wills and intents had already begun. They were convinced that it was best for me to settle down, to start a family, and to pursue a career. This was their heartfelt belief. If their intent had been strong enough, it could have significantly affected my navigation. They did not believe in the validity of my new approach to life. Their intent was pulling on mine like a magnetic field. This pull manifested as a distraction, triggering occasional insecurity and self-doubts. It chipped away at my convictions and acted to undermine the focus and strength of my intent. Consequently I spent a lot of energy counteracting this pull instead of having all my available attention on the present moment where navigation takes place.

99

In my experience it is futile to try changing other people's convictions. If we want to eliminate the interference of someone's conflicting intent, it is much more effective to remove ourselves from this person's sphere of influence, or better still, to become less conspicuous, less accessible.

Often it was enough to just listen more and talk less. Ultimately, I learned that it was not necessary to align anybody's intent with mine. The only worthwhile strategy in order to get beyond the world of problems was to align my intent with universal intent. This, of course, is the art of navigation proper.

Interacting with my family and friends showed me how much and how little I had changed. It was so easy to fall back into old patterns, so easy to feel self-important, annoyed, insecure, or bored. Nobody was particularly interested in my story. I sensed a big force field trying to straighten me out and make me forget. As a result, I wanted to leave again, the sooner the better.

Fortunately though, my newfound sobriety was rock solid, and it made all the difference. Against the background of trying to become a "man of knowledge," having stopped smoking and drinking seemed rather mundane, but it was something concrete I could hold on to. Besides keeping me clear and strong, it kept my intent in place and started to act as a catalyst for a series of other changes. My eating habits improved. I made healthier choices and developed a sense for the energy of food. The superficial pleasure principle that had once ruled me completely was broken. My priorities had changed.

The fact that these changes came about as a result of simply asserting my will had been empowering. I was nearly afraid to think about willpower at this point. I did not want to jinx anything, nor did I want to talk myself into another challenge. But my intent regarding the next goal was probably already set. Immersing myself in Carlos Castaneda's world had created an immense longing for the American Southwest, Mexico, and the Sonoran Desert. I did not want to simply go traveling again; I wanted to leave Germany for good. The familiarity with everything, my personal history, and the expectations of my family, however well intentioned, all seemed to work together to drown out my new dream, which I could not bear.

At moments I was desperate. Navigating life had felt so much easier and more exciting while traveling. My initial fascination with Germany's aura of cleanliness, comfort, and convenience faded fast. I was fighting the gravity of the collective intent, and I was afraid of getting stuck. I did not know how to navigate in a stationary situation and how to properly apply the warrior's way to my relationship with my parents. Even more frustrating was the prospect of having to work, most likely for years, until we had enough money to leave again.

Reluctantly I realized that now I had to deal with "real life," as my father put it. In his view it meant settling down, earning a living, paying taxes, and starting to save for my retirement. For me it meant having to make the best out of every situation, following my path impeccably, and above all, learning to be patient. This was definitely the hard part of navigation: applying my new principles to dealing with the "real life" of family and work and being patient.

Patience had been one of the biggest challenges of my life. I used to be thoroughly convinced that more important and worthwhile events were usually in the future. From the school bell, to birthdays, Christmas, and vacations, there was always something that I could hardly wait for. Later it was getting a driver's license, turning eighteen, finishing college, traveling, getting married, getting divorced, quitting a job, traveling again, etc. When the event finally arrived that I had longed for so badly, there were always more events in the future that nurtured my impatience. Now I was even impatiently longing to become a man of knowledge. This was particularly bizarre, since a man of knowledge knows for a fact that life happens only in the space of *now*, and therefore it is the now where he directs all his attention. With all his attention in the now, impatience is impossible. So, in a way, I was impatiently waiting for the end of impatience.

Being continuously invested in the future diverted a lot of energy away from my actual life. This meant that I did not have the totality of my energy available to deal with the present in the most effective way, and consequently my life could not unfold optimally. Apart from this, my impatience continuously created stress and frustration.

Why then was I so incredibly impatient all my life?

I suspect that some of the groundwork for my unwillingness to endure the now was laid in infancy. When I was hungry or my diapers were full, I learned that all I had to do was to express my discomfort and my mother would take care of it. I probably just never grew up. Most of my life I kept expressing my discomfort whenever it arose, as if there were a cosmic mommy or daddy who would keep changing my diapers if I only

101

continued to complain. While my needs as an infant could actually be met, my diapers could be changed and my stomach filled, my emerging needs and desires while growing older could not. Like everybody else around me I started to live increasingly in my mind. It was just too tempting. Nobody taught me how to use my mind properly. Instead of employing it only to solve problems, I lost myself in the virtual reality of thoughts. Instead of pruning my mind into a controlled and efficient tool for computation and problem solving, I allowed my thought process to turn into an unstoppable, self-generating orgy of mental masturbation.

Of course it was often entertaining, but while my stomach could be filled, my mind, if left to its own devices, was a bottomless pit. It never stopped generating new needs and desires. It continuously created fictitious realities that seemed more attractive than the present moment. While sitting at a red light, my mind imagined that the light could be green already, and impatience resulted. While trying to learn a new skill, my mind imagined that I should already perform better, and frustration resulted. While working to earn money, my mind imagined that I could be lying in a hammock on a tropical beach, and unhappiness resulted.

Instead of seeing through this dysfunctional mechanism, my intent was mostly set on increasing my personal power so I could fulfill as many of my artificial needs as possible. Despite having learned that a warrior does not need anything, I had never claimed this knowledge, and I could not make the connection. For me, not needing anything inevitably led to not having anything, even though there is no necessary correlation between the two. Actually, if I don't need anything, I have everything.

Learning to be patient was definitely not an easy matter. The root of the word patient means "to suffer," "to endure," and this does not immediately sound like a virtue. Who wants to suffer? It sounds more heroic to refuse to suffer and to refuse to endure, which, of course, is being impatient. I am probably not alone in having occasionally seen an element of strength and defiance in my cultivation of impatience. For the longest time patience had only had a positive connotation for me on a superficial and rational level. Deep down it felt like suppressing a natural dynamic and intensity. I did not want to suffer and endure; if anything, I wanted to transcend suffering.

Eventually I realized that I had misunderstood the value of patience.

My instincts had been right insofar as patience is not in and by itself descriptive of a transcendental state. It is instead an exercise of intent. By forcing myself to be patient I was pretending to disengage from the future, which entailed intending an emphasis on the present. Now that I find myself increasingly involved with the here and now, patience gradually became an empty concept. I do not think of myself as being more patient now, or more willing to endure. I am just more present and there is nothing to wait for in the present. Everything is here. I am simply rallying my attention around what *is*—instead of what could be, should be, or possibly will be.

∨ ∨ ∨

Unfortunately in those days I was neither present nor patient with my parents, but they loved and supported me anyway. My visit was harmonious for the most part, and after a few days I left for France.

In a response to a greeting card from Sri Lanka, my former employer, the bicycle tour operator, had offered my old job back upon my return. This was a navigational input I gladly followed. It had been the perfect job. I was to bicycle again with groups of happy people along the Loire River and the coastline of Brittany. Food and lodging would be absolutely exquisite and free, which allowed me to save all my earnings.

A little over a week later I was cycling by myself ahead of the group, my arms crossed over my chest against the cool morning air. It promised to be another glorious day, the last one for this group. In the afternoon we would be arriving in Angers, and tonight I would welcome the next group for the trip back to Orleans. It had been a perfect tour. Everything went smoothly, without any surprises. We all met at the Cheval Blanche, a beautiful little country hotel in Orleans. As always I knew within minutes of the orientation meeting who would be the complainer, finding flaws and problems everywhere; who would be the most appreciative, giving the biggest tip at the end; who would be the most competitive, challenging me to a bicycle race; and who would be the group clown, compulsively trying to be funny at all times. The groups of fifteen to eighteen mostly German tourists were usually quite varied, but never failed to produce a predictable dynamic, with these four positions always being filled.

The weather had been outstanding and the picnics in enchanted forest clearings and mysterious castle ruins a huge success. We visited some of the most fascinating of the over three hundred castles along the Loire River and meditated in monasteries that were over a thousand years old. I even coaxed the group into a silent late night tour of the medieval quarters of Loches to "allow ourselves to be pulled back in time." The food had been divine and every one of the hotels a unique experience. During the day we rode our comfortable tour bikes through some of the most beautiful and romantic scenery imaginable. Everything had been perfect—except me.

In the privacy of my mind and on the phone with Mona it was actually I who had become the complainer, finding flaws and problems everywhere. I did my utmost to run a smooth operation and provide everyone with a great experience, but my heart was not involved at all. In the past I had merged with my groups usually on the first day and won their hearts with my enthusiasm and passion for all aspects of my job. Now I needed all my energy to hide my disdain with everyone's "un-warrior-like" behavior, particularly with their obsession with alcohol, as I saw it. It seemed so unenlightened the way everybody celebrated the champagne and oyster picnics and the wine tastings, the aperitifs, beers, wines, digestives, and Armagnacs that accompanied the hours of dining every night. Some even didn't know any better than to smoke a cigarette between dinner courses or a big cigar with their Armagnac at the end. I seemed to have completely forgotten how much I had enjoyed all this myself in the past while I kept stubbornly nursing my mineral waters and my superficial sobriety. I felt ill prepared for this challenge. Oscillating between righteousness and temptations, I badly lacked wisdom.

∀   ∀   ∀

The cool morning air was refreshing. I often rode with my hands off the handlebars, and sometimes my mind was still dozing with my eyes half closed while my body seemed to merge with the bicycle, moving us along just fine. We were riding on a smoothly paved embankment with the river to our right and a row of willow trees to our left. The air was soft, saturated with the familiar scent of the slow-flowing water and the pungent fragrance of willows. The Loire River had been left to meander her own course through the lush and fertile valley, creating many picturesque islands. Besides passing the occasional fisherman, we did not encounter anyone this morning as the sun slowly burned off the last few patches of mist that were lingering in the shade. As confused as I now was with the social aspects of my job, I was enchanted with the natural beauty it allowed me to enjoy. The light changed markedly every day, becoming richer and brighter the closer we came to the Atlantic Ocean. When the sun finally broke clear from the treetops, I felt like I was breathing champagne, and a shiver of gratitude ran down my spine. There was a reason why over three hundred castles had been built along this river, and I was incredibly fortunate to be here.

"Why can't I just let go of myself and take pleasure from simply being here?" I wondered.

I slowed down, letting myself fall back into the group. Everyone seemed to be smiling this morning.

Of course I managed to complete and, to a large extent, enjoy all the tours I had committed to. But it had become blatantly obvious that something fundamental had changed. It was as if I had lost my innocence, or rather, come to the end of my grace period. My life had acquired a purpose and I could not help assessing everything I did in relation to this purpose. Some part of me was always monitoring how well I was doing on the path of the warrior, and another part was furiously defiant, constantly trying to bail out. As a totality I had been thrown into a limbo where I was to stay for many years to come. I was more disconnected from the social order than ever, unable to subscribe anymore to its goals and values. On the other hand, I felt light-years away from being an impeccable warrior, let alone a man of knowledge. What I saw in the mirror in those days, for the most part, was a confused and lonely pretender with dreams of being different and special. But I usually decided not to dwell too much on this part of my reflection and made sure my hair looked good instead. I used to have curly hair with the annoying tendency to get frizzy with humidity. As a result I must have spent hundreds of hours of my life dealing with it until I finally shaved it off in a rare flash of wisdom fifteen years later.

⌄ ⌄ ⌄

Mona had been working tirelessly and succeeded in organizing an art show with her work. The opening night was packed with many of her former colleagues and business partners. She received lots of praise and even a decent write-up in the local paper, but being an unknown and self-taught artist, she found it hard to find buyers for her paintings. When the show ended two weeks later she had sold one solitary piece and was utterly disappointed.

Without really having too many options, we decided to defy our frustrations, move to Munich, and find some "real work." I had been attending business school after all, and following a few explorative job interviews, I took a job as a consultant for a financial services and brokerage firm.

We settled in and started to "make" money. It was pretty straightforward. I called my target clientèle, made appointments, analyzed their "needs," suggested "solutions," and "sealed the deals." It went well, so well actually that I brought Mona into the business a few months later, and we sealed even more deals. Our navigational playing field was rather constrained. We tried to stay open to the input of intent, but our senses were dulled by the strain and monotony of our work. We did not engage much in social interaction. Mona was a natural loner, and since we were set on leaving again as soon as possible, I was no more motivated than Mona to connect with people on a deep enough level to make friends. Together with Yana, our newly adopted German Shepherd puppy, we spent most of our free time in nature.

I kept reading and re-reading all of Carlos Castaneda's books, relentlessly nourishing my unbending intent to gather enough personal power to find that elusive doorway into total freedom. Night after night, on my late walks with Yana through Munich's extensive parks, I often stood silently gazing into the darkness, beckoning and intending for magic to happen, just to relax into a smile at the sight of Yana, sitting patiently in front of me, her head tilted to the side, wondering.

My new line of work provided many great opportunities to hone my discipline, impeccability, and integrity. Perhaps the most challenging aspect was to deal appropriately with a significant gray area that became obvious soon. As a broker I was paid in commissions, and often the product that paid the highest commission was not the one that was in the client's best interest. I had to make significant ethical decisions on a daily basis. Fortunately, as a warrior, I had only one choice. I could not possibly cut corners. I had to aim for uncompromising integrity in every single case. This kept my commissions below the average for a little while, but my clients honored my approach and before long a growing referral base made our business take off.

After about eighteen months of intensive work we had saved our target amount of fifty thousand Deutschmarks. We hoped this would be enough fuel to propel us beyond Germany's gravitational field. As we were getting closer, I bought an old Mercedes delivery truck and began converting it into a motor home. This turned out to be great fun and distracted me from the tediousness of "deal making." I worked nearly every evening until late at night and all through the weekends for about three months. Since we were planning to travel through Central America, which we considered dangerous, our motor home ended up looking more like an armored vehicle than something meant for recreation. It had small barred windows, a detachable windshield screen, a full size roof rack, various secret compartments, padlocks everywhere, and an elaborate alarm system. Perhaps I had taken the warrior's way a little too far in this regard. Every time we wanted to test the "tank," as we lovingly called it, by camping in the Bavarian "wilderness" over the weekend, we got chased away by farmers, park rangers, or other concerned property owners. Unfortunately there wasn't any wilderness left in Germany.

At last, we gleefully quit our job, sold our few belongings, and erased all other traces we had left during the past two years. We were determined to embark on a warrior's pilgrimage, a one-way journey into adventure, magic, and transformation.

Our regular car was sold already and I was driving the "tank" all around Munich during the last few weeks before leaving for the port city of Bremen from where it was to be shipped to the U.S. On literally one of the last days, I drove down Leopoldstrasse, Munich's main boulevard, when I noticed a large poster in the English bookstore near the university. It announced the publication of Carlos Castaneda's latest book, *The Eagle's Gift*.

This was a gift indeed.

The hard part seemed over.

Hunting the Spirit

Yana was growling when she heard the pick-up truck approaching. We had not seen anybody for several weeks and became alarmed. With the help of forest service maps we had found a remote and beautiful campsite deep inside the Prescott National Forest in Central Arizona. It had been hard to get to, but the "tank" had braved all the rough patches and creek crossings of the abandoned mining road that we had followed for the last twenty miles. Only the doors and sides were slightly scratched from working our way through a thicket of dry bushes for about hundred yards after we had left the road. The flat, grassy area beside the creek where we had set up camp must have been a gold prospector's homestead a long time ago. There still were foundations, rusty metal pipes, dredging equipment, and, to our delight, a few old and gnarly apple trees that were bearing fruit.

The pick-up truck stopped. Mona and I looked at each other concerned.

"I don't like this," I said.

Yana got up and started to bark "Quiet, Yana!" I cut her off.

Whenever we had one of these remote encounters, we felt utterly vulnerable. Everybody was carrying guns, except us; and since we were non-residents, we could not really do much about it, legally at least. There seemed to be only one person in the pick-up truck that was now backing up through the bushes, aiming for another small clearing next to the creek about eighty yards downstream from us. After a while the engine was shut off, and we could hear a car door being slammed shut.

"I hope he is not planning to camp there," I muttered.

"He probably is." Mona shook her head in dismay.

"I need to see who it is," I said. "Come Yana, let's check him out. Try to look menacing!"

Always happy to go for a walk, Yana jumped up, grabbed a big piece of branch, and ran ahead.

"Menacing I said, you silly dog."

All she could think of was finding a new victim whom she could coerce into throwing sticks for her.

I put on my friendliest face and greeted the newcomer.

"Hi there, how are you doing; I'm Paul, nice to meet you. This is a great spot here isn't it?"

Yana dropped her stick in front of his feet.

"Howdy," he just shrugged, barely looking at me. He seemed to be equally annoyed to find us here, but he looked civilized enough to disperse some of my concerns.

I kept chatting on until he slowly warmed up and we both relaxed. He was indeed going to set up camp, and I decided to stick around a little bit to get to know him. Mona had joined us, bringing a cup of coffee as a welcoming token for John, as he gave his name. He had Native American features, and we learned that he was half Cherokee, which we found fascinating.

John and I became good friends over the next few weeks. It turned out that he was actually a fugitive of sorts. He said his wife had cheated on him, left him, and was now suing him for alimony. As a result he had split and was living in the woods, supporting himself off the land. He collected and sold firewood for gas money and found nearly all his food in the wild, fishing, hunting, and gathering plants. I had no reason to doubt his story. He seemed to be a nice guy, teaching me an enormous amount of practical knowledge. In the immediate vicinity of our campsite he was able to find watercress, dandelion greens, wild onions, raspberry leaves, and a variety of other edible plants and berries. He dug up roots, peeled and cooked young shoots from various bushes, and even made a kind of pasta from the sliced inner bark of a willow tree. There were no fish in our little creek, so he used a bow and arrow to hunt squirrels for meat. His squirrel stew was delicious. The meat was tender and tasted like chicken.

During the day we usually stayed to ourselves. John was hiking and busy providing for himself. Mona had begun crocheting colorfully ornamented purses and bags, or she was roaming the valley with Yana, collecting berries and greens. I had found a small cave halfway up a canyon where I spent most of my days recapitulating.

Recapitulation is a powerful technique a warrior uses to redeploy his energy to aid his navigation. It is a liberating and empowering exercise, greatly enhancing a navigator's awareness. Castaneda had put a particular emphasis on recapitulation, and I had been keen to get started. It entailed first making a list of all the people I ever met and interacted with. Starting at the present, I went all the way back to my earliest memories and came up with twenty-two handwritten pages of names. I had done this already during the trip across the country from New York to Arizona, but had waited to do the actual recapitulation until my navigation led me to a place that was conducive to the task. The little cave felt ideal, and after creating a comfortable sitting spot, I began.

Starting with the name on the top of the list, I made myself remember the most recent encounter with that person in as much detail as possible. Then while inhaling in a fanning motion from left to right, I attempted to recover all the energy and emotions I had invested in the encounter, and while exhaling from right to left, I ejected all the energy and emotions that were projected into me at the time. I continued until the remembered scene was completely free of charge.

To get a head start in this exercise of energetic redeployment, Castaneda suggested starting with all our sexual relationships, which hold the most energy. Skipping Mona because I did not want to detach from her, I went to work. It was an amazing experience. After nearly six weeks of spending at least four hours per day in the cave, I felt like a changed person. With practice, the recollections got more and more vivid and nearly attained the reality of lucid dreams. I ended up re-living scores of relationships with unbelievable intensity. The recapitulation of sexual encounters was often so realistic, complete with tactile and olfactory sensations and arousal, that I kept feeling guilty of having betrayed Mona when I came back from the cave.

Sometimes I was reluctant to let go of the memory. Exhaling all the emotions that Loretta, my first big love, had left in me and inhaling and reclaiming all that I had projected into her was painful. It felt more dramatic and irreversible than when we burned all our love letters together in a solemn ceremony after our relationship had ended. After recapitulating her, all emotions were gone. I had a hard time even holding on to her mental image. It seemed irrelevant. All my memories of her were still intact, of course, but they had been neutralized. Many years later, my second wife Victoria accidentally recapitulated me while we were still together. She did not know at the time that we were to skip the people we want to stay intimately involved with. As a result, our relationship was irreparably compromised and began to transform.

Besides redeploying and clearing energy, recapitulating also affords precious insights into our behavioral patterns. I refrained from consciously analyzing my recollections, but it was unavoidable to see the predictability and repetitiveness of all my social maneuvers. To see again and again how most of my behavior was driven by insecurity and fear of loneliness was a humbling experience.

❦ ❦ ❦

"I think I've eaten enough squirrels," John said one evening while we were sitting around his campfire.

"We still have some canned meat if you like," I offered.

"No thanks," he grinned, "there is no spirit in canned meat. I have seen plenty of deer tracks up the creek. Tomorrow morning I'll see if I can find a deer for us. With all of us eating, nothing will go to waste. If you want, you can come along, Paul."

I was excited. Going deer hunting with bow and arrow in Arizona with the son of a Cherokee Indian was a dream come true for me. Don Juan had taken Carlos on countless hunting trips while teaching him the warrior's way, and I couldn't help drawing parallels and feeling absolutely magical about this adventure.

There were quite a few deer in the area. Just the other day, a large buck had passed by my cave. I had been fascinated with these beautiful animals all my life. Growing up at the edge of a large forest, I spent a significant part of my childhood sitting in tree houses and observing life in the forest. Deer had always embodied the spirit of alertness and presence for me. In the forests of my childhood, the deer, with their silent intensity embodied the awareness of nature like no other being.

We left at dawn and quietly hiked up one of the canyons. John was carefully examining tracks and droppings along the way. At some point we sat down in the underbrush beside the trail and just waited motionless for at least an hour. Nothing happened and John called off the hunt for the day. The next morning we went again, following another trail.

"Over there," John whispered, pointing out two does that were leisurely grazing on the slope about three hundred yards away. "The smaller one is the right size," he continued. "Let's see if we can get close enough."

We were downwind from the does, but there wasn't enough cover, and eventually they spotted us and took off. We went every morning for over a week but never came close enough to a deer that John deemed to be the right size. He was conscientious and didn't want to waste meat or risk a shot that wouldn't kill instantly. I wasn't overly anxious for John to kill one of these magnificent creatures anyway. I loved the hunting experience, the patient stalking, the motionless waits, and crawling soundlessly over the rocky ground, inching our way closer to our prey. It felt so primordial, one hundred percent natural and fulfilling.

"Tomorrow I am going to take the rifle," John decided after a dinner of canned beef and beans that Mona had prepared for us after an unsuccessful evening hunt.

"Aren't you afraid somebody might hear the shots?" I asked, knowing that hunting season was not for another week.

"Well, I think we'll just have to take the risk," he shrugged.

We left at dawn again, hiking upstream along the creek. The ground was soft and moist, and we did not make a sound. We had walked barely half a mile when we turned around a bend and looked right into the eyes of a small doe. It just stood there on the trail, motionless, perhaps a hundred feet in front of us. John just nodded, lifted his rifle, aimed, and shot the doe right between the eyes. It shivered nearly imperceptibly and dropped straight to the ground.

John ran towards the animal and with a few quick moves he slit the throat and cut open the chest cavity, removing the heart. Holding the heart in his left hand he cut off the tip and offered it to me with his knife.

"Eat!" he just said. His eyes were glowing with pride and authority. I didn't feel I had a choice and took the tip of the heart from his knife and

113

ate it, raw and warm, literally seconds after it had stopped beating. John sliced off another piece for himself, put it into his mouth and chewed it slowly with his eyes closed.

"This is the way we honor the deer and take on its spirit," he explained. "It has to happen quickly."

Then he proceeded to gut the animal, and we buried the entrails a few yards away behind some bushes. John was moving fast now, seemingly concerned about the noise of the gunshot. We carried the carcass to a spot where the creek was deep enough so we could clean it out. When we were done, we brought it to a shady spot under a rocky ledge and hid it under a bush, covering it with branches.

"We'll come back in the evening to get it, when it is dark." John said, slightly nervous now. I didn't know at the time, but poaching is considered a serious crime, and I couldn't blame him anyway for not wanting to take any risks, particularly in his situation. We cleaned up as well as we could and started on our way back to camp.

Barely two hundred yards down the trail we ran into a group of three men who were scouting for deer tracks in preparation for hunting season. This was an incredibly unfortunate coincidence. We had not seen anybody for weeks. They had met Mona at the campsite and were friendly. We exchanged a few words and moved on. John was frantic now.

"They are going to find the deer, for sure," he said. "Damn it, they are hunters. They have their eyes on the ground. No matter how good we erased our footsteps and all the other traces. They'll find it."

He was basically running now and I tagged along, not knowing what to think. The moment we reached camp, John packed up, and half an hour later he was gone.

"What do you think we should do?" I asked Mona after I had filled her in.

"I don't think we have to leave," she answered. "You didn't do anything wrong, you don't even own a gun."

We decided to sit it out. Besides, we did not want to let the deer go to waste. That would seem like a terrible shame. I still felt the taste of its heart on my tongue. John had gotten me frightened though, and all day long we were nervously expecting the game warden to show up. I buried the shoes I had worn so I could not be connected to the "crime scene," in case there were still tracks we had overlooked. The three hunters came back after a few hours and left without giving us a clue. Nightfall came and went, and our concern shifted to what to do with the deer.

The next morning I went for a long walk along the creek with Yana, and when we came close to where the deer was hidden, I quietly gave her the command to "search the rabbit, Yana, where is the rabbit?" something she remembered well from our evenings in the parks of Munich. She immediately began sniffing and searching around, and within seconds she had found the deer carcass. I loudly pretended to be surprised at her find, in case a game warden had been staking out the area, but nothing happened. After having established my accidentally finding the carcass, I came back later with a knife and bags to skin and butcher the deer.

In the following days we fried, cooked, canned, smoked, and dried all the meat we could, and needless to say, for a long time to come, we did not have much of a craving for venison.

Meanwhile the nights were getting quite cold, and about two weeks later, when I had finished recapitulating my sexual relationships, we felt ready to leave for Mexico.

I had tasted the spirit and was hungry for more.

The Eagle and the Serpent

"Have you ever heard of an anthropologist named Carlos Castaneda? He wrote a few books about a Yaqui named Juan Matus?" I asked with apprehension.

Anselmo Valencia did not try to hide his annoyance. "Yes I've heard of him," he said angrily. "Someone gave me a book once. It is all nonsense. How can he write about the Yaqui? He doesn't know anything. He should have come to me. There are many Juan Matuses but no one knows about Carlos Castaneda. Many people already asked me that." Anselmo Valencia was the spiritual leader of the Pascua Yaqui Tribe west of Tucson. We had decided to pay him a visit while we were on the reservation.

I tried to appease him. "I am sorry. We are visiting from Germany, and the Yaqui have become quite famous over there because of these books."

"Germany, hmm," his face lit up. "Well, something good has come from all this," he said with a mischievous glint in his eyes. "Because of these books, suddenly everybody knew about the Yaqui, and Congress formally recognized our tribe in 1978. Without this Castaneda fellow this would not have happened. Maybe I should look him up and thank him, ha ha," he chuckled.

I wasn't really surprised by his reaction. Juan Matus had most likely not been don Juan's real name, and perhaps he hadn't even been a Yaqui. But while camping for a few days in the Saguaro National Monument, west of Tucson, I couldn't resist visiting the nearby Yaqui reservation. In my world at the time, I was in "holy land" now. Castaneda's books had become my bible for all practical purposes, my roadmap to salvation. Southern Arizona, the Sonoran Desert, and Mexico were magical places for me, oozing the spirit of don Juan. It was amazing, how strongly my intent affected my experience of reality. Just sleeping on the roof rack of our truck, surrounded by the towering Saguaro cacti and bathed in the starlight of the high desert was nearly enough to stop my world.

"This is where Carlos met don Juan," I told Mona while we drove by the Greyhound bus depot in Nogales next to the Mexican border. Retrospectively, my focus on the personal aspects of the Nagual's world seems naïve, but it also kept feeding my enthusiasm and allowed me to experience life as an ongoing treasure hunt.

I was excited to finally cross into Mexico. We had neither a particular itinerary, nor any concrete expectations. I just wanted to be as alert as possible and trust the spirit to guide me. Subconsciously, of course, I was intending to find a powerful sorcery teacher like don Juan.

An oversize Mexican flag was flapping in the afternoon breeze. At its center it depicted a fierce Eagle, perching on a cactus and clutching a serpent with its talon and beak. According to legend, the Aztec people had been commanded by their god Huitzilopochtli to build their capital at the precise spot where they would find an eagle with a serpent on top of a Nopal cactus. After two hundred years of wandering they saw this mythical eagle on a little island in a marshy lake that is now the *zócalo*, or main plaza, of Mexico City.

"Alemanes, Germans, *hola*, welcome in Mexico—nice Mercedes!" The Mexican customs officer examined our truck with visible appreciation. "Have a nice trip! *Buen viaje!*" He sent us off with a big smile.

I instantly fell in love with Mexico.

Even though the USA had felt somewhat lighter and definitely more open than Germany, crossing into Mexico had changed the music again in a good way. Near the border it still felt dense and somewhat aggressive, but the further we ventured into the interior, the more earthy, genuine, passionate, and powerful the energy became. Fortunately my Spanish was quite good, and with practice it quickly transformed into Mexican, enriched with plenty of colloquialisms that I picked up from truck drivers we met along the road. There were some idiosyncrasies that required adjustment, of course. Like the gas station attendant that claimed to have put five gallons more diesel into our tank than it holds. I just protested with a few hearty Mexican curse words and he apologized, and we all had a good laugh. Things like this just kept us on our toes, but they never spoiled our overall experience.

Most of the time we did not follow the tourist trail. We were on a different quest, and whenever it felt appropriate, I mentioned our interest in meeting *brujos* and *curanderos*, sorcerers and healers. This met with an interesting variety of reactions.

Some people just matter of factly gave us directions to "don Fernando" or "dona Maria" who had mysteriously healed their aunt from possession by the devil, or simply from backache.

Others just laughed: "Brujos? You believe in sorcerers? They are all con artists. They will just take your money."

Some were more practical: "Oh, you are lucky that you asked me. I know the most powerful sorcerer in the area. How much will you pay me if I bring you to him?"

Some got alarmed and nearly angry: "Brujos!" they said, hurriedly making the cross. "Holy mother of God, beloved Virgin of Guadalupe. What do you want with brujos? They work for the devil."

Most healers and brujos we ended up meeting did not bear any resemblance to the mental image I had of don Juan and his cohorts. More likely we found a toothless old man, surrounded by pictures and carvings of saints, crucifixes, and a variety of other Christian paraphernalia, thoroughly confused by our interest. Or equally likely, we were brought to an overweight and bad-smelling old woman with greedy eyes who wanted to sell us potions, herbs, or power crystals. Whenever we could establish a reasonable conversation with someone, I asked about Naguals, Toltecs, shape-shifting, or lucid dreaming, but usually I drew a blank on all accounts. Some turned unfriendly and even menacing upon my inquiries, and we left in a hurry.

A few encounters were quite remarkable though. Once, while we were traveling in the mountains of Michoacán we went to see Alejandro Montero who had been described to us as a powerful and knowledgeable curandero. He looked powerful indeed, a picture book sorcerer with piercing black eyes. When we arrived at his house, he stood by his garden door as if expecting us. He was polite and did not seem surprised by any of my questions. However, he kept repeating that, unfortunately, he cannot help us with our research, as he put it. He did not invite us into his house. Our whole meeting took place on the road by his garden door. At some point he asked us to please wait a moment and he went inside the house. When he returned, he was carrying a small birdcage with a large green parrot, which he wanted to sell to us. We were surprised and declined politely. Then Mona took out her camera and asked if she could a take picture of him with the parrot. Instead of answering he just shrugged, which we understood to mean that he didn't mind. Mona tried to push the camera button several times, but the shutter did not release. The first time she tried, I noticed a flicker in Alejandro's eyes, but he did not move or say anything. We all seemed frozen for a moment, and the mood became uncomfortable.

Without another word Alejandro turned around and disappeared into the house. We waited a few minutes but he did not return. Puzzled we got back into our truck. For a moment I was afraid that the engine wouldn't start, but it worked all right.

"What is wrong with the camera?" I asked as we were driving away.

"I don't know," Mona replied. "It was working fine this morning." She shrugged, aimed the camera at me, and pushed the button again. This time the shutter released without a problem.

"Wow!" we both said.

"This guy just stopped it." Mona added.

"He did it with his eyes. I could see it. Wow! He just stopped our camera with his eyes." I was in awe.

❦ ❦ ❦

While we stayed on a campground on the outskirts of Guadalajara, Mona came down with a bad stomach flu. I went to consult some herbalists at the central market and brought back a big bag of herbs, which I made into a tea that made her feel better. While she was recovering, I went back to the market several more times and became friendly with Benito, the Zapotec Indian who had sold me the herbs. We talked about many things, and of course, I asked him if he knew a bona fide sorcerer who would be willing to talk with me. He was evasive at first, but on my third visit he unexpectedly brought up the topic by himself:

"There is a powerful man you might be interested to meet," he said. "Nobody knows much about him. Most of the time he is in the mountains gathering plants. His name is Francisco Flores. His family lives here in town. I can bring you there if you like. Perhaps you are lucky and he is home."

"This is great." I was intrigued. "When do you think we could go?" I asked

"Actually," Benito hesitated for a moment, "it would be better to go see him in the daytime, and I cannot leave now. But if you want I can write down his address and you can take a taxi. It is not far from here." He seemed somewhat relieved by the idea of not coming along.

About twenty minutes later a taxi delivered me to the address that Benito had written on the paper. It was an old atrium-style townhouse with no street windows and a massive wooden door opening onto a cobblestone plaza. The sun was hot and the plaza deserted. Not even a dog was in sight. I stood in front of the door for a quite a while before I found the courage to ring the bell which sounded deep inside the house. It took a long time before I heard footsteps approaching.

The door opened slowly and a tall, exotic woman appeared from the dark background. She was perhaps in her mid forties, and her strong Indian features softened into a surprised smile when she saw me.

"Good afternoon," she greeted me in a deep and friendly voice. "What brings you here?"

There were a few steps leading to the door so I had to look up to her. "Good afternoon," I said. "I came here to see don Francisco Flores."

"Francisco?" she laughed, "Francisco will not be back for another week. But come in, come in by all means. You must tell us what you want from Francisco."

At this moment two gorgeous young women emerged from the dark hallway, flanking her. They were obviously sisters, both tall and strikingly beautiful. All three of them were smiling at me now, showing their dazzling white teeth, gesturing me to come in.

"Come in," they kept repeating, "Come in and have a cup of tea with us," they laughed, obviously aware of my increasing emotional turmoil. These women were unbelievably alluring, yet I could not move an inch. I felt painfully suspended, as if I were caught in a wicked little fairytale.

"Oh, oh no, thank you," I finally stuttered, blushing in embarrassment, "I'll come back another time then."

I started to back up towards the plaza, unable to take my eyes off the three women. They were still gesturing me to come in, alternately faking disappointment and smiling enticingly. There was something absolutely breathtaking about them, in the true sense of the word. The thought of following these women through the dark hallway into the depth of the house made me gasp for air. I was terrified, and I never dared to go back. But in another part of my brain I kept forever wondering what would have awaited me at the other end of the hallway.

Mona seemed glad that I didn't have tea with the "sirens of Guadalajara" as I had fondly filed them in my memory. I, on the other hand, regretted it, of course, but I began to suspect that I wasn't quite ready for real sorcery yet—not by a long shot actually. Any good-looking witch could just turn me into a frog at the drop of a hat. I was absolutely defenseless. I didn't need to see Francisco Flores. His daughters had done enough sorcery for me. They had exposed me as the coward that I really was.

What had made me run for the hills was my awareness that I was hopelessly susceptible to the beauty and sensuality of these women. But what I did not know at the time was that this susceptibility was not really my biggest weakness. I was a coward because I did not dare to own and accept this vulnerability. Courage in this encounter would not have meant to trust myself to stay in control in the witches' house. It would have been more courageous to give up control, to accept my vulnerability, to accept looking like a fool and to be turned into a frog, in a manner of speaking.

My instincts had not perceived any bodily danger. The sirens had felt entirely benevolent. They had only posed a threat to my need to be in control. My best guess is that at the other end of the hallway had waited a unique opportunity to let go of all that, to stop pretending and to just have tea with the witches, being entirely at their mercy. But this was not an option for my ego at the time, so it ran for the hills, dragging me along.

▿ ▿ ▿

Even though we knew that *A Journey to Ixtlan* had been a metaphor, we could not help but making it a part of our treasure hunt. There were three different Ixtlans in Mexico, as far as we knew, and we were determined to visit all of them. Perhaps something magical would happen if we found the right one.

Ixtlan del Rio was the first on our list and hard to miss. It is located between Tepic and Guadalajara. Federal Highway 15, Mexico's main north-south highway, passes right through the middle of town. It turned out to be a hot, dusty, and noisy place that did not tickle my imagination at all. I wanted to leave right away. Instead, we forced ourselves to cruise around town for a while and even decided to have lunch in a dubious-looking restaurant at the main plaza.

The food was actually quite good and the waiter friendly and talkative. When he learned that we had come all the way from Germany, he felt compelled to fill us in on all the tourist attractions in the area. It turned out that besides a beautiful old church and a few thermal springs, there was a temple from the Toltec culture, dedicated to Quetzalcoatl, the feathered serpent. The temple was regarded as the most significant archaeological site in northwestern Mexico.

I was instantly intrigued. Quetzalcoatl was arguably Mesoamerica's most important deity. He was the Aztec creator god and had been given many attributes by different cultures through the ages. The plumed serpent was the patron god of priesthood, of learning and knowledge, the god of the morning star and a symbol of death and resurrection. Incidentally, the final chapter of *The Eagle's Gift* was entitled "The Plumed Serpent." In its conclusion Castaneda describes his last encounter with don Juan and his warrior party before they all vanished into total awareness. The book ends with Castaneda's recollection of this monumental event:

"I saw don Juan taking the lead. And then there was only a line of exquisite lights in the sky. Something like a wind seemed to make the cluster of lights contract and wriggle. There was a massive glow on one end of the line of lights where don Juan was. I thought of the plumed serpent of the Toltec legend. And then the lights were gone."

❧ ❧ ❧

We were the only visitors at the temple site that afternoon. After roaming around the ruins for some time we sat silently in the shade of a large stone column. There was hardly a sound, and the rocks I was

123

leaning on still radiated the heat of the sun. I was wondering about all the battles and rituals they had witnessed for more than two thousand years. And I was wondering about the feathered serpent.

In most mythologies the serpent represents the earthly aspect of nature. Feathers on the other hand are symbols of the air, of heaven and spirit. As such, the feathered serpent of Mesoamerica essentially symbolizes the same concept as yin and yang in Asian philosophy. It expresses the two fundamental aspects that define human experience, earth and heaven, matter and mind, being and thinking.

A well-known example, illustrating this duality, is found in Genesis, the often misunderstood Judeo-Christian creation myth. Here, as well, the serpent represents nature, or more specifically, the evolutionary force of nature. As symbolized by the analogy in which the serpent tricks man into "eating from the tree of knowledge," natural evolution coaxes mankind into developing thinking and the resulting self-awareness. The latter is exemplified by Adam and Eve's perception of their own nakedness. As a result of being able to think and differentiate between good and bad, and of being self aware, the blissful experience of oneness with everything, or paradise, was forgotten.

This evolutionary adventure of thinking obviously became so central and paramount to human experience that the notion of universal connectedness was all but lost. All that was left was a deep and insatiable longing for mankind's timeless home base of oneness. No matter what the thinking mind conceives, this longing never seems to diminish. No matter how much wealth and power we accumulate, it can never make up for what we lost. In our fascination with the flight of thought, we became all feathers, creatures of the mind.

But the serpent never left. It speaks through our longing and guides us through our mythologies. Now that we know the power of feathers, we might as well remember our serpent body, which is the undifferentiated life that we are at our essence. We might be curious to see what happens if we remember that we are life itself that has grown the wings of consciousness. What else are gods good for if not to remind us of our true nature. In this light, Quetzalcoatl, the feathered serpent, was definitely inspiring.

▽   ▽   ▽

The sun was slowly moving down the western sky, and as the shadows were getting longer, the silence and serenity of the temple site grew more pronounced. I felt comfortable, not inclined to leave this magical place any time soon.

"Do you think that the eagle and the snake on the Mexican flag have anything to do with Quetzalcoatl?" Mona broke the silence.

"Hm, that is an interesting idea." I wondered. "Given that there are no flying snakes in the real world, I guess an eagle that is holding a snake is as close to a feathered serpent as you can get. Yes, I think you are right," I continued excited, "The omen that the Aztecs were looking for was most likely a symbol of Quetzalcoatl. And now the emblem of the Mexican flag looks like an eagle devouring a snake, which is much more in line with the deluded mentality of the Christian conquerors. For them snakes had always been a problem. Fascinating!"

The mental image of the fierce eagle on the Mexican flag made me think again of Castaneda's latest book, *The Eagle's Gift.* Its title refers to the rule of the Nagual, which is a set of core beliefs in don Juan's world. The most fundamental of these core beliefs states that the source and final destination of human awareness is a force resembling an eagle of infinite proportions. An eagle of infinite proportions and particularly its fierce and intensely conscious eyes would make the perfect archetype for universal awareness. This "Eagle" bestows awareness at birth, governs the destiny of individual awareness, and consumes awareness at death. However, in order to perpetuate awareness the Eagle has created an opening and granted each living being the power to go through this opening, keeping the flame of awareness. This opening and the power to go through is the Eagle's gift. The rule goes on to say that, "for the purpose of guiding living things to that opening, the Eagle has created the Nagual."

Perhaps the shortest formula of what it takes to make use of the Eagle's gift is found in an incantation that was given to Castaneda by one of don Juan's cohorts. The incantation was meant to provide him with strength and nurture his intent in difficult times:

125

I am already given to the power that rules my fate.
I cling to nothing, so I will have nothing to defend.
I have no thoughts, so I will see.
I fear nothing, so I will remember myself.
Detached and at ease,
I will dart past the Eagle to be free.

∨ ∨ ∨

Ixtlan de los Hervores was next on our list. It is a small town in the state of Michoacán, famous for its hot springs and geysers. We were curious to see what was awaiting us there when we left the main highway and turned onto a rural road for the last twenty miles or so. We had barely left the highway and were slowly driving through a small settlement when a rock hit our windshield with full force. It sounded like a gunshot and it was a miracle that the glass did not break. We stopped instantly and decided to turn around, assuming that it had been a bad omen and that this Ixtlan was not for us. The rock had clearly been thrown at the truck, but there was nobody around.

Occasionally we had encountered some unfriendly faces while driving through rural areas from people who mistook us for Americans. Whenever they found out that we were Germans, their attitudes changed dramatically. So, after the incident with the rock, we felt it was time to do something about this. In the next town we bought a set of stick-on letters and wrote "Somos Alemanes" (We are Germans) with big letters on the hood. We never had any more problems. It was interesting to watch the people, again and again, first stone faced when they saw us approaching, then their lips moving while they read "S-o-m-o-s A-l-e-m-a-n-e-s," and then, inevitably, a smile and friendly waving hands. Besides having mixed feelings about "Gringos," as U.S. citizens were commonly referred to, many Mexicans seemed to have a dubious affinity to Germany's fascist past, which occasionally brought about awkward conversations. Whatever the reasons were, this small and practical maneuver kept the stones off our windshield.

∨ ∨ ∨

Ixtlan de Juarez in the mountains northeast of Oaxaca had been my secret favorite from the start. From all I gathered from Castaneda's writings, Oaxaca seemed to have been one of the epicenters of the sorcerer's world. We found it to be a mesmerizing, magical, and exotic town, full of beautiful colonial architecture and brimming with indigenous life. Of the four months we traveled through the state of Oaxaca, we spent at least four weeks in the town itself.

Just like years later in Tula, I set all my intent on connecting to the elusive spirit of the Nagual, trying to find an opening, a point of departure. Countless hours I sat on park benches on the *zócalo*, the main plaza, where Castaneda had apparently met don Juan so many times. Other countless hours I roamed the Indian markets for the same reason. I was as silent and alert as I possibly could be, but no magic door ever opened, and no mysterious shaman ever recognized me as the long-awaited apprentice. But even though I did not find my savior in Oaxaca, nor the opening into total freedom, I spent weeks in alertness and presence that I experienced as a blissfully altered state.

Ixtlan de Juarez, a few hours up the road from Oaxaca to Veracruz, unfortunately did not meet my expectations. Our visit was utterly uneventful. It was not a pretty place and looked rather disjointed, not at all like the object of longing for an impeccable warrior like don Genaro, whose story was behind our quest to find his magical hometown. However, while roaming through the dusty streets and puzzling the locals with strange questions, we found out that a few hours east, deep in the rugged mountains of the eastern Sierra Madre, there was another Ixtlan. From the descriptions it sounded like a much more romantic place, and we were on our way.

It was an adventurous drive. The pavement ended soon, and the settlements grew sparse as the terrain got more and more rugged. We were pretty much on our own, and judging by the faces of the peasants we occasionally encountered, it was obvious that we were way off the tourist route. After a while, people did not even speak Spanish anymore when we asked for directions. We could have been concerned about our safety, but all we experienced was a sense of exhilaration. The mountain air was fresh and clear, and the dry and rocky landscape soon gave way to lushly forested mountains that stretched far into the distance. There were hundreds of miles of wilderness in front of us. This was pre-Columbian Mexico, powerful and raw, in a way I had never experienced it. As far as I was concerned, I was again in holy land.

Eventually we found Ixtlan. It was off the road, halfway down the side of a mountain, nestled in between two slopes, bathing in the late afternoon sun. It was just a small hamlet, a few houses, surrounded by fields, a picture book village, if there ever was one. We shut off the engine and sat next to an enchanting little spring by the side of the road for a timeless moment. The real Ixtlan, at long last. So we decided.

There was no way we would drive down that mountain, disturbing this idyllic scene with our screaming presence and asking senseless questions. It may be hard to explain, but we were incapable of going any further. We just kept sitting in silence, pondering the meaning of the metaphor that was Ixtlan. I felt strangely elated, even though this treasure hunt had not yielded anything concrete. In the metaphor, Ixtlan stands for the coziness of the familiar world that is lost upon awakening to the boundlessness of our true nature. But no matter how hard I tried, I could not understand why I would ever have a longing for the familiarity of the known once I had succeeded in "stopping the world" and reconnected with my essence.

As I was sitting there, gazing past Ixtlan into the darkening horizon behind the distant mountains, I realized that all that mattered to me at this moment was the journey—and I was in love with the journey.

Before we left we went to fill our water bottles at the little mineral spring that was bubbling out between two boulders just a few yards from the road. It was surrounded by trees and some flowering bushes. Next to the spring was a large flat vertical rock, about three feet high, with a carved relief that was covered with lichen and moss. As we looked closer we discovered, to our utter amazement, that it was an ancient rock carving of the feathered serpent.

Gathering Momentum

Our navigational odyssey through Mexico had been filled to the brim with adventures and magic. If I were to single out one event, however, that had the most direct impact on our lives, it would probably be an incident that happened on our last visit to Oaxaca. It was an insidious little event, not at all of the esoteric and magical kind that I had been consciously intending. We didn't even find out about it until weeks later, when we were already back in the U.S., visiting friends in Phoenix, Arizona.

While I was overseeing some repairs and a new paint job for our truck and learning a whole new level of colloquial Spanish in a Oaxacan car repair shop, Mona spent her days reading in a downtown café. Unfortunately the bathroom there was of the old-fashioned kind, where you had to scoop water out of a barrel to flush the toilet. There wasn't any soap either, and so it happened that the only tangible result of all our intending in Oaxaca was a bad case of hepatitis A. Mona realized it only in Phoenix, in our friends' bathroom, when the color of her stool, urine, and eyes told the story. A few days later my eyes matched hers. Luckily we managed not to infect our friends who generously let us camp in their garden and helped us to get through the ordeal.

Hepatitis is a unique disease, just as the affected liver is a uniquely complex organ. While I had a relatively smooth recovery after feeling miserable and debilitated for a few weeks, Mona went through hell. She felt absolutely wretched and emotionally devastated for nearly a month. The liver is intimately linked to our emotional states, and in Mona's case, her personality changed dramatically and never completely reverted. Even after all signs of the hepatitis were gone, she retained a severe and chronic homesickness that never left her. All she wanted was to go back home to the green meadows and perceived wholesomeness of Germany. We still spent nearly a year in the Western United States and Canada, but she never let go. Not only did she want to go back, but she had lost all taste for adventure. One year later, she succeeded in making us return to Germany, but our intents were no longer compatible and forced us apart. Following her own navigation and passion, Mona eventually became a successful artist.

Returning to Germany had not been part of my intent, and all I could think of now was gathering a fresh momentum.

▼ ▼ ▼

"Could you imagine living in America?" I heard myself asking.

Victoria's eyes widened in surprise and disbelief. "Yes," she nodded.

"Do you like dogs?" I asked quite seriously.

"Yes," she nodded again, still puzzled.

"Then everything will be all right," I said with total conviction. We fell into each other's arms one last time before I had to board the plane back to Munich. For a brief moment we forgot about the others, but nobody seemed to have noticed. I put on my sunglasses to hide my tears.

There was an empty row of seats in the rear of the airplane where I could be alone, and I sat down in a daze. I had not slept in over thirty hours, but when I closed my eyes, there was not even a thought of sleep. My whole body was vibrating as if I had been struck by lightning. And, in a way, that was exactly what had happened.

Only four days ago I had come to Budapest on an all-paid-for incentive tour. Upon my return to Germany I had again joined a financial brokerage and consulting firm where we were regularly treated to extravagant mini vacations by partner institutions as a reward and incentive for doing business with them.

The first time I saw Victoria was on the gallery of the Matthias Church, a thousand year old Budapest landmark. The church is an exquisite and powerful piece of religious architecture, steeped in history and tales of miracles. The church floor is about five feet below street level and as I descended into the interior my energy immediately shifted. It was dark, cool, and moist, and as my eyes adjusted they were drawn upwards by the sunlight coming through magnificent stained glass windows behind the gallery. That's when I saw her.

She stood in front of another part of our group that had arrived with an earlier plane, and I was awestruck. She was to be our main tour guide for the next four days. Completely mesmerized, I watched her coming down the stairs. A sparkling bundle of energy with long blonde hair, wide-set eyes, and high cheek bones, totally in control of my fifty-odd male colleagues that were following her. They all took off in a bus on a city tour, and I had to wait a few more hours until I saw her again, when our groups joined for a welcoming party in the Fisherman's Bastion, another historic landmark.

I was leaning against a stone column in the tower room where we were gathering, when suddenly our eyes met—and locked. Time was suspended, reminiscent of the moment before I somersaulted down the mountain with Loretta during our accident in the vineyard. Our souls plunged into each other and merged, changing the course of our lives. We fell in love in an instant.

But with over one hundred men jealously watching each other, it was not until late that evening that we finally had a few minutes alone to talk. We were all to meet at a dance club after dinner, and while everybody climbed into the buses, I quickly secured a ride with Victoria in her car. We had to let two of my colleagues sit in the back, but when we arrived at the club, she dropped them off at the entrance, and I stayed with her while she parked the car. After she had turned off the engine, we sat silent for a long moment, staring straight ahead, just feeling each other's presence.

"So, what are your dreams?" I broke the silence. "What do you want from life?"

"Peace . . . " she said dreamily, still looking through the windshield into the darkness. "A family, children, security . . . peace."

"Too bad," I sighed, "I love traveling, excitement, uncertainty . . . adventure, freedom."

My heart grew heavy.

But while we both kept looking ahead silently, as if following our words, as they drifted out into the night, our heads slowly started to pull together until they touched at the temples. A warm charge instantly

131

flooded my body and my heart, transcending all words and thoughts. A short while later we went into the club to join the others. Later that night we danced, and our fairytale began.

We only had a few secret moments together over the next few days. Victoria could not jeopardize her job, and I had to avoid detection by the alpha males of our corporate pack of wolves. One hundred men, away from home and family for four days, are capable of interesting dynamics, to say the least, particularly if combined with an unlimited supply of alcohol.

On our last evening, however, driven by our very own dynamics, we managed to stage an escape. Victoria claimed to have an academic deadline in connection with her doctoral thesis, which was plausible since she was also a research pharmacist at the local university. And I retired early with a headache. Nobody seemed suspicious.

What happened that night is beyond the scope of this story. Suffice it to say that the gods wanted to make absolutely sure that we had gotten the message. Early the next morning we went for a walk on the Margaret Island in the middle of the Danube River in central Budapest. The island is covered with beautiful parks and medieval ruins, recalling its past as a religious center in the Middle Ages. The morning sun was just beginning to burn off the lingering patches of mist; and in the shade, all the flowers and leaves were covered with dew. We were still vibrating from the ecstasy of the night and barely touching the ground.

But instead of simply succumbing to this exquisite lightness of being, I found myself talking compulsively for nearly two hours. Strangely driven and nearly unaware, I completely inundated poor Victoria with the Nagual's unabridged belief system, including the intricacies of the Eagle's Gift and the rule of the Nagual. As far as I could tell, she absorbed every word of it. Victoria's own recollection of this event had been quite different, though. Once she told me about a conversation she had with her best friend on that same day. Her friend, of course, wanted to know all the details.

"Wow, tell me everything! How is he?" she asked.

"Well," Victoria answered, "he is quite crazy, but I love him."

❧   ❧   ❧

I flew to Budapest at least every other weekend, and we married as soon as all the necessary paperwork was completed. It still took nearly a year until Victoria could leave Hungary, though. The country was still under communist rule at the time, and her emigration required navigating a great deal of bureaucracy.

Victoria was a powerful and passionate creature, and as a result of our joining forces, my life acquired an extraordinary degree of intensity. My longing to be with her during those initial periods of separation was so strong that it triggered my first spontaneous out-of-body experience.

One night, after a long phone conversation, I fell into a restless sleep. Some time later I woke up thirsty, got out of bed and went downstairs to drink a glass of water. Once downstairs, I was distracted and drawn to the window by a strange light on the outside. The light turned out to be just the regular streetlight in front of the apartment building, but it had an unusual halo that puzzled me. I tried to focus and rub my eyes several times, but to no avail. Then I suddenly remembered that I had read about this specific perceptual effect. It supposedly occurred during out-of-body experiences, and I got excited.

"If I am out of my body, then my physical body must still be lying in bed upstairs," I thought. My apartment was a split-level loft, and as soon as I had completed that thought I found myself floating just above the upstairs guardrail, looking towards my bed. Sure enough, there I was, curled up in a fetal position, fast asleep. It was a disconcerting and unpleasant sight, and I never got used to it, even after having had countless such experiences over the years. I always perceived my body as a lifeless piece of flesh, terrifying and unattractive when seen from this vantage point. I got used to quickly averting my attention, whenever I caught sight of it.

I stayed conscious and completely aware that I was dreaming. Trying to make use of it, I decided to go out. I walked out the door and down the hallway to the elevator. After battling with it for a while, I finally found myself downstairs, and I walked out into the street. At this time things were no longer recognizable. The street turned into a desert scene and with my last bit of dreaming awareness I decided to fly, which I enjoyed tremendously for a few moments. Then my experience became an ordinary dream where I was no longer aware that I was dreaming.

Shortly after that I woke up. Now obsessed, I tried all night to leave my body again, but I did not have the energy. At one point I lifted out a few inches, just enough to look at one of the paintings on my bedroom wall, but I was pulled back instantaneously like on a rubber band.

Now I was on a mission. Every night, just before falling asleep, I programmed myself to leave my body. I even connected a timer to my tape recorder, so it would start at two or three o'clock in the morning with suggestions like: "I am dreaming now, I am aware that I am dreaming, and I am free to leave my body." I tried many different variants and different times, with or without music or sound effects, but with painfully little success. I did learn however, that there was no need to open my door or use the elevator once I was out of my body. I could just think myself to wherever I wanted to be, or float through walls, if I was so inclined. Floating through ceilings and walls became a personal favorite of mine. It always produced a titillating tingle throughout my body.

Despite all my efforts, these experiences remained a rare occurrence until several years later when I had harnessed more of the specific energy it seemed to require. Once I was no longer separated from Victoria, which had somehow stirred my energy body out of its housing, my astral excursions ceased altogether. We burned up the necessary energy in other, less esoteric ways.

With all this new excitement, my quest for freedom and my intent to go back to America both found themselves somewhat on the back burner, but they were definitely not forgotten. Victoria had a powerful intent of her own and was happy to align it with mine. But to generate a strong momentum, we still had to integrate our respective belief systems. I had never allowed myself to intend abundance. Perhaps I did not trust my indulgent nature or I simply lacked confidence, but in my worldview at the time, abundance, particularly material abundance, was antagonistic to "true" freedom and spiritual development. Victoria did not have this constraint. For her, freedom and material abundance were mutually inclusive, and she was not afraid of anything, nor did she lack confidence. Her intent and her energetic resources afforded us the means to integrate all aspects of freedom, material and transcendental.

It was indeed amazing, how Victoria's power affected my life. I was never known to be ambitious, particularly in terms of material success.

Once my basic needs for food and shelter were met, I was usually already on the lookout for two trees to put up my hammock. Embarking on the warrior's path had introduced the power and beauty of impeccability into my life, but it had not affected my worldly ambitions.

Victoria never put any pressure on me, nor did she seem to have any particular expectations. She was always humble and grateful for what life provided us with. It was just her energetic mass and presence and the silent strength and focus of her intent that manifested the rapid increase of our material resources. She provided the horsepower; I was just driving the car. Her more obvious participation in generating income was maintaining contact with my growing client base. Nearly every day she spent an hour or two on the phone injecting her energy into the link between me and my customers. As a result I was able to produce the fourth highest business volume in a highly competitive company with hundreds of consultants after less than three years. And we even managed to spend at least three months on vacation every year, traveling extensively. We indulged in all sorts of mundane pleasures to our hearts content. We owned a twelve cylinder Jaguar, my dream car at the time, had thousand dollar dinners in the world's best restaurants, and, after I obtained a pilot's license, we flew all over Europe in a small private airplane.

And within just a few years we got it all out of our system. It all had felt great and empowering at the time, but we were never any happier than before or after those years. The mechanics of the mind had become blatantly obvious; it was completely insatiable and always wanted more. While flying around in our single engine Cessna, we quickly became annoyed with the noise level and lack of speed when traveling long distances, and we began dreaming of a Lear Jet. While eating the second time in a celebrated dining temple with its Three Michelin Stars, the experience was less spectacular than the first time, and we were disappointed.

We made many acquaintances with other high-rollers. I remember a rather typical conversation we had with my client and friend Frank, a highly successful surgeon, and his wife Gabi. We were visiting them in their vacation home in Marbella, Spain. They were in a terrible mood, having just arrived from Thailand.

"Can you believe this?" Frank was beside himself. "We stayed in this resort near Phuket that had been voted number one in the world, $1,600 dollars a night. Sixteen-hundred dollars!" he repeated, looking at us aghast. "They didn't even have 24 hour room service." Frank's eyes widened in disbelief.

"And the towels," Gabi added, "remember the towels, Frank? You get better towels in every Holiday Inn," she added in disgust.

⌄ ⌄ ⌄

I considered it a true blessing that we were able to manifest all these experiences. They provided precious first-hand knowledge and proof that the mind and its mundane pursuits cannot lead to happiness and freedom. Being able to immerse ourselves so thoroughly in the world of material abundance and sense gratification was also an indispensable step to aligning both our intents. I lost my fear that money would corrupt my soul, and Victoria readily expanded her concept of abundance beyond the material towards a more transcendental dimension. She had read most of Castaneda's books at this point, but so far they had failed to inspire her much. She still mainly trusted my navigation, and only later, after reading Taisha Abelar's book, *A Sorcerer's Crossing*, did she establish her own link with this myth.

⌄ ⌄ ⌄

I had made sure that I found out immediately whenever Castaneda had written a new book. To that end I resorted to calling his editor in New York at regular intervals. His publisher at the time was Simon and Schuster and his editor, Michael Korda, was kind enough to indulge me. With his help, I was in possession of the next two books the minute they came off press. I am deeply grateful to Michael Korda, particularly because he was gracious enough to put me in touch with Tracy Kramer, Castaneda's agent, once he was promoted to editor-in-chief of Simon and Schuster and no longer handled Castaneda's literary affairs. It was my subsequent connection with Tracy that led me to the Nagual himself in the end.

Navigation not only entails the cultivation of one's receptive capacities of awareness, alertness, internal silence, and presence, but also has a proactive side as well. It always needs to be supported by unbending intent, the cultivation of energy, and a good dose of persistence. One has to broadcast one's interests clearly, and then listen and watch intently for the response and guidance.

Immersing ourselves in the abundance of our newfound wealth had, of course, been pleasant. But it was never any better than the abundance of life we had experienced before and after this financial windfall. It was just as fascinating and rewarding, or challenging and humbling as any other phase of our lives. And it was just as magical, as illustrated by the following story, which would become a navigational blueprint for the rest of my life.

During our last summer in Europe we went on a plane trip through France. Our dear friends Robert and Edith were courageous enough to come along. My pilot's license was still fairly new, and this was going to be our first extended cross-country flight. From Munich we flew straight to the Loire Valley and visited some of my favorite old haunts. From there we took the Cessna up north and then around the whole country in a counterclockwise circle. We stopped at Mont St. Michel, explored all of Brittany, including some of the islands, and then flew down the Atlantic Coast to Biarritz. As we were getting ready to leave Biarritz for Carcassonne I learned during the weather briefing that a big low pressure system was moving in from the west, and that we only had a narrow window to leave immediately, or we would be stuck in Biarritz for at least three days. We decided to go for it, and within minutes we were in the air.

As soon as we had reached cruising altitude, we could see the weather front with its huge thunderheads, and it was approaching fast. Strong gusts of wind were already shaking our little plane, and I was getting concerned. The front was moving much faster than the weathermen had predicted, and I decided to deviate from the original flight plan and steer away from the Pyrenees, the mountain range that separates France from Spain.

Before long, a cloud cover pulled over the blue sky and rogue clouds forced me to descend to a lower flight level. I was only licensed to fly by visual rules and had to stay in the clear. With the encroaching clouds and the lower altitude, my field of vision became smaller and smaller,

137

and before long I had lost my orientation. I still had instrument bearings and could calculate our position, but the closeness to the hilly ground required all my attention.

The map did not show an alternate airport anywhere in the area and the ground was too rugged for an emergency landing. Robert was sitting next to me, filming everything with his video camera, seemingly unaware of the increasing danger.

"Wow, did you see the lightning bolt over there? I think I got it on video," Robert said excitedly, turning to Edith.

"Cool," I just managed to squeeze past the lump in my throat. "Just put your seat belt back on, would you please," I added with a forced smile. I did not want them to know how terrified I was. Robert and Edith had left their baby that was just a few months old in the care of Edith's parents. I remembered how her mother had grabbed my arm with both hands before we took off, her eyes burning with concern. "Please be careful," she had said, her fingers digging into my arm. "Please, bring them back safely."

"Wow!" everybody exclaimed at the same time. "Jesus," Edith gasped, "there is lightning everywhere." Victoria put her hand on my shoulder. She knew how I felt and that I had no more control.

At this point we were entirely surrounded by the weather system. Fortunately I could still see the ground and a few miles ahead. The wind constantly changed directions and whipped us around like a toy. Black thunderheads with lightning bolts appeared in all directions. Robert was still filming and nobody said a word. I became strangely calm. Another part of me took over, just like it had way back in Weligama, when the attacking mob of fishermen began throwing rocks at us and started to approach our house.

There was no more worry now and navigation became utterly simple. I flew just high enough to avoid obstacles from the ground, and I aimed the plane towards the brightest spot in the sky. All I did, and all I could do, was flying towards the light. It kept changing. Sometimes it was to the right, and sometimes to the left, or straight ahead. If the wind gusts became too violent, I slowed down, otherwise we went full throttle. That was all. There were hardly any thoughts. A strange peace came over all of us. I looked around and everybody seemed to be in the same space.

I don't remember how long we danced with the storm. At some point the contrast between the black thunderheads and the whiteness straight ahead was sharp and defined. The wind roared, making the speedometer needle jump erratically. The closer we got to the whiteness, the brighter it became, and the louder the wind roared. Then, suddenly, there was a moment of stillness. The plane dropped markedly and was picked up again. The direction of the wind changed nearly one hundred eighty degrees, and in a matter of seconds we were literally spit out into a deep blue sky with not a cloud in sight. Random gusts still shook us up a few times, as if patting us on the shoulder.

Within minutes we had our bearings again. We were barely off course. Carcassonne was straight ahead, less than thirty minutes to touchdown. And a few hours later we sat on the main square of one of the world's most authentic medieval cities, as if we had popped out of a wormhole.

It provided the perfect backdrop for our reflections on one of the most dramatic navigational lessons ever.

The Power of Silence

After four years of gathering momentum and aligning our intent, Victoria and I felt it was time to jump. I sold my business, and Mona, with whom we had stayed friends, took over most of our belongings. This time we left Germany for good. Two years prior we had initiated immigration procedures into the United States and our Green Cards were ready.

We had been traveling extensively during these four years and spent time together in all the places that I felt passionate about, particularly France, Spain, India, Nepal, the American Southwest, and Mexico. Traveling and living in many different places had shaped my personality, and sharing these places with Victoria had seemed important in our quest to merge and integrate our intent. Before making our home in the New World, we went to explore Thailand, a country that was new to both of us.

"*Sawatdee Kaa!*" "Welcome!" was the first Thai word I learned from the beautiful hostess at Bangkok airport. We felt welcome in Thailand indeed. It was 1989, and the Thai must have been the friendliest and sweetest people in the world. Everybody was smiling, even at customs, at immigration, the policeman, the taxi driver, and of course, every employee at the hotel. Bangkok was steaming hot, but everybody was smiling.

We were smiling too, and we had every reason. Life had been incredibly generous with us. Ever since I had engaged in this organic and interactive relationship with life, I felt supported, nourished, and embraced. I loved following the warrior's path because it inspired me and spoke to my heart. There was such beauty in intending impeccability and integrity. I believe however, that the abundance and generosity of life that I was experiencing were not so much tied to the effort of intending and following principles, but rather the result of simply honoring and acknowledging the aliveness of life, every step of the way. Ultimately, looking life in the eye with recognition seems to be all that is truly necessary.

While navigating Bangkok, we were inevitably guided into the cool serenity of the countless Buddhist temples. Particularly Victoria developed a strong affinity to everything Buddhist right from the start. The contrast was striking and compelling. Bangkok is a huge metropolis, with all its traffic and frenzy aggravated by the tropical climate. Stepping into the silent, cool, and incense-flavored sacredness of a temple felt like instant nirvana. Especially if everybody is smiling at you, elflike nuns and meditating monks alike, and, most endearing, all the little "baby monks," young boys of all ages in their oversized saffron robes and their round little shaved heads. We loved those temples. And if we ever tired of the enchanting serenity, we signed up for a session of serious Thai massage that was offered in some of the temple compounds.

When we weren't in the temples, we were cruising through the Klongs, a seemingly endless maze of enchanting waterways, fed by the mighty Chao Phraya River. The Klongs were a world of their own, with floating markets, houseboat villages, and stilted teak mansions. The air was filled with the intoxicating scent of tropical flowers and water plants and with the laughter of children jumping into the cooling floods from just about everywhere. We were so enamored with this magical water world that we seriously considered buying one of these stilted houses and moving there.

From Bangkok we went to explore Thailand's fabled islands in the Andaman Sea. Following a friend's recommendation we started with Ko Phi Phi, an apparent jewel among tropical islands and among the top five must- see yachting destinations worldwide, according to a yachting mag-azine at the time. We were curious, and it was incidentally on my thirty-sixth birthday when we arrived there on the early morning boat from Phuket. I had been sitting at the front of the boat for most of the ride, dreamily enjoying the gentle up-and-down motion as we were plowing through the waves. My feet were dangling on both sides of the bow, and whenever we rode up a bigger wave, I let my head fall backwards with the motion, and I took in a deep breath, inhaling the sun. As we turned around the steep cliff that shields Ko Phi Phi's beaches and landing dock from the West, I was just listening to Puccini arias through my headphones. The captain turned down the engines and made the boat glide leisurely around the cliff into the bay.

Flanked by two massive vertical limestone formations that were covered with tropical flora like stones with moss, emerged a picture book South Sea island scene with dazzling white sandy beaches, palm-thatched huts, and colorful fishing boats. Countless coconut trees were leaning into the bright turquoise bay, and the water was so clear that we could easily see the bottom, at least forty feet below us, and all the tropical fish in between. It was utterly breathtaking, and tears streamed down my cheeks as I tried to cope with the impact of so much beauty. I have had many magnificent moments in my life, but nothing ever came close to the experience of floating into Ko Phi Phi's Ton Say Bay on the morning of my thirty-sixth birthday. My sense of gratitude was boundless.

Upon arrival we loaded our bags onto a smaller boat, and together with a handful of fellow travelers, we headed to Long Beach, as our friend had recommended

"Lon Bee, Lon Bee, Lon Beee..!" the operator of our small long-tail boat shouted a few times in unmistakable Thai English, and off we went, sputtering across the bay to our final destination. Long Beach, a spectacular stretch of white sand shielded by a coral reef, was lined with a row of quaint little bungalows. I jumped off the boat as soon as we arrived to have a head start on getting accommodations.

"You are lucky, my man!" the friendly young guy at the reception greeted me with a high-five. "We have only one bungalow left," he went on, as he handed me the key in exchange for my passport. I looked at the key. The number was carved and burned into a small wooden tablet to which it was attached. The number of our bungalow was thirty-six. Smiling from ear to ear I walked back down to the boat to help Victoria with the bags.

"We got the last one," I reported happily. "Guess what number it is."

"Four?"

I shook my head.

"Then it is probably thirty-six," Victoria said laughing.

"Yep," I held up the key and performed a little dance in the sand. "This is a good omen," I added emphatically, not even sure what I exactly meant by that.

There was absolutely nothing wrong with Ko Phi Phi in those days. It had not been overly developed yet, but there was enough infrastructure to enjoy the good life to your heart's content, which still was undoubtedly a specialty of mine, and Victoria was an all too willing partner. One day was as blissful as the next. We made many friends. We played and snorkeled in the turquoise water, got massages under the coconut palms, or went deep-sea fishing. We hired a boat and went on adventurous overnight trips to small neighboring islands. We feasted and danced in the many restaurants and beach bars, most of them operated by Europeans. We climbed the limestone cliffs and dove in underwater caves. And occasionally we managed to enhance our perception of the breathtaking natural beauty by snacking on hallucinogenic mushrooms. In short, we were in heaven.

One day we hiked to the other side of the island with our beach bags and put up our hammocks in the shade, in front of a few scattered beach bungalows. I dozed off reading, and when I woke up I noticed that the bungalow next to my hammock incidentally was also numbered thirty-six. This was intriguing and I put Victoria's attention on it. There were towels drying on a line, showing that it was occupied.

"I am curious who lives there," I said. "We have to stay here until they show up."

I was sure that there was an important clue in this synchronicity.

Towards the end of the afternoon the occupants of the bungalow, two young men and a woman, showed up.

"Hi guys, I hope we are not encroaching too much," I said apologetically. "We'll be leaving in a minute.

"Oh, no worries," they laughed, "you are welcome to stay."

All three came to greet us. "Hi, I'm Jack." "I am Bruce." "Dawn." They introduced themselves with hearty handshakes. All three were from Alaska where they worked seasonally as herring spotters. We had never heard of it and were fascinated to learn more about this apparently dangerous profession. Herring spotting in Alaska entailed flying small airplanes in usually rough weather conditions to supply fishing fleets with visual information on fish movement.

I had been playing with the idea of turning my passion for flying into more than a pastime, and naturally I thought that the synchronicity of our meeting might point in this direction. But it all seemed too farfetched. We chatted for a while longer, mostly exchanging travel tales. All three of them were genuine, good-natured people, and we liked them a lot. We decided to go scuba diving together a few days later, and we met several times by chance in the village, but nothing tangible transpired that felt like a compelling navigational input. Eventually they left the island, and we forgot about them.

Several months later I quite literally bumped into Dawn on Khao San Road in Bangkok. I was just stepping out onto the street from our hotel, looking backwards to Victoria, when I accidentally collided with Dawn who was walking on the sidewalk. We were both stunned. "Dawn," I exclaimed, holding her by both shoulders.

"Paul, Victoria, what a surprise!" She was clearly stunned as well.

"Wow, how good to see you. Where are Jack and Bruce? How are you doing? What have you been up to?" I blurted out.

"I was just going to have breakfast next door. Why don't you join me and we can catch up?" Dawn suggested.

It was not exactly a miracle to run into someone you know on Khao San Road, Bangkok's "Backpacker's Central," lined with cheap hotels, coffee shops, restaurants, travel agencies, and anything else a budget traveler might need. But bumping into each other like that, particularly after the serendipity of our initial meeting, definitely made all my bells ring.

Dawn had split from the guys soon after they left Ko Phi Phi. She had just arrived from Suan Mokkh, a Buddhist monastery near Surat Thani in Southern Thailand where she had attended a ten-day silent meditation retreat. Her eyes were shining, and she was overflowing with superlatives describing her experience.

"This was the best thing I ever did," she said with conviction.

Victoria was thrilled. She couldn't stop asking questions.

"Tell me everything," she insisted. "You had to be completely silent for ten days? How could you deal with this? How many people were there? Where did you sleep? What did you eat? How many people quit? What if you never meditated before?"

I became increasingly uncomfortable. Victoria had read a book about the life of a Buddhist nun that fascinated her, and I was concerned that her interest in Buddhism might pull us apart. On the surface, my shamanic belief system and the warrior's path did not seem to have much in common with Buddhism, and I did not see how it could be compatible. I instinctively liked everything about it, though. I loved the temples, the monks, the nuns, the serenity, and the beauty and peacefulness that it radiated.

"We should go too," Victoria looked at me excited. "There is a retreat every month, from the first to the tenth. It is practically free. We should definitely go."

"We'll see," was all I could say. "Let's just see what happens. Maybe at the end, just before we fly back."

I was well aware that the synchronicity of us running into Dawn was a navigational imperative, and it was obvious that we should go to Suan Mokkh. But for now, I couldn't help wishing that something would still prevent it from happening. Strangely enough, with all my ambitions to become a man of knowledge, I was afraid to go to a meditation retreat.

Nothing prevented it from happening though, and barely two weeks before our return flight to Germany we arrived at the monastery. We had been traveling extensively. Besides Ko Phi Phi, we explored half a dozen other islands, each with its own beauty and charm. We had had a particularly magical and adventurous time in the northwestern corner of Thailand around Mae Hong Son, an area commonly referred to as the opium triangle, where we rented an all-terrain motorcycle and rode through the hill tribes region across the borders into Burma and Laos. We spent weeks exploring beautiful Chiang Mai and the north of Thailand. We trekked through caves, stayed in mountain monasteries and with hill tribes. We even ventured into the border regions with Cambodia, and we took the train to Singapore all the way through Malaysia. We left no stone unturned during those six months in Southeast Asia to make sure we had the time of our life.

Just prior to our arrival at the monastery we had spent three weeks on Ko Phangan, another island paradise off Thailand's east coast. Ko Phangan was even more laid back than Ko Phi Phi, and we had rented a beach hut at a remote and absolutely gorgeous beach where clothing was optional and the supply of hallucinogenic mushrooms abundant.

After all that it seemed like a good idea to sober up, and a silent meditation retreat sounded perfect, at least in theory. Practicing internal silence had not been on our agenda recently. But I was still wary of the change it might bring. Victoria and I were going to be housed in separate quarters, and we would not even have eye contact for ten days.

"What if one of us can't bear it and wants to leave?" I asked her as we sat waiting for the introductory talk on the evening before the retreat.

"Don't worry so much," Victoria just laughed. "Everything will be fine. It is only ten days," she added, squeezing my hand reassuringly. "Only ten days."

"I love you," I said, as we finally retreated to our separate quarters for the night. "Whatever happens, I love you. Don't worry about me. I will be fine," I assured her, while we hugged for a long time.

"I love you too," Victoria pulled me tight. Suddenly there was a glint of fear in her eyes too.

And then I was alone with myself.

ᴠ　ᴠ　ᴠ

Our accommodations were basic. My room was plain, about eight-by-six feet, with a concrete shelf three feet off the floor that served as a bed. For comfort I had a straw mat and my folded-up towel as a pillow. We were informed that the absence of softness makes sure that we only sleep as much as our body really needs.

At 4 AM a large bell was rung, which came as a relief. I had been lying awake for hours and was glad to get up. There was a large bath hall where about twenty-five men crowded and splashed water around, attempting to get proficient in monastic bathing rites. Everyone was trying hard not to make accidental eye contact, which gave the impression that we were all angry at each other.

At 4:30 AM we gathered in the meditation hall and started the day with listening to a few short instructions, a Buddhist reading, and half an hour of meditation. We continued with yoga, more instructions, and more meditation. There was a breakfast at 8 AM, then more meditation and a vegetarian lunch at 12:30 PM, which was the last meal of the day. The time from after lunch until bedtime at 9 PM we spent in sitting, standing, or walking meditation, listening to instructions, resting, and doing cleaning chores.

The meditation that is practiced at Suan Mokkh is called Anāpānasati, which means "mindfulness of breathing." Basically, the attention is kept on the breath, or more specifically on the area just below the nostrils, where the breath enters and leaves the body. Whatever happens as a result of trying to keep the attention on the breath, whether physically, emotionally, or mentally, is just observed, not rejected, analyzed, or engaged in. The purpose of this exercise is essentially to develop an "observing self."

Usually we find our identity within our mental and emotional processes. The goal of meditation is first to develop an observing awareness that is always present while we are perceiving and experiencing, and then to shift our sense of identity into this observing awareness. This shift is experienced as an awakening, not unlike the shift that occurs when an ordinary dream turns into a lucid dream. The moment we become fully aware that we are dreaming, our sense of identity shifts from the dreamed to the dreamer.

Initially my concentration was basically non-existent. I couldn't keep my attention on my breathing for more than a few seconds. Instead of calming down, my mind went into overdrive. I couldn't sit still. Walking meditation felt ridiculous. My body was in pain. I couldn't sleep at night. I was angry and miserable, and I was constantly thinking how I could get out of this and why this retreat was not for me. I tried to find clues in Victoria's face about how she was doing, but to no avail, which aggravated me even further.

After a few days, though, my agony gradually gave way to acquiescence, and my internal dialogue slowly quieted down. Eventually I was able to just sit with my breathing and watch the thoughts come through my mind. I started to be intrigued by the randomness and redundancy of my thinking and by my emotional ups and downs. I noticed how short breathing affected my mind differently than long and deep breathing, and how my thoughts triggered my emotions. I found it truly amazing that I usually let all this random activity go completely unobserved and unchecked.

I also started to admire the poise and peaceful radiance of the resident

148

monks and nuns, who guided us through the retreat. The head monk and founder of Suan Mokkh was Adjarn Buddhadasa who was eighty-four years old at the time. He was regarded as a national treasure in Thailand. Our main teachers were a young American monk named Santicaro and an even younger American nun named Dhamma Dena. They had come from a monastery in Burma. Both were brilliant, literally, but I was absolutely in awe with Dhamma Dena. Often, she was the first sight when I opened my eyes after a long meditation, and what I perceived, particularly in the first moment, was the epitome of radiance and beauty. Dhamma Dena with her serene presence, her genuine smile, her total lack of pretense, and with her clear and peaceful eyes accentuated by her shaved head, forever changed my ideal of female beauty.

The serenity and peace of Suan Mokkh penetrated deeper and deeper, and I experienced moments of stillness and presence that were without precedence in my life. And when the eleventh day came and the retreat concluded, I was neither happy nor sad. It just happened. Already on the evening of day ten we had begun speaking again, and after an initial awkwardness, words just started to pour out of everybody.

On day eleven we had our last breakfast, and then we quietly left, took a taxi to Surat Thani and the train to Bangkok. Everything was different. Everything was amazing. We felt like newborns, or like tourists from another world. I found myself touching things and getting excited about the most mundane sounds. We did not talk much during the train ride. It seemed to take up a lot of energy, so did thinking. It didn't take any time at all for the train to reach Bangkok, and we suddenly found ourselves in a hotel room that, in all its simplicity, seemed extravagantly luxurious. We were intrigued by the huge soft white bed, and then we touched and smelled each other and through our eyes we saw each other's soul and a shiver went down my spine. And then we began to discover our bodies in the most sensual embrace imaginable.

We kept up our practice of Anāpānasati for a long time and tried to stay mindful in whatever we did. This new state of being felt incredibly precious and unlike anything we had ever encountered. Particularly after having experienced the most pleasurable six months of our lives, we would have never expected to find a whole new level of happiness. We were simply in awe and knew now without a doubt that there is no substitute for the true bliss that comes with inner peace.

There is nothing like the power of silence.

Dreaming Awake

When we weren't sleeping we meditated during the whole flight to Los Angeles. Even as we were getting off the plane and while standing in line at immigration we tried to concentrate on our breathing. We also had agreed to switch from speaking German to English the moment we left Germany. Our emigration was a big opportunity, and we wanted to do everything right to facilitate the best possible momentum for a completely fresh start. I was obsessed with fresh starts, new beginnings, rebirths—anything new and different. I had been trying to run away from myself since I could think.

"This time for sure!" I thought.

I wanted to leave my old persona behind and slip into my intended warrior self, devoid of personal history, daring, mindful, levelheaded, and impeccable. Speaking a new language would help, and if I lost my focus, I could always bring my attention to my breathing.

Nice try. By the time we were through with immigration, about two hours later, we had not only lost our focus, but were profusely venting our frustration in German.

"Damn it, I can't believe they are putting us through this ordeal again. We've done all this already at the embassy in Frankfurt," I fumed.

"Unbelievable, after twelve hours of flight, this is ridiculous," Victoria agreed.

Well, everything went fine, and we re-grouped, and lost it again a little while later. We re-grouped again and lost it and re-grouped and lost it— and pretty much lost it. We spoke German with each other, and most of the time we were about as mindful as everybody else.

But we were in Los Angeles, and we had Green Cards. The sale of my business had left us with a few hundred thousand dollars in cash and ten years of follow-up commissions, totaling another few hundred thousand dollars. And if that was not enough, Victoria was a pharmacist with a doctoral degree, a profession in high demand, which provided us with additional security and peace of mind. We were young, healthy, and much in love. So we should have been really happy, unabashedly happy.

But we weren't, not yet at least—not ever really. At this particular moment, the universe had thrown us a little curve ball in form of a tax audit back in Germany. It had probably been triggered by our emigration. And as we were settling into our new existence, as we were visiting friends and shopping for a motor home, and as we were trying to remember our breathing every so often, an auditor from the German tax authorities was sitting in our accountant's office back in Munich, going through four years of returns. It took him four weeks, and he came up with nothing, nothing at all.

My stupid mind, however, jumped at the opportunity to create four weeks of worry, four weeks of lying awake at night many times, trying to remember possible problems, oversights, invalid deductions, and scores of dire consequences. There is no rational explanation for the insanity of my mental fixation on this audit. I had done my returns as thoroughly as I could and might as well have had some faith. But no, four weeks of worry set the tone for my new life in the new world, compliments of my mind, happy to be back in problem mode after I had caught him off guard with a silent retreat.

∀ ∀ ∀

The plan was to stay as open as possible and just navigate along in our motor home until a particular place drew us in. Victoria had a strong affinity to the Pacific coast and we spent a considerable amount of time exploring it. This was a lot of fun. We started in San Diego and ended up in Vancouver about two months later. By that time we enjoyed traveling so much that we were not in any hurry to settle down. We spent the summer in British Columbia, and on our way back south we nearly got caught by Lopez Island in the Puget Sound off Seattle. It had felt so peaceful and magical that we found ourselves looking for property.

We were sitting on a fallen log in a clearing of old growth forest, overlooking a quiet bay. The afternoon sun broke through the trees in thick rays and was playing with the ferns. The property we were looking at was exceptionally beautiful and surprisingly affordable. My mind was already starting to build a house between the trees.

"I think we should build on wooden pillars here," I mused aloud, "so we are at the same level with the trees."

Victoria was gazing dreamily over the bay, nodding absentmindedly.

"We could have a little hand elevator to haul the groceries up," I continued.

Then two things happened at the same time, a helicopter flew over the clearing and the ants that had been crawling into my pants started biting.

Victoria looked up startled and frowned.

The mood was broken, the peace was gone. We left the property, and we left Lopez Island.

"How about making a full circle?" I suggested while we were driving along the Oregon Dunes. "We go down to San Diego again and then across to Florida, up to Newfoundland, across to Vancouver and then check out Hawaii. What do think?"

"Sure, why not." Victoria didn't seem overly excited. She was slightly ambiguous about the life on the road, but she had no better idea.

Towards the end of October we drove into Mendocino on the Northern Californian coast. We stopped to walk around and to get some groceries. It was a most beautiful and quaint little artist community, surrounded by ancient Redwood forests, rivers, cliffs, beaches, and the endless ocean. Colorful Victorian houses were framed by beds of fall flowers and fragrant herbs. Sitting on a small plateau and buffered by the wild headlands, the village was defiantly jutting out into the vastness of the deep blue Pacific Ocean, looking onto a splatter of tiny rock islands that were breaking the waves. On one side it was flanked by a lighthouse and on the other by a white sandy bay that was created by the Mendocino River as it emerged out of the forest.

The day we arrived was one of those incredible Indian summer days that seem to expand time indefinitely, and we didn't stand a chance. It was love at first sight for Victoria, and I was happy to see her so excited. We decided to stay around a few days, and before we knew it, we had made an offer on a bed and breakfast inn the next day, as if we were in a trance. Nobody had made an offer on the inn for several months, so we started low. But it just so happened that on that particular weekend two other, higher offers were made, preventing us from becoming inn-keepers. But now we were on a roll, and a few days later we made another offer on an undeveloped piece of property at the Navarro River mouth. The offer was accepted, and we had settled down before we even realized.

Now all our energy poured into the creation of our new home. It felt great that we could actually build it from the ground up. The land was still completely raw and pristine. There was no water and no electricity, and the property was not even zoned correctly. The actual building site was so overgrown with blackberry bushes that it was impossible to enter at first. We had to climb on a tree and literally go out on a limb to see what the place was all about. Well, it definitely was a view property, as they say. It was all about the view.

I think we spent hours on that limb the first time we looked at the site. The view was magnificent. The Navarro River meets the ocean between two high cliffs, perhaps a mile apart. We were sitting on the inside of the northern cliff and were looking onto the entire river mouth, the bay, and the southern coastline. To the left we could see deep into the Redwood forests of the river valley. Straight ahead, on the opposite side, a rugged cliff slowly surrendered to the ocean, boulder-by-boulder, rock-island-by-rock-island. About seventy feet below was a broad sandy beach, scattered with driftwood, and separating the river from the sea during the summer months. Beyond the cliff on our side, accentuated by twisted juniper trees on the headlands, was the vast Pacific Ocean, shimmering in a deep northern blue and the brilliant white of the breaking waves.

We camped on the property for two months, clearing it with a machete, measuring, dowsing, and drawing plans. At first I located the spot where the living room couch would have to be, point zero so to speak, the optimal point in reference to the view. And then we let the energy of the land guide us how to built the house around that spot. Our site was naturally oriented towards the southeast due to a curve in the otherwise westerly coastline. This was fortunate because it shielded us from the prevalent and cold northwesterly winds, and it allowed us to install a magical dimension by calibrating the house to face exactly southeast, even corrected by the magnetic variation. Southeast had been the favorite direction of don Juan, and for me it was a mythical direction, symbolically pointing to the opening I was navigating towards. When the plans were finished, we drilled for water. A generous spirit rewarded my dowsing efforts, and we hit an underground stream exactly on my birthday. The well was a gusher, which was quite rare in the area. Our pump was producing about forty gallons a minute, and we were never able to run it dry.

Everything went smoothly, perhaps a little slower than I had wanted, but within a year and a half we were sitting on the couch that had materialized exactly where we had dreamt it. I had involved myself in every part of the construction, from landscaping with a small bulldozer to the finishing carpentry with the help of Robert, my magical carpenter friend.

"I warn you Paul," he had said at the beginning, "I am used to building for the elves. It is going to take longer and cost more than if you hire someone else."

What he meant was that he finishes his carpentry even where it will not be visible in the end, like on the backside or inside of everything he works on. I loved the idea. It sounded like something don Juan could have come up with. Robert gave the house its soul with his impeccable spirit, and I felt privileged to learn from him.

The entire building project was a dream come true—a dream I did not even know I had. As it grew out of the plans into three dimensions, the house gradually acquired the energy of a sensory organ. A big and comfortable sensory organ, that is. While the floor levels stepped downwards with the slope, the shed roof rose up towards the sky. And where the living room met the patio, an eight-foot high folding glass wall slid all the way to the side, uniting the inside with the outdoors. When the glass wall was open, which it was most of the time, all this delightful southeasterly energy flooded the house. Sitting on the living room couch felt like being at the center of a parabolic antenna, energizing my longing, rather than giving me the peace and rest I thought I had found. Facing the southeast, we lived with the rising sun and the rising moon. The rising was relentless and did not let us settle down.

155

We kept landscaping and planting, created a pathway to the beach, built tree houses and a recapitulation cave, and we explored the area extensively. After several months of gazing into the horizon my lucid dreaming began to intensify, particularly after reading Taisha Abelar's book *A Sorcerer's Crossing.* I had begun to harness my sexual energy and was soon having out-of-body experiences four to five times a week. I had unfortunately found out that I had much more frequent lucid dreams when I did not allow my sexual energy to disperse the usual way.

I set the alarm clock for three o'clock every morning, got up, drank a sip of water, and ate half a cracker to slightly awaken my metabolism. Then I lay down on top of a sleeping bag on one of the wooden benches of our sauna. I used the sauna room because it was isolated and quiet. I had built it myself out of soft, fragrant cedar wood, getting carried away with the router, softening and rounding every conceivable edge. It was very cozy, and I liked it immensely. As soon as I lay there on my side in total darkness, I intended my body to fall asleep while I willed my mind to stay awake. After some undeterminable time I frequently awoke to the sensation of a buzzing ring of energy moving up and down around my body. As the buzzing subsided, I knew that I was in a lucid dream state. I was fully aware and conscious, but I could not move. I needed to think myself out of my body. Sometimes I could not do it, and my physical body moved with my efforts, waking me up. With practice, however, I learned to get out, and then I always followed the same routine. I floated through the two walls that separated me from the patio and deck, and then I took off.

No matter what I had planned beforehand, most of the time I just wanted to fly as soon as I was out. I flew down to the beach or into the river valley, high over the hill behind us or through unrecognizable landscapes, always fully conscious for a large part of the adventure. I was absolutely addicted to the exhilaration of flying and defying gravity. After a while I either drifted into a regular dream or I woke up in the sauna. Whenever I awoke after one of these astral journeys, I was brimming with energy and wellbeing. Most of the time I did not go back to bed but went on early-morning hikes or to meditate on top of the hill behind our house.

After several dozen flying adventures, I discovered the sexual dimension of lucid dreaming and naturally became addicted instantly. One night, while flying around, I saw a naked woman stepping out from behind a tree, and I suddenly understood that I actually had control over my dream. This led to intensive experimentations and an even increased motivation to spend my nights in the sauna room. Even though I was entirely conscious while out and about, dream control and volition were difficult to maintain, and my adventures were mostly a mix of control and arbitrary events.

Taisha Abelar's work had strongly affected Victoria too, and she had finally positively connected to this myth on her own terms. She was intrigued by recapitulation and wanted to explore it for herself. However, she felt that it would be easier to muster the discipline for an extended recapitulation if we would go away temporarily, to a mountain retreat or somewhere else secluded. Finding a retreat where I could hone my dreaming attention and where Victoria could recapitulate undisturbed, sounded like an enjoyable navigation project. And while Victoria was occupied with a visit from her mother, I embarked on this new treasure hunt.

I began by intending to get the first cue in dreaming, and as soon as I was out of my body the next time, I thought about finding a place for our project. Instantly I was hovering above my meditation spot on top of the hill, and then I woke up. It was getting light already, so I physically hiked up the hill and sat down on my spot, awaiting the sunrise as silent and alert as possible. The unfolding scenery was awe inspiring, and it took a while until my eyes were willing to close. From up here I had a 360-degree view of one of the most spectacular coastlines along the West Coast.

The moment the first sunrays hit my closed eyes, a small gust of wind startled me from behind. I was concentrating on my breathing, waiting for a vision or a cue that would tell me where to go, but nothing happened. The only thing that kept forcing itself into my awareness was the wind. It had a nagging and pushy quality this morning, and I was just on verge of getting annoyed when it dawned on me that I also had the choice of going along with it. I had come up here to find out where to go, so why not let the wind tell me. The moment I formed this thought a really strong gust nearly blew off my hat.

Immediately I returned to the house to get my compass, and as soon as I was back up on the hill, I determined exactly in which direction the wind was pushing me. Then I used the precise heading and drew a straight line onto a map. The first town that the line crossed was Yuma, Arizona. This had been one of the most capricious navigational maneuvers I ever performed, but it felt compelling and logical at the time. So I packed my bags and headed to Yuma to start on my quest. Yuma was not a bad starting place at all. Supposedly it had been don Juan's home town.

"Yuma?" Victoria frowned. "That doesn't sound too exciting. Isn't it terribly hot?"

"It is just a starting point," I laughed, trying to disperse her concerns. "Let me just play with this and see where it leads."

I was in my element again. Before long I was driving attentively through Yuma, listening and looking, watching for synchronicities or anything else that stood out, keeping myself always in reception mode so as not to miss a cue. To avoid becoming too obsessive with my treasure hunt I had bought a high quality Nikon camera for the trip. This would give me something else to do. Since I was tuned into my environment anyway, I took pictures of everything that caught my eye along the way.

I felt much in harmony with the world, and it talked to me extensively. From Yuma I was first led to Tucson, Patagonia, and Bisbee, all in Arizona, and then into Mexico. Navigating like this is definitely not an exact science, but it is far from being arbitrary. Even though I focused predominantly on my environment, my navigational guidance did not come entirely from the outside; it appeared to come from life itself, which was just as much inside of me as it was everywhere else. More than anything, navigating seemed to involve aligning my inside with the outside, so to speak. As such, I couldn't really define it as finding and following the cues and signs of life, but as a total and uncompromising alignment with life. This, of course, entails relinquishing any personal agenda that one may have, which ultimately is a complete surrender.

Still falling short of allowing a complete surrender I was navigating one cue, sign, and hunch at a time. Some were more compelling than others. At one point I came to a stop sign in Bisbee and did not know which way to turn, so I just sat there and waited. Suddenly somebody honked behind me, and in reflex I went left, which brought me to Mexico.

Bisbee I had found because I went to investigate the source of a sparkling reflection in the morning sun while I was meditating in the Saguaro National Monument near Tucson. It turned out to be the shaving mirror of a hiker who was camping a few miles away from where I sat. When I found him, I learned that he was from Bisbee, and he kept telling me what a great place it was. It wasn't really, and it certainly did not draw me in for longer than a night.

My treasure hunt took me all the way to Alamos in Sonora, Mexico, where the road ended, literally, at least the pavement. Coming from Guaymas and Navajoa, the sky had been cloudless and deep blue all day, but as I came over the last hill, a few miles outside of Alamos, I stared straight into a huge black thunderhead with a magnificent semicircle rainbow framing the town. From a navigational perspective it was nearly a joke. Not a shadow of a doubt: I had arrived.

Alamos is an old silver mining town and now a national historic monument, and it had even been declared "Pueblo Magico" or "magical village" by the government. It looked so perfectly quaint, colonial, and quintessentially Mexican that it was nearly corny. On Sundays the "rancheros" came to town on horseback, walking around the main plaza in their sombreros, playing guitar and singing, while groups of young girls were trailing them, laughing and flirting.

I checked into a gorgeous hacienda-style hotel, and as I walked out onto the street, a woman offered me her services as a tourist guide. She was well mannered, and I immediately liked her.

"Good afternoon, Senor," she addressed me with a broad smile. "My name is Maria Gutierrez; I am working for the visitor's bureau. If you are interested, I can organize a tour of the historical buildings and residences for you."

"This is kind of you," I replied. "I am actually looking for a house to rent here, a nice and quiet house, if possible."

She thought for a moment and said, "There are quite a few houses for rent, and one is particularly beautiful. If you want I can get the keys, and we can go there right now. It is only about five minutes from here."

The house was absolutely perfect for our purpose. It was a classical colonial one story building, located on a quiet cobblestone street, with three rooms and a large kitchen, built around a beautifully tiled courtyard with a small fountain and a huge mango tree. Two large sunken, windowless, and cool bedrooms with separate baths looked like the ideal setting for our endeavor. With Maria's help I contacted the owner and rented the house for a period of six months. Victoria sounded excited when I called her and described everything. Mission accomplished.

After finding a temporary tenant for our house in Mendocino we moved to Alamos and went right to work. Victoria had already made a list for her recapitulation, and she pretty much vanished into her room from day one. She had amazing discipline. If her mind was set on something, she never deviated. It was incomprehensible though that we never discussed the possible repercussions of her recapitulating me and our relationship. It was a mysterious and ominous oversight.

While Victoria went to work, unraveling her energetic entanglements, I set up my room for dreaming. Since I usually did not do much spontaneous dreaming in bed, I had to prepare specific places for this purpose. I built a cozy little dream nest on the floor, in a corner behind a Spanish screen, and I hung up a hammock and a separate contraption that allowed me to dangle from the ceiling in a sitting posture. I wanted to experiment to learn how different positions would affect my dreaming experience. I would go into my room at any given time, get comfortable in one of the positions and then go through the routines that brought about my coveted astral adventures. More often than not, I just fell asleep. Since I could only sleep and dream so much, I spent a lot of time reading, cooking, shopping, and wandering around town.

As time went by, our retreat in Alamos evolved into an emotional pressure cooker. On top of the perceptual and emotional intensity that came with our activities, the weather was becoming blazingly hot, and occasional monsoon thunderstorms were so violent that the streets turned into raging rivers. My walks through the village at odd times often felt so ethereal and magical that I had a hard time differentiating them from my lucid dreams. And being absorbed as we were in our rather unusual exercises, we found it more and more difficult to connect with each other when we met for meals or during arbitrary breaks on the courtyard patio.

When we had to end our retreat after about four months because Victoria needed to fly to Hungary to attend to a family matter, we were actually quite relieved. This attempted crash course in sorcery had not exactly been a honeymoon. Victoria's thorough recapitulation had affected our level of intimacy profoundly, and we had to re-invent our relationship.

ᵥ ᵥ ᵥ

We were on our way to the Los Angeles airport as we stopped in Tucson for the night. After driving all day, we were utterly exhausted, and all we wanted was a shower and a good night's sleep. We were just ready to go to bed when the local evening news on television announced that this night was the yearly peak in meteorite shower activity, and that the show was going to be spectacular.

"Did you hear that?" I asked Victoria, who was in the bathroom.

"Yes, something about meteorite showers tonight." She sounded tired.

"We should have a look," I suggested, "just for half an hour or so. You want to come?"

"OK, whatever," she answered, shrugging her shoulders while she came out of the bathroom.

We drove up to Gates Pass, which was just fifteen minutes from our motel. There we were shielded from the city lights and had a magnificent view of the night sky. Tucson is very conscious of light pollution because of the large number of astronomical observatories that use the clear high desert skies in the area.

"Let's climb up those rocks, just a little bit," I said as we had parked the car. Suddenly we weren't tired anymore. The evening was exquisite. The air was refreshingly cool and clear, and all the rocks around us were radiating a pleasant warmth after having been baked all day by the sun. There were quite a few people scattered around, sitting on boulders and looking at the sky. Even as we were climbing up a few hundred feet we could already see shooting stars right and left, and we had to be careful not to slip in the darkness with all the distraction.

As soon as we had made ourselves comfortable on a nice flat boulder, the fireworks really began.

"Wooow ... .Oh my god ... ... Jesus, did you see this one?.....oooh ... . yoooh ... ." It was impossible to keep quiet. I had never seen anything like it. There weren't just a few shooting stars streaking down the sky.

They were all over, seemingly coming from all directions, crossing the sky from one side to the other. Huge ones. Some exploded midway into several smaller pieces "Unbelievable!"

Gradually we quieted down and just witnessed this spectacle in silent awe. The boulder below us generously released its soothing warm energy, keeping us comfortable while we gazed at infinity, at billions of stars and the brilliant band of the Milky Way. The fireworks of burning and exploding meteorites went on for a long time, making us shudder again and again with its unsolicited splendor.

"I think I want to come back to Tucson after I drop you off at the airport." was all I could say after we were back at the motel. We had not spoken a word on our way back down from Gates Pass.

"Yes," I reiterated, "that solves the problem of where I am going to live until you come back."

I did not really want to go to Mendocino at the moment, particularly not by myself. And we had a tenant in the house anyway, who would not be too happy to move out yet.

"Yes," Victoria agreed, "you like the desert, don't you?" She did not seem too interested.

Yes, I liked the desert. Tucson had seduced me in one single evening and my life there would evolve as spectacularly as the meteorite shower had promised. I moved into "The Promontory," a happy, pink, and beautifully landscaped apartment oasis. It was a sprawling complex with several pools and Jacuzzis, a fitness center, and yoga and aerobics classes. But despite all the amenities, my spacious ground floor apartment was private and quiet. I went right back into dreaming mode. To create the ideal environment, I used tin foil and duct tape to hermetically seal one of my two rooms against light from the outside until it was perfectly dark. This way I could live around the clock and use the room at any time of the day for dreaming. I bought half a dozen books on lucid dreaming and astral projection and, true to my compulsive nature, focused obsessively on honing my dreaming awareness.

"So what are you doing all day alone?" Victoria asked during one of our phone conversations.

"I try to keep my mind on dreaming," I said truthfully. "Reading about it helps a lot. You have no idea how many books there are on this topic.

They aren't all good, but most of them are stimulating and helpful in one way or another. And whenever I feel like it, I go into my darkroom and try to get out of my body. It's really working great," I reported excitedly.

It was indeed working great, and the few months I was alone in Tucson were the best in my life as far as dreaming was concerned. I had finally acquired a degree of control over my dream journeys that allowed me to go beyond just indulging in fantasies and sense gratification. I pursued many personal knowledge projects, communicated with conscious forms of energy I encountered "out there," and I broadcast my intent.

Out of the body is an interesting place, to say the least. Broadcasting my intent in dreaming meant that I was actually going through the subjective experience of calling out the word "intent" as loud as possible while standing next to my sleeping body in total clarity of mind. I was used to voicing or even yelling "intent" while in normal waking state. It was my way of beckoning freedom, my prayer for liberation. Naturally I had no clear concept of freedom. I did not know what liberation really meant or entailed. The emotional charge that went into the calling of "intent" was a kind of definitive resolve, a declaration of readiness for whatever the universe had in store for me, an attempt to drown out the concerns of the ego, a "yes" at all cost.

Nothing could have prepared me for what happened when I yelled "intent" in dream space, though. I yelled at the top of my dream lungs, and I instantly felt that I had gotten the attention of the entire universe. After a moment of total silence an echo of monumental proportions came my way. I felt a myriad of awarenesses turning towards me, an infinity of invisible eyes and ears, something entirely beyond my comprehension, and I immediately fled back into my waking state. I rushed out of the apartment where I slowly solidified in the reassuring sunlight and the calming desert breeze.

163

Once, shortly after separating from my body, I was sucked into an opening that had formed in the wall in front of me. After a short flight through a tunnel that seemed streaked with luminous fibers, I was spit out onto a meadow. As I was trying to orient myself, I felt drawn to a house in the distance and soon found myself floating towards it at an increasing speed. I was unable to resist the pull and, within seconds, I literally popped into a man who was standing in one of the rooms of the house, and who was engaged in a conversation with his wife, as I realized instantaneously. I had completely taken over his body and mind, and the woman who was now in front of me, stared into my eyes, looking startled and concerned.

"Are you all right? What is going on? Speak to me!" She shook me by the shoulders.

I desperately tried to wiggle back out of her husband's body. I was getting terribly embarrassed and did not know what to do. Finally I managed to wake up in my room, and I hoped that the woman had her husband back, unharmed. I instantly felt that I had had a connection with this man, which I later understood as cyclic. In general, dream space did not appear to be homogeneous. There were several different levels of vibration, or different levels of solidity, that I was able to differentiate. The space or world, in which I had popped into my cyclic counterpart, felt decidedly like a parallel universe and quite different from the dreamscapes I normally encountered.

My most profound dreaming experience happened shortly after I had so boldly broadcast my intent into "hyperspace." I had just left my body again and was looking around the room, contemplating what to do. Volition during these conscious dream states continued to be a challenge. I could basically do what I wanted, but most of the time nothing came to mind. In this particular instance, I was unexpectedly made to experience a profound shift of consciousness and instantaneously all differentiation was gone. Then I reverted back to my normal state, where I felt distinct and separate from everything else. Again I dissolved into undifferentiated awareness. It was an experience of oneness, and yet oneness did not feel like a correct description because there was no sense of one, there was just total, universal awareness which was I. Then I shifted back to my separate state again. While in my normal, separated state, however, I had no notion of just having experienced universal awareness, and when I was the universe itself again, I had no notion of the separate state. There was no apparent connection between the two. Only in retrospect did I notice that I had been oscillating back and forth between these two states of awareness for an indeterminate amount of time, back and forth, individual and universal, separate and one, differentiated and undifferentiated, back and forth, back and forth . . . until all of a sudden a realization formed and took hold, expressing itself in a most unusual explosion of laughter. It was as if the realization and the laughter had its origin in the oscillation itself, in a reality between those two states. I had never known this kind of laughter. It was a total, complete, quintessential laughter, starting at my core and exploding outward into infinity, an all-consuming and all-knowing laughter. It was not my separate self that was laughing, nor was it the universal awareness. Rather than being the result of a realization, the laughter felt like the realization itself.

"How could we have forgotten?" "How could we have so completely forgotten?" This is hilarious!" were the first thoughts that came to my mind as the laughter finally abated. And then I woke up.

ᵛ ᵛ ᵛ

Once Victoria returned from Europe we realized that we wanted to stay in Arizona. After several months of soul-searching, we concluded that we would never move back to northern California, and with a heavy heart we sold our Mendocino property to our tenant. After that, our attention turned towards finding our new home in Tucson. Following an energetic map that I had created of the area, we found a beautiful property in the Catalina foothills on the north side of town. It was totally private, bordered by a seasonal creek, and surrounded by several acres of lush desert vegetation. Everything felt right about it, including the current owners who had a pleasant energy. We spent a few hours on the grounds, discussing all the details, and finally agreed to let the owners know the next morning if we would buy it.

Now all that was needed was to get a green light from the universe, so to speak. As the sun was setting I drove back to the house. I parked my car at a distance so nobody would see me. Then I secretly approached the back side of the property through the dry creek bed and found a place about fifteen feet from the fence where I could sit down comfortably, without being visible from the house. I had a good view of the back patio and the pool area with its two magnificent date palms, several large Saguaro cacti, honeysuckle bushes, and a variety of other plants. The house looked gorgeous against the evening sky. It was an authentic burnt-adobe structure with shaded patios and fountains, perfectly adapted to the hot desert climate. But we needed an omen. Buying a house was a significant and far reaching decision, and we would not go forward if it was not supported by the spirit.

I sat on the warm desert floor, leaning against a mesquite tree and waited curiously. Anything could happen. A sudden thunderstorm could drench me. Snakes, scorpions, spiders, mosquitoes, gnats, ants, all could easily turn into unfavorable omens, not to speak of the mountain lions that were fairly common in the foothills.

I noticed how quiet it was. The rustling of the evening breeze and the distant howl of a coyote was all I could hear at the moment. The light came on in the kitchen. The owners were probably preparing their dinner.

Suddenly, in a soundless swoop, a big owl dropped out of the date palm and landed on the edge of the roof. It fluffed its feathers and stared directly in my direction. It was a gorgeous animal, about a foot and a half tall, and I was excited. "Thank you!" I said to the twilight in front of me. I was moved. This was a great sign. Owls had only positive connotations for me. I couldn't even imagine a more meaningful symbol as an answer to my quest. Owls represented wisdom, mystery, and magic for me and all throughout mythology. And while I was still musing about my good fortune, a second owl swooped out of the tree and landed next to the first one. Then, even before I could get excited, the first owl took off and flew straight towards me, perching on a fencepost, barely fifteen feet away from me. I held my breath. Only moments later, the second owl followed, and as it landed on the same post, it immediately began mating with its partner.

I have no idea how long these two beautiful creatures performed this extraordinary spectacle right in front of me. I was absolutely spellbound and time was not part of my reality at this magical moment. Whatever had responded to my request for an omen, was not only extremely generous, but also had an exquisite sense of humor. It goes without saying that we bought the house, and we were glad we did. Incidentally, the day we moved in, four owls, the parents and their two chicks from the previous year, sat lined up on the lowest branch of the date palm, greeting us. We all became good friends.

❧ ❧ ❧

Tucson held what the meteorite shower and the mating owls had promised. It brought a refreshed sense of clarity and intensity into our endeavors, and at long last, it would finally deliver us into the Nagual's world. Among the many good things that happened was my meeting Brian, one of my neighbors at "The Promontory." He was a psychologist and we met regularly at the pool or in the Jacuzzi, having long and interesting conversations about his work.

"Why don't you go back to school and get a degree in psychology yourself," He suggested one day after I had confided in him that I wished I had studied psychology rather than business.

"Me, going back to school?" I laughed. "Not in this lifetime." I brushed off his idea, still having vivid memories of sitting through boring lectures and cramming for exam after exam. It didn't really compare well with spending my days with lucid dreaming, yoga and aerobics classes, and the luxury of unlimited leisure.

"Maybe you should just check out the psychology department at the university here, or even sit in during one of the lectures. It is a great school. You might like it," Brian kept insisting. As a matter of fact, he seemed to have made it a project to get me back to school. Every time we met, he found a way to keep the topic alive, and eventually I went to check out the psychology department at the University of Arizona. I was instantly hooked.

I loved the campus, the architecture, the grounds, the energy . . . everything. The psychology department had a heavy leaning towards cognitive psychology and a brand-new program in cognitive sciences, an interdisciplinary study of the mind. It combined the approaches of several disciplines, including psychology, philosophy, anthropology, linguistics, computer science, and cognitive neuroscience to gain comprehensive insights into cognition and consciousness. I went to the admissions department at the end of my first visit and was enrolled for the next semester. I had run into open doors everywhere I went. Brian kept pushing me, Victoria was encouraging and enthusiastically supportive, bureaucratic hurdles dissipated before my eyes, and synchronicities abounded. This was another navigational "no-brainer," pulling me inescapably into years of the most intense mental activity imaginable.

Contrary to my initial concerns about the rigors of going back to school, I was actually in heaven. The meteorite shower had not only been a good omen, but also a fitting analogy of my mental state during the time I lived in Tucson. Diving head-on into this high-powered interdisciplinary dissection of the human mind created ongoing celestial fireworks in my head. The in-depth exploration of topics such as perception, language development, artificial intelligence, cognitive neuroscience, and the philosophy of knowledge, was fascinating. Since most of my fellow students were about half my age, I became friends with many of the professors, which, of course, intensified my involvement even further. As a special bonus and as the highlight of my academic fever-dream, I became involved in the first international conference "Towards a Scientific Basis for Consciousness, Tucson I" in the spring of 1994. The conference marked the first major gathering devoted entirely to unlocking the mysteries of consciousness from a scientific perspective. It explored the whole spectrum of approaches from philosophy of mind and dream research, to neuropsychology, pharmacology, and molecular dynamics, to neural networks, phenomenological accounts, and even the physics of reality. Among the participants and presenters were Nobel Prize winners and academic luminaries from all over the world.

Day after day, for a whole week, I absorbed every bit of knowledge I could get my brain cells on, from early-morning lectures to late-night poster sessions; and the resulting high powered my studies all the way to the end. I surprised myself by graduating summa cum laude and probably would have pursued an academic career if the Nagual had not unintentionally rescued me. Not that there is anything wrong with academic pursuits, but I found that there is an ultimately fatal danger in believing the findings and fabrications of our thinking mind to be fundamental facts and truths. The more sophisticated the acrobatics of the mind, the more convincing and compelling they are to us. Particularly in retrospect, it became clear to me that the attempt to understand the human mind and consciousness only makes sense as a pragmatic pursuit, to develop artificial intelligence and robotics, for example, or for the sheer enjoyment of knowledge. To pursue knowledge in order to find existential truths and to understand life and the universe, I found to be utter folly.

"You have to develop a *romance* with knowledge," was the Nagual's tenet on this topic, which strikes me as a most elegant way out of this dilemma. A romance with knowledge makes me think of the aesthetical dimension of knowledge, of beauty, love, and passion, of knowledge for knowledge's sake, without any claim to truth. As it happened, I was rescued from searching for the truth, and eventually I let it go completely; I got it out of my system. And even though this result was rather unexpected, it was worth all my efforts.

Interestingly, after nearly twenty years of my own intense explorations, and after studying the human mind in the most scientific and systematic way available, I was basically back to my original realization, that in order to understand our mind and the world it perceives, we would have to be smarter than our mind. This, of course, is a paradox and leaves us with no truly fundamental knowledge. I had found out the hard way that the more I learned, the less I really knew. But unlike when I was in my twenties back in Sri Lanka, this realization produced neither hedonism nor cynicism.

Letting go of the idea that I am able to understand life liberated me to live it more fully, more experientially, organically, intuitively, interactively, and directly.

Maybe we *are* smarter than our minds after all.

The Nagual's World

"How did you like *The Art of Dreaming*?" Tracy asked during one of our phone conversations.

"Oh ... hm ... it felt somehow different than all the other books actually, don't you think?" I responded. "I don't know how to explain. The whole mood is different, as if someone else had written it."

"Really?" Tracy's raised voice startled me. He sounded nearly alarmed.

"Well, I love the book; it is powerful, of course. I was just surprised." I tried not to make it sound like a criticism.

Tracy Kramer was Carlos Castaneda's literary agent, and I had called him occasionally to find out when the next book would be available. Now I was giving some feedback as he had suggested. I never dared to ask about anything else, fearing to be rebuffed, but in the back of my mind I always hoped to find some kind of inroad into the world of the Nagual through Tracy.

The Art of Dreaming had indeed struck me as carrying a different intent than all the previous eight books by Castaneda. I found it to be much more ominous and less abstract and transcendental than I cared for. I never got quite used to this new mood, but it did not prevent me from appreciating its premise. With its extensive and detailed description of sophisticated dreaming techniques, it brought my experimentation with lucid dream states to a whole new level. The practice of accessing different layers of reality by passing through so called "gates of dreaming" was entirely original and led to profound insights into the potential of the human experience. On some occasions, using these techniques brought about conscious dreams that felt so solid and real that they were indistinguishable from everyday reality. This left me confused upon waking up and convinced me that the "real world" is in fact nothing but

TRIALS AND TRIBULATIONS

a collective dream, appearing so solid only because it is dreamt by over six billion people simultaneously.

During another one of my exploratory phone calls to Tracy Kramer's office I talked to one of his colleagues, Renata Murez, who informed me about an upcoming workshop in Mexico City.

"Carlos is probably not going to be there," she said, "but Florinda Donner, Taisha Abelar, and Carol Tiggs will be. You should definitely come, if you can make it."

"Of course, I'll be there. Thank you much for letting me know," I said happily.

"Yes, yes, yes, yes!" I threw up my fist in celebration after I had put the phone down. "You can be sure I'll be there."

I could hardly believe this was happening. On the surface level I had nearly resigned myself to never making an actual connection with the Nagual or any of his cohorts. I was also somewhat ambiguous about needing anything or anybody on my journey towards freedom. I certainly did not like to think of myself as a desperate follower or "groupie," spending his life searching for a guru and savior. Carlos Castaneda had written nine books to date, Florinda Donner three, and Taisha Abelar one. This added up to a vast body of knowledge and practical wisdom—more than sufficient, if I would only use it all and put it into practice.

I had not been desperate by any means, but I was ecstatic nevertheless that finally a door had opened. But I also was immediately apprehensive; my worry-loving mind would not have it any other way.

"Do you think these people are for real?" I asked Victoria. "I have a hard time imagining Florinda and Taisha giving a workshop. A workshop—on what? Sorcery?"

"Well, you will know in a few weeks," she answered.

"You don't want to come?" I asked incredulously, "Taisha Abelar will be there."

"No, no, it's ok, you go ahead and check it out," Victoria said. "It is quite a lot of money for both of us. But you should definitely go."

I was surprised, but also somewhat relieved. I expected Victoria to be much more critical, and if the "real" people did not live up to our expectations, she might be more inclined than me to deconstruct this myth, which had pretty much become the basis of my entire worldview.

172

∀ ∀ ∀

My first encounter with the real-life world of the Nagual took place in the auditorium of the Anthropological Museum in Mexico City. The venue was appropriate. Many of the artifacts, particularly in the Toltec exhibit, held great significance in my world at the time. I had been to the museum many times during previous visits to Mexico City, and, naturally, I spent most of the afternoon there before the introductory talk to saturate myself with the energy of the ancient symbols and artifacts and to shift into magic mode. In the morning I had met with the local organizer of the workshop, a likable and well-spoken young man named Marcos Antonio Karam. He was the director of "Casa Tibet," the Tibetan Buddhist Institute in Mexico City. He was a personal friend of the Dalai Lama. I instantly felt a deep connection and kinship with Tony and was delighted every time we met during my many subsequent visits. Only later I found out that "Tony Lama," as he was fondly called by the Nagual, had been chosen as his heir apparent, the lineage bearer and next Nagual, but Tony never took on this role and eventually fell out of favor.

The auditorium filled early. Many workshop attendants had lined up to get a front seat. I ended up in the center, about ten rows from the stage. There were perhaps three hundred people in attendance.

"Hi, my name is Luis Marquez," a friendly young man, who sat to my right, introduced himself. "I am from Puerto Rico, where are you from?"

I introduced myself and told him about my background, and we kept chatting until the lecture began. Luis turned out to be the brother of Talia Bey, one of the Nagual's closest associates. More than anything, he had come to the workshop to see his sister. She had terminated all contact with her family during the process of re-inventing herself as an impersonal warrior in the world of the Nagual. Unfortunately for him, she was not going to be at this workshop.

Then, suddenly, all eyes turned to a side entrance as the protagonists emerged into the auditorium.

Here they were. Finally the myth had some faces, and instantly my mind went to work, judging and processing everything. Previously superhuman, magical beings like Florinda Donner, Taisha Abelar, and the nagual woman Carol Tiggs had turned into humans. Florinda was my instant favorite. She looked at least as fascinating as I had imagined her. Her face was elfish, mischievous, all-knowing, and incredibly alive. Florinda sparkled and her charismatic presence single-handedly pulled me through this process of adjustment, dispersing any doubts I might have had about everyone's authenticity. I didn't really know what to think of the rest of the group, and probably this was a good thing. Taisha appeared rather non-nondescript and obscure, not showing much of herself, which gave her a detached and somewhat mysterious aura. Both these women were trim and light. Carol Tiggs seemed heavy in comparison. She was pretty, with a soft, even face and a well formed body, but her energy appeared denser than that of the two others, and her self-confident demeanor bordered on arrogance. Besides the witches, who all looked to be in their late forties, there were three female and two male apprentices. The three female apprentices, also known as the "Chacmools," were Renata Murez, Nyei Murez, and Kylie Lundahl. They looked like impeccable apprentices, keenly avoiding showing a personal face. The two male apprentices were Lorenzo Drake and Julius Renard. They were referred to as the "Elements." Julius, as I found out later, was actually Tracy Kramer, Castaneda's agent.

The group felt distinct from the audience. Their appearance was otherworldly, even alien. The females all had short hair and were dressed androgynously. The males were unobtrusive and low-key, appearing to have only a symbolic role. All introduced themselves, or were introduced, in the case of the males.

Then the witches took to the stage, and over the next three hours they spun their mythical web. Some of their stories were outlandish, like don Juan and the old sorcerers being trapped in some distant layer of reality, and about inorganic beings that are preying on human energy like psychic parasites, keeping humanity's awareness from growing. Having spent considerable time in conscious dream states, I had developed quite an expanded worldview and could not readily discard any of these scenarios. I was actually quite excited to share in the inter-subjectivity of such an enhanced view of reality. This was all interesting stuff. But no matter how esoteric some of the precepts were, the practical maneuvers that the witches proposed were rock solid and sound.

The main message that I received out of this and many other

workshops was always the same: To access our totality and our full potential, we have to raise and cultivate our awareness. The tools and strategies to achieve this goal were discipline, impeccability, internal silence, and the "Magical Passes" or "Tensegrity." The overriding goal of this and all subsequent workshops was to teach us "Tensegrity," a series of movements designed to raise our awareness by reconfiguring and redistributing our energy. The term *Tensegrity* is short for tensional integrity. Borrowed from architecture, it refers to a structural balance where everything is working together in synergy. Tension and compression, push and pull, are optimized as in the case of a geodesic dome, for example, creating a self-supporting structure of immense stability.

The Magical Passes, for the most part, were aimed at creating this tensional integrity, optimal synergy, and dynamic balance in the practitioner. In the Nagual's world there was no differentiation between body and mind. Body and mind were considered an undivided entity. There was, however, another dualism we were made aware of, the dualism between our mind-body and our energy-body. The mind-body is the familiar entity with which we normally operate in the world. The energy-body, from which we have become estranged, is the energetic twin of this entity, but it is not governed by a self-reflective mind. As such it is our gateway into infinity, in a manner of speaking. To re-connect with our energy-body was necessary in order to reach our totality and our evolutionary destiny. The Nagual's perception was, as I understood it from the witches, that the best way to re-unite with our energy-bodies was through optimizing the integrity of our mind-bodies. To reach this goal, Tensegrity had become his strategy of choice. The movements were mostly bypassing the thinking mind, which in its current form was seen as the main obstacle between us and our true unified self.

This strategy felt compelling, and I committed myself to the Magical Passes with my usual compulsiveness. For two full days following the introductory lecture, we were instructed in Tensegrity by the Chacmools. The movements were straightforward and easy to learn. They resembled an esoteric form of Kung Fu. Usually we were only given a minimal rationale for each movement in order to pacify the mind without engaging it too much. This was definitely the overriding formula governing all the instruction coming from the Nagual through the witches and the Chacmools:

"How can we be optimally affected and motivated to change, without engaging the thinking mind?"

Movements had to be the answer. It was certainly not an entirely new concept. Yoga and Qigong probably evolved along a similar intent. But both movement forms are now, more often than not, practiced outside the evolutionary and transcendental context in which they originated. They have been hijacked by the fitness movement of modern societies for the most part, and their intent has been altered and weakened as a result. I still think that these ancient oriental movement systems have a powerful evolutionary potential, but in direct comparison with Tensegrity, they lacked originality and the magical component that I found so enticing. The Magical Passes were incredibly alive and instantly began to enhance my energetic perception of the world.

Even though there was a huge difference between how I had envisioned the Nagual's world and how I experienced it during this first real encounter, I was not disappointed. The transition into this new chapter of my magical journey had been compelling and powerful.

⌄ ⌄ ⌄

"Did you get a chance to talk with Florinda and Taisha?" Victoria asked when I was back in Tucson.

"No, not really," I answered, "they were all keen to deflect everything personal. No personal questions, no personal contact. The emphasis was exclusively on the Magical Passes. Of course, I was curious, but there was no room for this kind of interaction."

I gave Victoria a detailed account of everything that had transpired during the workshop, but despite my obvious excitement she did not seem inclined to join me for any of the upcoming meetings. She had actually intensified her Buddhist meditation practice and planned to attend some silent retreats instead. We did not perceive this to be much of a conflict any more. There were vast differences in mood, terminology, and practice in our respective belief systems at the time, but ultimately they both aimed at achieving a state of internal silence. As far as we knew, the underlying intent of both systems was to guide us into the experience of silent awareness, of becoming able to be fully conscious without having to think. In Buddhist terminology this experience is often called emptiness, because it is empty of thought. In the Nagual's world it was usually referred to as infinity. I guess, I preferred the term infinity, maybe because it sounded like a lot more than emptiness to my unenlightened mind. Besides, in the Nagual's world, the journey into silence, his road to infinity, seemed surprisingly attractive, magical, and enchanting. It did not occur to me at the time that the Nagual might actually have intended a little detour.

Whatever it was, it motivated me enough to practice Tensegrity every morning and evening for up to three hours a day. Nearly every month the witches and the Chacmools offered another workshop, and I did not miss a single one. I traveled to Hawaii, California, Colorado, Arizona, New York, Spain and Germany, and many more times to Mexico City to learn an ever-growing number of movements that my body absorbed like a sponge.

After several months of this saturation, one night I found myself doing an entirely original movement over and over in one of my dreams until I became lucid. I realized then that this movement was pertinent to me, and after practicing it a few more times in the dream, I woke myself up so I could execute the movement in my waking state. This way, I was sure to capture it as precisely as possible. From then on I incorporated it into my practice. I had never done this movement before, but it was similar to other Magical Passes, insofar as its intent seemed to be to redeploy energy, in this case to my midsection.

The more I saturated myself with Tensegrity the more it entered my dream-states, and more individualized movements appeared over time. It seemed that my body's own intelligence was making use of this technique, and I wondered if this effect was a hidden intent of Tensegrity. In any case, the fact that my body had created some Magical Passes all by itself, without the interference of my mind, had only increased my trust in the integrity of the Magical Passes in general.

No dramatic changes occurred as a result of my intensive practice, but my body, as well as my will, acquired a hardness, definition, and determination that I had not known before. By the time I finally met the Nagual himself in August of that same year, I had allowed myself to be wholeheartedly re-configured by the Magical Passes. I was committed to his world with skin and bones.

⌄   ⌄   ⌄

Some bizarre car trouble in the middle of the desert caused me to arrive late to the introductory meeting. Carlos Castaneda had already begun to talk when I opened the door and my eyes fell on him. He stood on a small podium, about thirty feet away from the door against the back wall of the room. It was the beginning of a three-week intensive Tensegrity seminar he would be teaching himself. The setting was the Culver City High School Cafeteria, which had been available in August, and which was inconspicuous enough for our "sorcery summer theater." Carlos was a bundle of energy. Without any doing on my part, my perception suddenly zoomed in on him as if I were looking through a telescope. There he was, clearly the Miguel I remembered from Bandarawela, but noticeably trimmer and more athletic. His full, dark silvered hair was boyishly disheveled, and he was wearing new white tennis shoes, a new pair of dark blue Levi's and a pocketless blue dress shirt that was flawlessly ironed, perhaps even starched. His arms were gesticulating, describing something funny. He seemed bouncy, weightless, and his face had an intense, impish smile. He made me think of a naughty little boy and an old wizard at the same time. And on the top of his forehead I perceived two short protrusions that immediately disappeared as I took a second look. For a split second he had looked much more like Pan or Mephisto than the Miguel I remembered. He looked like the same person, but he had lost a lot of weight.

I forgot both thoughts as I became engrossed in what he was saying.

"How is it possible," he asked, "that we are all so obsessed with ourselves? 'Me, me, me, I, I, I,' is all we ever think about. We go to our grave, thinking 'me, me, me,' and at no time in our lives are we giving it up."

Then he went on to explain that all the energy and awareness that is necessary to see beyond the "me" is being consumed by the "flyers," a collective inorganic entity that thrives on the specific energy we are producing when we are focused on ourselves, like worry, fear, anger, despair, envy, etc.

"What makes us so sure that we are on top of the food chain?" he continued. "How can we be so sure? Just because we are not aware of a predator does not mean that we cannot be prey. How conscious are chickens that they basically exist only to supply us with eggs and meat."

"We have to get out of the chicken coop," he asserted vigorously, "and Tensegrity is going to help us."

It was genius. The idea of inorganic "flyers" keeping us like pets or livestock and preventing us from ever using our energy to explore our true potential was genius. The flyers supposedly had taken over our minds, putting our internal dialogue under their control. The only strategy for the being that had been hijacked in such a manner was to try anything possible to shut off that internal dialogue and to gather the strength and the resolve to shake off this "foreign installation," as the Nagual called these predators.

"That is the true purpose of Tensegrity."

The scenario was indeed genius. It is impossible to prove wrong, which makes it a definite possibility. And in the end it does not even matter if it is true or not, because the maintenance of health and vigor and the attainment of silent awareness are in our best interest anyway. But perhaps it is useful, or even easier to engage our intent against a "foreign installation" than just towards awakening to our evolutionary destiny.

I loved the man instantly—his Pan-like impishness, disheveled hair, tennis shoes and all.

He was an exquisite storyteller, delightful, fierce, and engaging. His sense for drama could make us shiver or fill our eyes with tears at the drop of a hat. The Chacmools did the bulk of the Tensegrity instruction, but the Nagual was present every single day, assisting with the Magical Passes, talking, teaching, and making us laugh.

179

Tensegrity was the main focus of the seminar, of course, but again and again, the importance of recapitulation was stressed.

"Recapitulation is mandatory. Nothing goes without recapitulation on the warrior's path," he said repeatedly.

The other recurring theme was impeccability.

"Impeccability is of overriding importance. It is the decision to always act the best way we can and then do a little bit more. If nothing is "too much" any more, we are in the realm of impeccability. In this realm we take everything as a challenge, no matter what happens. If it defeats us, we waste no time in laments and move on. Impeccability is fluidity. It knows no regrets. We just have to be impeccable and state our intent. The rest happens."

Many components of the Nagual's worldview related to a perceptual element he called the "assemblage point," an area of special intensity in our overall energy field where perception takes place. He maintained that, when viewed energetically, humans appear like a luminous cocoon, defined more or less in size by the reach of their outstretched arms. The cocoon is buzzing with a myriad of energetic filaments or emanations, and the assemblage point appears as a small area of intense luminosity on the periphery of the cocoon. Perception happens as the assemblage point aligns emanations on the outside of the cocoon with the corresponding emanations on the inside. The world that is assembled in this way naturally depends on the position of the assemblage point.

Apparently, when we are born, the position of the assemblage point is still undefined, but through the collective pull it gradually moves towards the same place as in everyone around us. This way we all share the same reality. Later, the assemblage point usually only moves in dreams, under the influence of certain drugs, and with trauma or intense pain. Otherwise, it is fixed by our fellowmen and our internal dialogue. The internal dialogue is the process that constantly strengthens the position of the assemblage point.

Ultimately, all of the Nagual's teachings aim at moving the assemblage point in a controlled fashion, thus accessing the entire field of human perceptual possibilities, which he understood to be our birthright. Internal silence is the key requisite to free our perception from its habitual setting, so to speak. Conscious dreaming, stalking, the Magical Passes, and intent are all tools to move the assemblage point, and the art of stalking and intent are again used to fix and stabilize it in a new position. Stalking is a form of controlled behavior that aims to create a new and coherent subjectivity, similar to acting. However, while acting usually entails only pretending to be someone else, stalking entails becoming someone else. It follows that true stalking requires relinquishing one's specific identity.

I had already been familiar and intrigued with the audacity of the Nagual's worldview from his written work. But hearing him expound it in so many new and charismatic ways finally brought it completely to life. His charm, wit, and vibrating presence were outright addictive. He made no claims or promises, but most of us were more than willing to follow his navigation. All limitations seemed off. It promised to be the ultimate adventure:

"Navigating on the sea of awareness? Count me in!"

⌄   ⌄   ⌄

While driving back to Tucson I pondered about the fact that I never had found an opening to ask the Nagual about our encounter in Sri Lanka. But with his relentless emphasis on avoiding anything personal, particularly any mention of our personal history, it would have reeked too much of self-importance and me, me, me. So I let it rest and hoped that he would approach me himself in due time, whenever the energy was right.

While I spent three weeks in the magical kingdom of the Nagual, Victoria had attended a four-week silent meditation retreat. Sorcery met Buddhism as we re-united at the Tucson airport at the end of her retreat. Our assemblage points were definitely in different positions. I had cut my hair short and was charged with defiance, passion, and determination. Victoria seemed vulnerable in comparison, highly sensitive and aware. She was wide open while I was more closed. Her eyes reflected concern.

"So, this is how you look now?" was one of her first questions.

It was incomprehensible that we could have moved this far apart. The overriding objective of both our belief systems was to attain internal silence, to reach a state of pure alert awareness. And yet, looking in Victoria's eyes, it seemed that we had moved in opposite directions. Was it possible that such divergent paths could lead to the same result?

It was a profound chasm that had opened between us. We had not just spent a few weeks apart. We both had wholeheartedly committed to vastly different spiritual paths for nearly eight months. While Victoria had aimed at observing and quieting her internal dialogue, I had changed it, and through Tensegrity I had engaged my whole body in my quest to evolve. While she intended her self out of the picture, I intended more than anything to claim my birthright. Unfortunately, both of us had fallen prey to a form of spiritual materialism. We were clearly each holding strong positions and ended up confronting each other, and in retrospect it is obvious that we were both being fooled by our minds. In the Nagual's terms, the flyers were having a field day with both of us.

In any case, as we faced each other across this chasm on that fateful day, the spirit decided to intervene with a beautiful display of personal synchronicities, and we both jumped across the abyss. Ultimately it was our deep love and affection that had created the synchronicities and the navigational imperative to jump. We let go of our holdings. For a precious little while, Buddhism and sorcery were both forgotten. What a refreshing reprieve.

▿   ▿   ▿

Things changed as a result of our letting go. We shared harmoniously and found a beautiful synergy. Everything began to work together—my academic studies of cognition and consciousness, the Buddhist principles of non-attachment and emptiness, and the magical mood, the passion, determination, and defiance of the Nagual's world.

Shortly after these events I received an invitation to attend a private practice session with the Nagual in Los Angeles. To my surprise and delight, Victoria was interested too, and the invitation was extended to her.

These private practice sessions usually took place on Sundays in a Santa Monica yoga studio and were free of charge. For nearly a year, Victoria and I flew in from Tucson every weekend, until we moved to Los Angeles in the summer of 1996. The practice group consisted on average of about twenty-five dedicated Tensegrity practitioners and was by invitation only. The invitation list changed frequently which kept everybody on their toes. It sometimes seemed arbitrary and cruel when some of us fell off the list, but it was hard to beat as a motivating strategy to encourage impeccability and discipline. As a result I pretty much followed the Nagual's suggestions to the letter.

One of his guidelines was not to treat our relationship with him in a personal way. He would often start a session by encouraging us to give him a cue or starting point. Rubbing his hands together in exaggerated expectation, he would begin by asking in a secretive voice:

"So, what's new? Tell me! Hm . . . Hm . . . Hm . . . ?" he glanced around the room mischievously. "Tell me a story, but without I or me? Tell me something truly interesting that has nothing to do with you!"

If someone was brave enough to volunteer, the Nagual would often use what was said to make a point or even develop a theme for the session. He told endless stories himself, usually highlighting human folly and the general insanity of the social order. He was an exquisite storyteller and always kept us laughing, basically at ourselves. Another frequent ploy was to expose and attack our self-importance by telling exaggerated or even fictitious stories about one of us that were severely embarrassing. For example, he might say that he had learned that John would masturbate up to five times every day, or that Jane had a bad hemorrhoid problem.

Often the witches and other immediate cohorts or Tensegrity instructors were also present at these Sunday sessions, and the atmosphere was always immensely charged and powerfully addictive. There was a marked change in everybody's energy level after every one of these two-hour sessions. All our eyes were usually shining intensely while leaving the yoga studio. Sometimes I perceived a strong tingling around my solar plexus area, or a pressure at the base of my neck, not unlike the sensation that occurs before the onset of a shift in awareness as caused by psychotropic agents like LSD or Mescaline. The mere proximity of the Nagual undoubtedly caused a shift in the assemblage point. Naturally we tried to prolong this state by spending time with the other session participants and by practicing the Magical Passes. Soon all our friends were from this inner circle of practitioners and particularly after moving to Los Angeles, we were permanently absorbed in a magical bubble, upheld by the force of the Nagual.

In addition to the Sunday sessions, large-scale Tensegrity workshops continued to be offered nearly every month in various locations of the Americas and Europe, sometimes with more than a thousand participants. Gradually I became involved in staffing these workshops, predominantly providing security, which meant to shield the Nagual, the witches, and especially Nury, the "Blue Scout," from the curiosity of workshop participants. At other times, I was asked to provide simultaneous translations of the talks to the usually large German contingent, and during a workshop in Berlin I was entrusted with the entire logistics. The most consistent and direct relationship I had was with Florinda, with whom I met quite frequently on various projects.

The Nagual's world had a number of clearly discernible parameters. Most fundamentally there was the paradigm of the assemblage point and the predatory scenario involving the flyers. In response to this there were the behavioral elements of defiance, impeccability, internal silence, and unbending intent; and there were the practical maneuvers of stalking, dreaming, and the Magical Passes. The fabric that tied all these elements together was the art of navigation.

Having had the privilege of spending countless hours in the inner world of the Nagual, it became patently obvious that nothing ever happened in his world that had not been the direct result of navigation. Every major action or decision by the Nagual was directly elicited or confirmed by navigational means. Undoubtedly, the Nagual was the master navigator, but his closest cohorts, particularly the witches and Nury, served as extended sensory organs, funneling navigational data his way. His intent may have changed over the years, and it was certainly influenced by his personality and idiosyncrasies, but his navigational maneuvers I have never perceived as anything but impeccable.

Uncompromising navigation may often look capricious from the outside, because most of us have forgotten how to perceive energetically and how to move through the world intuitively. To perceive energetically, we have to suspend labeling and interpreting everything around us. If we succeed, we find ourselves immersed in a kaleidoscope of energy configurations. Some of these energy configurations feel neutral, some feel attractive, and others repelling. As navigators we would naturally move away from repelling and towards attractive energies, much like I operated while flying our little airplane through the system of thunderstorms in the South of France. In order to determine what feels right, a navigator has only his or her impeccability.

As far as I could see, the Nagual was indeed uncompromising. If it became apparent that somebody's energy did not fit, he let that person go, and unless dictated by a navigational imperative or intent, as he called it, there was no second chance. One of his main pursuits was the molding of a coherent group of "warrior-travelers." He was intrigued by the concept of critical mass. An experiment with ants that he had come across, showed that the insects would behave erratically as long as their number was kept below a critical mass, in this case around fifty. Once the critical mass was reached, the whole group suddenly would organize and work together effectively. The Nagual speculated that if he could facilitate the formation of an energetically coherent group of practitioners and reach a critical mass, a collective shift in awareness would result. He continually experimented with us, like an energetic conductor with his orchestra. While we were practicing Tensegrity in small groups, he would move around between us, changing our positions in the room as if we were chess figures, until it felt just right. Whenever I was in his presence, my perception was that his exclusive intent was to navigate impeccably and create the optimal conditions to raise our awareness, individually and collectively. If he could not make us shift as a group, he at least wanted to bring us to the "border" individually.

Examples of the Nagual's energetic conducting were his pairing of Victoria and Renata on the basis of their cyclicity and of David and me on the basis of our complementariness. For the longest time he tried to integrate me into his innermost circle. Every outing I had with Florinda was carefully choreographed, and every time I was paired with a male or female member of his closest associates, but to no avail. There was never any chemistry, no fit at all. As a matter of fact, while I was sitting once on stage with Taisha Abelar, translating her talk at a workshop in Berlin, a giant steel bar crashed from the ceiling to the floor, fortunately not injuring anybody, but conveying to me in a rather chilling way that I did not really belong with them. This was a genuine dilemma for me at the time. While I was totally committed to the Nagual's world, I was also aware that I did not really fit. At the height of my enthusiasm I actually believed that eventually we would be able to slip into a collective dream as a group and go travel the sea of awareness. My only concern was that I was not at ease with my travel companions. And to travel through infinity with the wrong crowd sounded like a really bad trip.

185

❧ ❧ ❧

Even my relationship with the Nagual himself was strangely ambiguous. It was not so much that I liked some aspects of him and disliked others. It was more that I became aware of a split in myself.

One part of me was frequently frustrated by him and another part adored him unconditionally. The frustrated part was my usual self that wanted recognition, praise, special status, and promotion. It was the needy, self-reflective, insecure, disconnected, mind-controlled, flyer-feeding part of me that often resented the Nagual for failing to recognize my "specialness." On this mundane level, he was like the head coach, the team leader, the boss, and it was easy and convenient to find fault with him. Once my hubris even drove me to question his judgment in regard to the staffing of a Tensegrity workshop. We were having lunch at the Versailles, discussing a powerful four-day workshop that had just concluded. Lorenzo Drake had introduced a new series of Magical Passes, and the Nagual praised his performance.

"Lorenzo was fabulous, don't you think?" the Nagual beamed.

"Yes," I said, "but I was even more impressed with Julius. There was no ego at all in his demonstration, and his movements were incredibly precise."

The Nagual just looked at me with his unfathomably deep eyes, making me lose my thread for a moment. But I was driven. I never understood why he favored Lorenzo so much who struck me as quite an egomaniac while Julius always seemed unassuming and impeccable, like the quintessential warrior. I kept on ranting why I thought that Julius would have been the better choice to introduce the new movement series until the Nagual finally shut me off with a single forceful glance. The atmosphere at the table cooled considerably and his hug at the conclusion of our lunch meeting did not feel very cordial.

Fortunately my outburst did not terminate my apprenticeship. All that came out of my daring dissent were the Nagual's opening remarks at the beginning of our next group session:

"In case you don't know, we are not a democracy here. We do not navigate by consensus," he proclaimed with a mischievous glance in my direction. I doubt that anybody else had a clue what he was referring to, but I got the point.

It was challenging to suspend judgment, personal concerns, and any form of self-reflection while with the Nagual and the witches. Since none of us was quite ready to transcend our individual ego at the time, we ended up suppressing and transferring it. The most noticeable expression of this dynamic was a form of collective egomania that took on monumental proportions within our little world. With each other we pretended to be selfless warriors on an evolutionary quest for freedom, but as a group we felt unabashedly special. In our minds we were the chosen ones, the only ones that knew. We were the ones that were getting ready to leave the sinking ship of this despicably ignorant social order all around us. Despite all our efforts, our internal dialogues were anything but silent for most of the time. Our heads were filled with disdain for the social order, with stories of specialness, with concerns on how to advance in the hierarchy of our myth, and with hopes of being delivered by the Nagual. All of those thought processes caused more tension, fear, and frustration than peace and happiness, and the Nagual was obviously at the center of this dynamic.

But there was another part of me that had nothing to do with any of this. It was a fleeting and elusive part that felt more like a memory than an aspect of my personality. Or perhaps I should say that I am aware of this part more in retrospect then when it was actually present. It happened many times that I communicated with the Nagual with this other part of myself. It just did not register much in my rational mind. Whenever my thought processes stopped, which fortunately happened quite frequently in the Nagual's presence, I was flooded with a wave of unconditional affection and gratitude towards him, and all I could see in his glowing eyes was boundless affection as well. Particularly after some of his phenomenal and mind-stopping talks before a large audience during workshops, I just stood in awe and total silence, and suddenly I found myself in his embrace as he walked off the stage. These were literally timeless moments, and I felt that immensities transpired between us every time. I understood completely without having a single thought.

I also remember such timeless events at the Versailles during lunch meetings or during the occasional chance encounter. Once, the Nagual asked me to sit at his table, and while holding both my hands, he pulled me into his vision of what he called "the wheel of time." It was, in essence, a metaphorical rendering of his perception of reality as a presentation of countless parallel universes. He saw the possibility of "jumping grooves," as he called it; I understood it as switching lives or universes. His fascination with the mystery of awareness was absolutely genuine and pure, and again I bathed in this mutual experience of unconditional affection and silent understanding. He must have talked for nearly an hour but I was not aware of a single minute having passed. During these instances I felt enveloped in a bubble of energy that blocked out everything else. I never experienced this with anybody else. There was never an unfitting interruption; even outside sound seemed to be shielded off.

Another memorable event of this nature occurred only a few months before the Nagual's departure. While running a few errands, I passed a Nordstrom department store in my neighborhood, and suddenly I had the impulse to run in to get some shoelaces of all things. I had needed them for a long time, but in that moment it had just popped into my mind out of the blue. I was in a hurry and rushed inside, and as I reached the shoe department I saw the Nagual sitting in one of the chairs, and my momentum was so strong that I literally fell into the chair next to him, before I even said hello. I was afraid I had startled him but he showed no sign of surprise. His smile of recognition emerged slowly from a very deep place.

"Nagual . . . I am sorry . . . I don't know . . . I just fell into this chair. How are you?" I asked confused and still out of breath.

Now I saw Talia at a shoe rack nearby, holding a pair of designer shoes in her hands, greeting me with a faint smile.

"Talia is helping me to find a pair of shoes," the Nagual answered.

And then we just sat there for an indeterminate amount of time doing small talk, or not even talking at all. I kept touching his arm or shoulder whenever I addressed him. His eyes were extremely deep and warm. Talia did not interfere and at some point I said good bye, got up, and left the store, completely forgetting about the shoelaces.

188

Later I found out that the Nagual had felt that he was getting ready to leave the world, and he had always joked with us, or so we thought, that when he was to leave, he would do so in his favorite suit and a pair of brand new shoes. It certainly felt as if my energy body had gotten wind of this event and managed to communicate to him that we weren't quite ready yet to be on our own.

The last time I saw him was at a dinner party at the Pandora Avenue compound that he shared with Florinda and Taisha. Some of the apprentices were performing "sorcery theater" sketches for everybody's entertainment before dinner. The sketches were all written by the performers and always highlighted the folly and insanity of the social order and the self-obsessed human mind. Nobody was a professional actor, so sorcery theater provided a good practice in stalking and humility.

The dinner was sumptuous and healthy. Florinda and Taisha had been cooking all day. Sugar was an absolute "no-no" in the Nagual's world, so I was especially delighted when Florinda took me aside after the meal and shared some of her secret stash of chocolate with me. She was not made to follow rules, and neither was I, apparently.

The last one of these timeless moments occurred a little later that evening when the Nagual led me into a corner, and as the bubble closed around us he asked me the most unusual and unexpected questions about karma, damnation, redemption, death, and even god. I was dumbfounded and had a profound cognitive dissonance. These weren't concepts I expected to even be part of his vocabulary. Fortunately his questions were mostly rhetorical and he answered them himself. I would not have known what to say. But as always during these events I felt that the surface communication was nearly irrelevant and something else transpired that could not be captured by my cognition. It was not so much that I was silent and therefore able to connect with the Nagual in a different way. It feels more appropriate to say that the internal silence allowed an entirely different part of me to surface. This different part of me was completely in sync with the Nagual and knowledge was just shared instead of exchanged or dissected.

∨ ∨ ∨

We were not informed about the Nagual's rapidly declining health, but it should have been obvious that things were coming to an end. Except it wasn't. We took him for granted, just like we do it with everything and everyone else. His frequent remarks that he is running out of time we just understood as a teaching tool to keep us on our toes. David and I went to his house a few more times, but the Nagual never came out of his quarters anymore, and we spent time with the witches instead. On the last occasion, Florinda gave me a copy of the "Magical Passes," the

Nagual's latest book, which he had dedicated to me:

> *To Felix,*
> *Don't lose your step, ever,*
> *Carlos Castaneda*

A few months prior I had finally received my new name "Felix," signifying that I apparently had outgrown my old self and that I was part of the sorceric family, for better or for worse. Choosing "Felix" as a name for me was very much in line with the Nagual's sense of humor and his navigational mode of operation. He obviously had not forgotten our encounter in Bandarawela and even remembered the name of the parrot we had entrusted into his care. Once I asked Florinda about it, and she confirmed it so nonchalantly that I wasn't sure if she was just humoring me. She did not want to dwell on the topic but she mentioned that Nury had actually suggested my new name to the Nagual. It is a strange and powerful thing to take on a new name and trying to live its intent. Felix means "the lucky one," and I considered it a beautiful gift that I vowed never to take for granted.

The last time I saw Nury, she presented me with a Swiss watch as a token of her gratitude for my guarding her with so much dedication all this time. It was at the end of a workshop, and I did not have time to unwrap the gift until I came home late at night. When I finally opened the box and took out the watch, the hands showed exactly five minutes to midnight. It was to be her farewell present.

▿ ▿ ▿

It must be hard to understand for an outsider what it meant for some of us to see this myth coming to an end. Just as I felt enveloped by a magical energetic bubble during some of my encounters with the Nagual, there was a continuous energy field around us all the time while the myth was still alive. It grew in intensity so gradually that I never became fully conscious of its force and extent. Only after the Nagual had died and the field collapsed did I notice how strong it had been. The most noticeable element of this energy field was the incredible prevalence of synchronicities. In retrospect my whole life at the time seemed scripted. Life was as smooth as if it had been rehearsed. Signs, omens, and any conceivable form of navigational guidance were everywhere. If I went to see friends, I took it for granted that there was always a parking spot, or that one just opened in front of their houses when I arrived. Or, I could be thinking of someone, and sure enough, the phone rang and that person called. Everything talked to me. Bird calls, car horns, billboards, license plates, anything could stand out in my field of perception to highlight a thought or trigger an action, always making perfect sense. It was a beautiful dance with reality, and subconsciously I took it to be the result of my own increased personal power.

Well, it wasn't. When the Nagual died and the witches left, the field collapsed and nothing was the same anymore. The music was gone. The dance had ended. I was on my own, or nearly on my own. All my fellow apprentices together could not bring back the music, nor could Carol Tiggs, who had stayed behind. Of course, life went on, and I just let the momentum of the implosion carry me. As far as navigation was concerned, it looked like I had to start from scratch. Rather than feeling thrown into the water and being forced to swim, I felt like I was being pulled out of the water, being forced to walk. It was the end of the magic carpet ride. The carpet was gone, and gravity was back.

And I was holding on to a few handwritten words on the inside of a book cover:

"Don't lose your step, ever!"

Part III

A NEW ERA

Sometimes with the bones of the black sticks
left when the fire has gone out
someone has written something new in the
ashes of your life.
You are not leaving. Even as the light fades
quickly. You are arriving.

DAVID WHYTE
The Journey

The End of Certainty

The full moon was no longer visible through the window in David's apartment, but it illuminated everything outside. The leaves of the large tree next to the house were glittering in a silverish light as the evening breeze gently moved through them. I knew the flock of parrots that was roosting under the foliage would be restless tonight. The roofs, the houses, even the fast-moving cars on the freeway to my left, everything reflected the cool mysterious light onto our faces. The air seemed strangely fluorescent. I instinctively took a long, deep breath. What a magnificent evening.

David had been silent for while now. He rested his case.

My body felt like stretching and doing a few Tensegrity movements after sitting nearly motionless for what had seemed like an eternity, but it was getting late, and I still had a long drive ahead of me.

"Well, Dave, I'll be taking off now," I said, getting out of my chair. I walked to the open window, still marveling at the fluorescent quality of the night outside.

"It was so good to see you again," I said from the depth of my heart.

"Likewise, likewise," David nodded emphatically.

He had gotten up too, and we hugged good-bye at the door.

"We should stay in touch," I suggested.

"Absolutely," Dave nodded again.

"Thanks for the tea and all," I called back over my shoulder while walking down the hall to the elevator.

"Of course."

"Bye."

"Give my love to Carmela."

"I will, bye."

∀ ∀ ∀

The elevator opens with a loud "bing" and I step inside. The floor feels elastic, prompting me to gently bounce up and down a few times. I smile. A slight pull and change in gravity as it starts to move. "Bing" again as the doors open on the ground level. Pink frames around the glass doors in front of me. A deep breath in the fluorescent air outside. The moon above. I am looking up, squinting.

My car, big, white, friendly, familiar. More "bing," reminding me of the seat belt. Gently rolling through empty streets. Bigger streets. Many cars. The night air blowing through the window. Pleasant. Driving up the ramp onto the elevated freeway. The ocean far to my right, lit by the moon. Vast. Another ocean of city lights to my left. Many cars. All different shapes and lights. Ten lanes. Beautiful. Unbelievably beautiful. Everything is breathing the fluorescence. Buildings, billboards, hillsides. Eight lanes now, gently curving. A motorcycle, passing fast. Exhilarating. Roaring sound. So many sounds, all fused together and changing, always changing. My hand is playing with the wind outside the window, diverting the air into my face. The ocean is gone now. Only lights. And a few stars. There are mountains far to my left. A maze of overpasses flowing with lights. So beautiful. Industrial landscapes, breathing fluorescence. Long straight stretches. Going fast. Exhilarating. Flying along. Breathing deeply. Signs. Off-ramp. Slowing to a stop. Silence. Only the ticking of the direction lights. Empty streets. Street lights. Fast food places. Malls. Quiet streets. Lush gardens. Home. Silence. Deep silence. Steps. Light inside. Carmela smiling. I embrace her happily.

∀ ∀ ∀

My meeting with David had been a monumental experience. Everything had worked together just perfectly to produce the biggest cognitive dissonance of my life. As a result, my mind had lost its footing, in a manner of speaking, and would never be quite the same. None of David's revelations had actually been a real surprise. It was the poignancy and precision, and particularly the timing and setting of the event that had made it so magical and powerful. I had been well aware that the Nagual maintained intimate and sexual relationships with most of his closest female cohorts, while preaching abstinence and celibacy to us. I always assumed that a large part of his story contained a considerable amount of creativity and creative intent to enhance the factual components. And I had had my own problems with some of his idiosyncrasies and with the less transcendental aspects of his pursuits. But as long as all these elements had only been assumptions, speculations, and occasional inconsistencies, they were easily suppressed and readily forgotten.

When David put it all together, however, and it was all fleshed out with facts and details, it became an entirely valid and comprehensive story of its own. In this story, conventional ethics had consistently been violated, and from a conventional point of view, not much good could have possibly come out of an association with Carlos Castaneda. Period.

So, for all practical purposes, David's story, illuminating the mundane aspects of the Nagual's world, was true. But so was the story of my own experiences, of the years of breathing the magic, of the practical value of recapitulation, Tensegrity, impeccability, intent, and above all, the excitement and joy of navigating in harmony with the universe. The apartment itself was still steeped in the memory of countless hours of practicing Magical Passes and sorcery theater. It was still oozing the scent of years of unbending intent and my deep longing for transformation. And the magnificently rising full moon, in a generous gesture of the spirit, had served as a magnifier, an exclamation point, highlighting this unique opportunity and holding it in place.

The opportunity, of course, as counterintuitive as it may feel to our dualistic mind, was to let both truths be true, to forsake certainty; to let these two irreconcilable stories form the pillars of a gateway into silence and freedom. And to walk right through. End of story.

"Thank you!"

∀   ∀   ∀

Even though this event brought about the longest period of sustained inner silence and peace that I had ever experienced, it did not quite set me free. The Nagual and his magical force field were gone, and I felt seriously underpowered. But nothing was forgotten. Just like I had done it all these years, I kept practicing Tensegrity every day, and I tried to be impeccable with everything I did. There was nobody checking on me, and nobody kept me on my toes. It just seemed to be the most natural and effective way of being. I was utterly disoriented, perhaps even disillusioned after eighteen years of single-minded pursuit, but I still felt fiercely determined. I just didn't know any more to what end. Perhaps "just for the hell of it." The Nagual would have liked that.

The cognitive dissonance that was triggered by the events at David's apartment had brought my apprenticeship to a definite conclusion though. I felt transformed. There was an element of peace in my life that I had not known before. The outer signs of my transformation were a new name, a new wife, a new vocation, a new home, and even a new car.

Victoria and I had gradually drifted apart after moving into different apartments upon our arrival in Los Angeles. Initially we still dated each other, which was actually quite exciting after over ten years of marriage. I would pick her up, or vice versa, and after dinner or a movie we would invite each other up for the proverbial "cup of coffee." But eventually she moved in with the Nagual's female cohorts, and, for both of us, our focus was completely on the dynamics of our magical world. In the end, these dynamics pulled us irreversibly apart, at least in the conventional sense. On a deeper level, however, we were fortunate enough to stay connected. We have kept sharing and rejoicing in each other's navigational tales throughout all these years since, and Victoria's continued input and unfalteringly supportive intent has been, and still is, invaluable for my journey.

▿   ▿   ▿

Shortly after moving to Los Angeles I began to study Oriental Medicine, first just out of curiosity and soon with an ever-increasing passion. Originally, I had planned to work towards an academic teaching position in my field of cognitive psychology, but the beauty of the energetic paradigm on which Oriental Medicine, and particularly acupuncture, is based, soon eclipsed my fascination with psychology and cognition. Carol Tiggs was an acupuncturist, and several of my fellow apprentices were studying acupuncture as well. It was a natural fit. As an acupuncturist one works with the energetic matrix that is underlying the physical body, and over time this greatly facilitates the perception of energy at large, which was a cornerstone of my emerging worldview.

Carmela had originally just been a fellow student who caught my attention because of her apparent cyclicity with Renata, Victoria, and Carol Tiggs. In my world at the time, this was a significant discovery, and I felt compelled to act on it. My initial impulse had been to recruit Carmela into our myth by inviting her to a seminar. But I had no idea how to go about this. I had never even had so much as eye contact with her, and how was I going to explain my rationale for inviting her. It also occurred to me that I could try to seduce her in true sorceric style, as a warrior's task, so to speak. This seemed to have been a common practice in the world of the Nagual, when it came to recruiting female warriors. At the time, I was definitely not in the mood to initiate a social order relationship, romantic or sexual. I felt complete in my dedication and single-minded pursuit of our magical group endeavor. It had been a tremendous and painful effort to transform the relationship that Victoria and I had shared. So, in the Nagual's terms, for once in my life, I needed a woman like a hole in the head.

Seducing Carmela as a means to integrate her into the myth admittedly sounded intriguing, but I did not give myself the slightest chance. She was an attractive young woman, sixteen years younger than me, and she had just recently gotten married. I only saw her once a week during a single lecture, and so far she had not even acknowledged my existence. I decided that this task would require a real sorcerer and not just a wannabe who was probably past his prime as far as seducing beautiful young women was concerned. Consequently, I put the idea completely out of my head.

Intent, however, had its own designs, and arranged for us the following semester to have the same time slot during our internship in the herbal pharmacy of our school clinic. The herbal pharmacy was an olfactory wonderland with hundreds of exotic herbs emitting a most distinct and wholesome symphony of scents that saturated the entire campus. Originally, I had only come to the college out of curiosity, to take a few introductory courses on meridian theory and the energetics of Oriental Medicine, but the bewitching scent wafting out of the pharmacy had been so addictive that I ended up staying for the whole four-year program.

Carmela and I were filling prescriptions for the clinic, weighing, chopping, sifting, and researching herbs together, and naturally we became acquainted. I was somewhat startled by her warm personality when we talked the first time. There was not a trace of pretense in her, and I liked her immensely. We quickly became friends. On one particular occasion, we were both asked to cut a large quantity of earthworms into small pieces. Besides plants, Chinese herbs include various minerals and animal parts. Earthworms are sometimes used as an ingredient in formulas that clear heat or lower blood pressure. Since finding long earthworms in their teapot might irritate unsuspecting patients, especially if they reconstitute once the herbal mix is boiled in water, the worms are generally cut into small pieces to better blend in with the rest of the formula.

As it happened, Carmela and I were both sitting on low stools in the back corner of the pharmacy, diligently cutting worms with scissors while joking and laughing about our bizarre little assignment. Our bodies were nearly touching and the uniqueness of our situation developed its own magical momentum. On one level we felt like children, playing in a sandbox, doing forbidden things, and on another level we were utterly content and wished the assignment would last forever.

"I like cutting up worms with you," Carmela said innocently with a broad smile.

"Me too," I answered after a slight pause, "very much so."

Soon we were inseparable during the few hours per week when we had a common curriculum, and one day, while talking about different bodywork modalities, we agreed to work on each other sometime. This was common practice among acupuncture students since different forms of bodywork like Shiatsu, Reiki, and Tuina are part of Oriental Medicine. We were both licensed massage therapists with a regular client base and had traded with other fellow students before. So, at least on the surface, there was nothing out of the ordinary with Carmela agreeing to come to my apartment one Thursday afternoon, after lectures, for a Shiatsu treatment. I had a professionally set-up treatment room that was separated from the general living area, and I was professionally dressed in a white shirt and white pants as she arrived. Somehow I thought she wouldn't show up, but she was exactly on time.

I had developed my own style of bodywork, combining elements of Sports Massage, Shiatsu, and Reiki, and I gave all I had, as professionally and impeccably as possible. The following Thursday, Carmela reciprocated, and soon Thursday became my favorite day of the week. After each session we hugged good-bye, and every week the hugs lasted just a little bit longer. Several months went by and we seemed oblivious to what was happening to us, until on one of those Thursdays, after a particularly long hug, our lips touched as if by accident. We laughed it off and continued as if nothing had happened. But during the next session, quite on reflex and outside of my control, I accidentally kissed Carmela's toes while I was stretching her leg. She did not pull them back, and as a result, all professionalism, reason, and prudence went out the window. And it was a big window. I scooped her off the table, naked as she was under the sheet, and carried her upstairs into my den, where we broke all the rules.

A few weeks later we went to a sweat lodge that was run by a Native American medicine man high up in the Santa Monica Mountains. There was no moon that night and the depth and brilliance of the star-studded vastness that awaited us as we emerged from the lodge was beyond description. The purifying ceremony had been intense, and we felt extremely present and lucid. The night was crystal clear and cold at this elevation, and the heat was leaving our bodies fast. As we dressed, I gave Carmela my padded leather jacket to keep her warm. It was too big for her, of course, and she looked absolutely adorable. My heart opened wide, and a wave of the most intense longing swept through me as I pulled her closer into my arms. The fragrant smoke of the ceremony was still on her skin and hair. I could smell leather and sage brush and the pure, sweet scent of her breath as we kissed and pulled even closer together. There was absolutely nothing missing in this primordial and timeless moment on that mountaintop. And I was falling deeply in love.

This had definitely not been in the book. For all I knew, warriors don't fall prey to personal love affairs. All a warrior intended was the boundless affection he or she feels towards fellow warriors as they face infinity together, shoulder to shoulder, liberated, and ready to face the unknown. Or, there was the love affair a warrior develops with the earth itself as his eyes are opened to the true nature of things. But the overflowing love I felt towards this incredibly delightful little creature in my oversized leather jacket was not in the book. I was sure of that.

Had I lost my step already?

201

But even while I was pondering my fate and the unfathomable workings of intent, an even bigger event made the floor simply drop away from under my feet. Within weeks of Carmela and me falling into each other and off the pages of the book, Carlos Castaneda was gone, and the book was closed.

Now what?

∨　∨　∨

Our myth had imploded, and as the dust finally settled, I found myself living in a little house in a nondescript neighborhood in Long Beach with Carmela, walking her two big dogs three times a day. The bubble had burst, and I could not see the magic any more. I had lost my momentum and direction and needed to reinvent myself every single day. Our group of fellow apprentices had dispersed quickly, having fallen victim to power struggles and other insanities. Only a small group of friends remained, and all had to reinvent their lives as well. Carmela who had managed to dissolve her marriage effortlessly and harmoniously was as sweet, loving, and supportive as anyone can be, and I was determined to make her happiness my new purpose. My link with intent seemed all but gone. I had no more conscious navigational perception, and in a rare moment of clarity, I decided from the bottom of my heart to simply follow Carmela's lead instead. No expectations, no questions asked.

This was truly the end of me as I knew myself.

All my adult life and particularly the previous eighteen years I had been governed by principles and dogma. My world had been full of opinions, convictions, and rules. Even if I did not always follow the dos and don'ts of my belief system, I always knew what was right and wrong. I don't know how Mona and Victoria had been able to put up with my enthusiastic righteousness and dogmatic pursuits. Never had I been able to let go of my beliefs, and never could I have subordinated myself to anyone, including the Nagual. And now, suddenly and unsolicited, I decided to surrender to Carmela's lead, wherever she would take us. It simply happened. And what looked like an act of defeat and failure, as the ridicule of many of my former cohorts suggested, turned out to be one of the most powerful decisions of my life.

Not that Carmela made following her lead difficult. We seemed to be like two sides of a coin to begin with and lived together in a total absence of friction or disagreement. She went out of her way to make me happy, and the only time I remember that my new attitude was even tested was after I had gotten excited about buying a new motorcycle one day.

"I am thinking about buying a new motorcycle," I began while we were having dinner. "You know, I had my bike in the shop today, and while I was waiting for it to be serviced, I saw this brand new special edition Honda Shadow in the showroom. It's a dream, absolutely beautiful. I'd like to show it to you tomorrow."

"Sure," Carmela answered with a smile, "I didn't know you wanted a new motorcycle."

"Well," I had to smile too, "maybe we don't really need it, but wait until you see it. You'll love it too. I guarantee."

The next day, as we drove to look at the motorcycle, we passed by a large Chrysler car dealership. In passing, Carmela pointed to a brand new silver LHS model that was prominently displayed.

"Look," she said, "isn't that the car you liked so much when we rented it last month. Remember? While we were in San Francisco for the Tensegrity workshop?"

"Oh yeah," I answered. "Do you want us to have a look?"

"Sure, why not?" Carmela seemed excited.

We both had indeed liked the car very much while we drove it around Northern California after the workshop.

"Hi, my name is Greg; let me know if you have any questions."

We barely had a minute to look at the car before the salesman arrived, and he did not wait for our questions. Without having any serious intentions we ended up playfully haggling with Greg for a while. He went through his whole routine and finally asked:

"OK, what is your bottom line? How much would you be willing to pay per month for a three-year lease?"

I didn't even think much and just named an amount about one hundred dollars less than what we had arrived at after a while of back-and-forth. I basically wanted to end the game. A wave of annoyance went through his face.

"Let me see what I can do. " His smile was gone now as he walked off.

I looked at Carmela with a slight frown.

203

"You think we should rather buy a car than a new motorcycle, it seems."

"Whatever you want to do, my love," she said, caressing my hand. "A motorcycle is fine with me too."

It doesn't get much more subtle, but it was obvious what she would prefer, and she was right. We needed a new car much more at the time than a new motorcycle.

"Let's see what he comes up with." I tried not to think anything as we waited for Greg to return.

His beaming smile and thumbs up sign, as he emerged out of the sales office, abruptly ended my motorcycle dream.

"You got it guys," he declared. "I didn't think we could do it, but . . . " And he went into a lengthy story that was supposed to make us feel truly special and extraordinarily lucky.

We knew the game, of course, but after doing the math, we realized that it was indeed a great deal. And so it happened that we never even made it to the motorcycle dealership and drove home with a new car instead.

"Look, isn't that the car you liked so much when we rented it last month?" was all she had said.

I liked this new dynamic and celebrated it by printing a big sign that I pinned to the wall above my desk. All it said in bold red letters was: "Carmela Rules!"

❧ ❧ ❧

Only a few months ago I had been a fierce warrior, guarding the witches and attending secret, magical meetings with the Nagual. I had been readying myself to leave this wretched plane of existence, to navigate the sea of awareness into parallel universes. I had had nothing but contempt for social order pursuits, and particularly for romantic love affairs. I had been living one long lucid dream, awash with synchronicities and magic. And now...?

All my convictions and certainty were gone. I felt that I didn't know anything anymore. I couldn't even think straight outside the most basic daily concerns. I had no energy for dreaming, no ambitions, and no plans. The only point of reference in my life at the time was Carmela, whom I loved dearly. But there was a part of me that was unable to rejoice in our love. For years, the Nagual had discouraged and ridiculed conventional love in the harshest terms, which led to the dissolution of many relationships, including the one I had had with Victoria. He had been on a mission when it came to love, and he usually distorted the term with scorn and contempt. And even though he was gone now, this sentiment regarding love was still strong in me, and sometimes I couldn't help but wonder if I had not simply relapsed and indeed lost my step.

As a result, and for the most part, I was neither happy nor unhappy in those days,

I just was.

The Intent of the Drawing Tide

The Nagual had been right, of course. There was something intrinsically wrong with the love that can turn into hatred at the drop of a hat—the "I love you, if you love me" kind that we all know so well, the needy and exclusive love that clings and wants to possess. He wanted us to consider unconditional love instead, or as he called it, the true affection of an impeccable warrior. He urged us relentlessly to write each other "blank checks of affection" as he called it. But while his guidance regarding all other aspects of the warrior's path was always powerfully alive and compelling, I did not find the same to be true for the concept of unconditional love. The element of the heart had been strangely underpowered in our magical kingdom. There was passion, of course, the passion for freedom and for unfolding our true potential. There was even the idea of awakening to selfless affection for our fellow warriors, as we were all preparing to face infinity. But there always was the disdain for the social order at large. Compassion was not in the vocabulary of the sorcerers. I never felt a decisive knock on my heart to open unconditionally, to allow for all-inclusive and all-transcending love to flow through.

Interestingly, the heart was never much emphasized in Tensegrity either. In our attempt to reconfigure and redeploy energy throughout the body with hundreds of different Magical Passes, we mostly ignored the heart. In the energetic paradigm of Oriental Medicine, there are five distinct energy centers that govern all physiological and emotional processes, and a large part of Tensegrity dealt with balancing and strengthening these energy centers. I spent countless hours doing movements designed to energize the centers that correspond to psychological functions like will power and motivation, courage and confidence, steadiness and persistence, or the ability to let go. But there were few movements that focused on the heart and the associated emotions of joy, love, and compassion.

Apparently this specific emphasis, or rather lack thereof, had left its mark on many of us apprentices. Howard Y. Lee, an accomplished energy healer and Kung Fu master, had been Carlos Castaneda's martial arts teacher for many years. The Nagual even dedicated one of his books, *The Fire from Within*, to Howard:

"I want to express my admiration and gratitude to a masterful teacher, H.Y.L., for helping me restore my energy, and for teaching me an alternate way to plenitude and wellbeing."

Naturally, many of us became acquainted with Howard who made no secret of his observation that all Tensegrity practitioners he had met, consistently had heart energy issues, either presenting as stagnation or outright deficiencies. His observation did not pertain to the physical heart, but to the functional entity as recognized in energy medicine. In simple terms, we all had a closed heart, in one way or other.

Carol Tiggs, the only member of the Nagual's innermost circle who had stayed behind to coach a group of apprentices to continue teaching Tensegrity, had declared a major change in intent and practice soon after Carlos Castaneda's death. According to the Nagual's own words, his only motivating force had always been fear, the fear of losing his link with intent. He had been terrified to lose his step and fall back into a life of being disconnected from the source. It had been his understanding that as warriors on a quest for total freedom, we only have a limited amount of leeway in life, and that we could easily fall off the train, in a manner of speaking, and never catch up again. In this scenario his driving force had to be fear.

Carol had been in fundamental disagreement with this predilection of the Nagual, and she had made a tremendous effort to introduce love as the new motivating force for anyone continuing along the warrior's path, the love for life, the love for freedom, and the love for love itself. Tensegrity was taught with a new emphasis, and even the rigorous contempt for conventional love and affection was abandoned.

I feel that it is important to see our common personal love relationships without self deception for what they really are: fueled by biological imperatives, intrinsically selfish, possessive, and usually exclusive. But despite all this they may well carry the seed of awakening to the love that is the essence of life itself. To stomp out this timid attempt of ordinary love in order to go on a search for the real thing could prove to be a mistake, as in "throwing out the baby with the bathwater." We might be better off to keep that little bit of imperfect love we find in ourselves and intend it to unfold while letting go of everything that stands in its way.

∀ ∀ ∀

Did the Nagual throw out the baby with the bathwater? Was his teaching flawed because he did not open our hearts?

I don't know. I cannot see him in terms of right or wrong. To me he was a force of nature that woke me up from a small and predictable dream and took me on a journey of awareness that appeared to have infinite possibilities. And possibilities require making choices. Maybe opening our heart is a choice we have to make ourselves. A warrior's journey definitely has to follow a path with heart, but it may not be the path *of* the heart.

According to the Nagual, a path with heart is a path that makes for a joyful journey; it is a path we are one with, a path that makes us strong. And only on a path with heart are we at our best.

He writes: "It is the consistent choice of the path with heart which makes a warrior different from the average man. He knows that a path has heart when he is one with it, when he experiences a great peace and pleasure traversing its length."

Without a doubt, to follow a path with heart is the only way to go, but depending on one's predilection and intent, it can lead into many different directions. In the end, the Nagual's path led him to pursue the bold attempt to depart from this world alive and intact. He perceived our reality as a collective dream, and he saw the possibility to shift into a separate collective dream as a group. As consummate lucid dreamers, he and his cohorts lived in a world of parallel universes, and even if this attempt was utterly audacious, it did not seem impossible.

I was fascinated and intrigued by the Nagual's intent, but I did not share it. He had led me on an unprecedented journey of awareness and understanding, but at the bottom of my heart, I had no interest in perpetuating my individual self. My own journey, even my dreaming practice, had shaped my intent differently. Over the years I have been afforded a few profound glimpses of something that I perceived to be the essential nature of reality. These incidences have defined my most fundamental yearning and intent.

One was definitely the experience of undifferentiated and unreflective awareness, or oneness, that I had during my explorative dream practices in Tucson. The resulting understanding could only express itself in the deepest and most genuine release of laughter imaginable, and it changed my worldview forever. More than anything, it did not allow me to take seriously anymore the idea that I am an exclusively separate entity. So, to put all my intent into perpetuating my individual self seemed counterintuitive, to say the least.

Another experience that influenced my intent had to do with the phenomenon of compassion. Over the years my navigation had guided me to integrate Buddhist wisdom and strategies into my journey. I had mainly been interested in Buddhism for its meditation techniques that are intended to silence and control our compulsive internal dialogue, or to "tame the monkey mind," as a Zen metaphor describes this process. But besides the taming of the monkey mind with mindfulness and meditation, the practice of compassion is considered equally indispensable on the path to awakening and enlightenment. Compassion had never resonated with me much, particularly not as a spiritual teaching. As long as I saw it as something I had to generate in myself, even if I did not feel it, compassion seemed empty. I never considered it to be much more than a hollow, though noble, ethical duty, like charity. I also thought of it as being in the same category as pity, which I found an undesirable emotion, coming from a perception of superiority and being injurious to the spirit.

One day all this changed, however, unexpectedly, and in the most unlikely of circumstances. I was by myself, cleaning our house in Tucson and listening to Beethoven's Ninth Symphony. The volume was at maximum, and I was having a good time. Beethoven is my favorite classic composer, and parts of his Ninth Symphony definitely have the potential of moving my assemblage point. The vocals had never been my favorite part, though. They felt disruptive and even unmelodious to my ear, often pulling me out of my ecstasy. On this day, however, they did not disturb me, and I even found myself singing along with the German lyrics of the Ode to Joy.

" . . . . . . Joy, daughter of Elysium . . . all men will become brothers under your gentle wing. Be embraced, Millions! This kiss for all the world! Joy, beautiful spark of Gods! Daughter of Elysium, Joy, beautiful spark of Gods!"

And as I sang along praising joy over and over in my native tongue, as I celebrated happiness and joy with the chorus on the top of my lungs, I suddenly cracked open, and as the symphony powerfully concluded, I stood in the middle of the room crying my heart out. Without any effort on my part, my heart and mind had suddenly popped open like a soap bubble, making me feel and understand how every single one of our six billion fellow humans just strives to be happy, in whatever way possible. It was as if I saw billions of eyes longing for happiness, billions of arms desperately reaching for joy like children for their mother. We were all the same, so much the same . . . A dam broke and I burst into an ocean of love, embracing everyone and everything. There was no strain, no effort, no differentiation, just unconditional love.

It was then that I realized that true compassion cannot be practiced. It has to emerge by itself out of understanding and deep insight. But just as with patience, behaving compassionately can be a powerful exercise of intent that does not share the detrimental aspects of pity. It has to be expressed in gestures and action and not displayed as an attitude. And as such, practicing compassion can go far beyond relieving incidental suffering. It will prepare the way for our awakening, for the remembering of our essential oneness.

Perhaps the most defining incidence in this context happened once while I was meditating in the desert outside our house in Tucson, Arizona. My favorite meditation spot was on a large, smooth boulder in the middle of a seasonal creek that ran through a corner of our property. Save for a few weeks during the monsoon season, the creek, or wash as it is called locally, was dry most of the year. It was bordered by lush desert vegetation, and it had an energy and life of its own. Clear of fences or other human-made obstacles it served as a natural animal path for all the large desert wildlife. Coyote, deer, wild boar, and the occasional big cats, all used the wash to come down from the mountains on their nightly excursions.

Naturally, the wash was full of boulders, some of them carved and shaped beautifully through the ages by the intermittent stream. My favorite rock was right in the center of the wash, creating a small island behind it, where a healthy mesquite tree had been able to put down its roots. The branches of the tree provided shade for most of the day, creating the perfect resting or meditation place with an unobstructed view of the magnificent Catalina Mountains, rising over nine thousand feet to the North. I had spent countless hours on this magical spot, particularly in the late afternoon or during moonlit nights. The wash was usually a few degrees cooler than the surrounding desert. Especially in the evenings, one could feel the heavier cool air flowing through the wash down from the mountains like a stream, and in the enhanced sensitivity and awareness during meditation, this could be quite an experience.

Here I was, just getting comfortable in my meditation pose, enjoying the last rays of the sun that was about to set behind the Tucson Mountains to my left. The wash was only about thirty feet wide and fairly deep around this particular spot, and the brush-covered banks drowned out the last faint murmurs of civilization. I felt the thick cool mountain air gently washing over me, alerting my senses to the separate world of the wash as it awoke in the twilight. My eyes were half closed while I focused my attention on my breathing, and in no time I merged with the rock, the wash, and the fragrant desert around me.

At some point my eyes opened on their own account, and I found myself getting out of my pose and looking around. There was no discernible thought, and it was only when I took my first step away from the boulder that I noticed the change. Everything had come to life around me, or rather, I suddenly realized that everything around me had always been alive, but I had failed to see it. I hardly dared to put my foot down. Everything, absolutely everything around me was alive, collectively and individually at the same time. I walked slowly up the wash in the most gingerly fashion, apologizing loudly to the world around me. "I'm sorry, I'm so sorry," I kept repeating from the deepest place of my heart.

Sorry not so much for stepping onto everything now, but sorry for all the previous times, and for all my life that I had been so painfully unaware of the consciousness I was trampling on all the time. The awareness around me was so intense that I felt like I was walking on a gigantic eyeball, for lack of a better analogy. I held my head down in shame as if it would help to avoid the gaze of the world. Like a bull in a china shop I had been trampling around my busy little life, completely oblivious to the most fundamental reality of all. Everything, absolutely everything, is aware, infused with awareness, made of awareness, aware, alive, and looking at me, aware of me, and most astoundingly, seemingly delighted to see me awake. There was not a trace of judgment coming my way, not even the faintest sign of reproach or blame. I had been trampling through the face of the world all my life, my senses plugged tight with an endless stream of thoughts, ideas, and concerns. But all the world did in return now that it had finally gotten through to me, was rejoice in delight and welcome me home with boundless affection. All I could see and feel was love.

⌄　⌄　⌄

It did not last. Thoughts came rushing in, trying to understand and effectively canceling out my perception. I don't have any recollection of the transition back to my usual awareness. When I climbed up the banks of the wash towards the house, I was still conscious of my every move, but I was already alone again. The aliveness had vanished like a mirage. I kept looking around, beckoning, staring, focusing on my breathing, but to no avail. In retrospect, my attempts to reconnect with the mind of the world, remind me of staring at one of those "Magic Eye" stereograms that reveal a three dimensional image if you cross your eyes just right. But no matter how I crossed my eyes and stretched my mind, the connection was gone.

213

None of these incidences lasted nor did they ever repeat themselves. If I were to think of life as a game, a treasure hunt of sorts, I had only been allowed to pick up the scents, the respective scents of oneness, compassion, and universal love. It had been a good sustained sampling every time, and now it was seemingly up to me to find and follow the trail.

However, my thinking mind had little interest in following this trail. It could not deny that all three instances had been profound and compelling. It could not possibly make an argument against moving towards the bliss of oneness and unconditional love. But it was even more keenly aware of its own fate in this scenario. In the end there was simply no room for the self-reflective mental construct that I took to be my identity. It was either/or—and therefore my thinking mind could not be trusted to guide me in the right direction. I had to rely on older instincts and on the trickery of intent to play this game.

❥   ❥   ❥

Intent is the magic wand.

I never cease to be intrigued by the power of intent. Intent is the intrinsic psychological algorithm that shapes our lives like nothing else, whether we are conscious of it or not. In a computer analogy, I think of our individual intent as the collection of programs and processes that are running in the background: the specific browser we have installed, the virus software, pop-up blockers, spyware protection, cookies, desktop gadgets, word processors, creative programs, communication software, etc. All of them, individually and in unison, are shaping our computer experience. Some programs we chose consciously, some were pre-installed, and some were downloaded or uploaded without our knowledge.

But while we usually buy a new computer every few years, and while we can restart, clean up, tune up, and defragment our computers with the click of a mouse, it is much more difficult to streamline our lives. The algorithms and programs in life are our beliefs and our thought patterns. Collectively, they form our intent, which shapes our life. Conflicting beliefs and thought patterns can have the same effect in life as conflicting programs have for our computer experience: frustration, inefficiency, and crashes.

As we become aware of this mechanism, however, we can turn it to our advantage, and intent becomes the most powerful tool imaginable, a veritable magic wand that empowers us to customize our reality. Of course, we can only affect our individual intent, and it would seem wise to align it with the collective intent of our species and with the intent of the universe at large, if we are aiming for ultimate peace and fulfillment.

As part of the all-creating universal consciousness, we are co-creating our reality through the power of our beliefs and the associated thought patterns. In order to live the best life we can possibly imagine, we have to create and cultivate a belief system and its inherent intent that will manifest that life. We can try to "reboot" our "operating system" with silent retreats, baptisms, sweat lodges, and other transformative rituals, but chances are that some old patterns, programs, and convictions will prevail. Recapitulation is an excellent technique to take inventory and clean up in the process. In addition, we can utilize more contemporary techniques like Neuro-Linguistic Programming, Subliminal Messaging, Vision Boards, or Mind Movies to re-program and overwrite our mostly subconscious conditioning.

These contemporary methods of re-defining and honing our intent are based on what has been termed the "law of attraction," a concept that was widely popularized in recent years. It basically states that beliefs, thoughts, and actions have an energy that attracts like energy. I prefer to think of it as the law of manifestation, or the law of co-creation. The concept of attraction puts an unnecessary and counterintuitive division between us and the universe, essentially preventing our spiritual evolution. Using this law or dynamic of co-creation has two main components.

First, we have to know what we want to manifest, bearing in mind that it would not be prudent to formulate a personal intent that conflicts with what we perceive to be universal intent. And second, we want to expose our subconscious mind to a maximum of genuine mental and emotional energy that pertains to our intent. Ideally, we want to feel as if the intended state or object had already manifested. Most manifestation techniques work by flooding our subconscious perception with a script and/or imagery that describes and represents what we are intending. The more emotional energy we connect with the new script the better, since it determines the strength of the associated new neural connections we are creating while reprogramming ourselves.

The actual steps leading to the intended state are best left up to the universe and then discovered by using navigational strategies. Essentially, intent is the destination that we are programming into our personal navigation system.

215

▼ ▼ ▼

The collapse of our myth and the resulting cognitive dissonance had rebooted my life, but I did not exactly feel reborn as a result. The exhilaration that I associate with rebirth was definitely missing. My emotional state resembled limbo more than anything else. I felt suspended, running in idle, and before shifting into gear, something wanted to know what for and to what end. It would have been a perfect time to define and powerfully cultivate a new intent, but that was not what happened. My assertive and powerful intent cultivating part had vanished together with the concept of certainty, and my first real decision had been to let Carmela chart the course of our lives. And the more I think about it, the clearer it becomes that this was one of the most significant decisions I ever made. For the first time in my life it was not all about me. And this, of course, is a powerful intent in itself.

I don't recall ever having to shift into gear. After peacefully idling for a little while, the car started rolling all by itself, imperceptibly at first, but soon gaining a beautiful momentum. Unbeknownst to me at the time I had finally connected to the ethereal and elusive gravitational field of the universe itself. I had encountered the "drawing tide," an image taken from one of my favorite poems by David Whyte, the *Song for the Salmon*:

> . . . But now that I have spoken of that great sea,
>   the ocean of longing shifts through me,
>   the blessed inner star of navigation moves in the dark sky above,
>   and I am ready like the young salmon to leave his river,
>   blessed with hunger for a great journey on the drawing tide.

The incredibly fascinating and magical world of the Nagual had driven my journey for so many years with the promise of adventure, freedom, personal power, and even the impossible audacity of defying death. It had forcefully enticed me into single-mindedly pursuing the warrior's way of discipline and impeccability, and it had guided me into a vastly expanded understanding of life and awareness.

But ultimately it took the demise and deconstruction of the Nagual's world to crack my mirror of self-reflection. I needed to let go of everything I believed in to finally connect directly with life and the intent of the universe at large. It was when I found myself floating in intergalactic space, far away from any source of gravity, that the suppressed memory of unconditional love dared to awake. And it resonated through the cracks in the mirror, connecting with the universal ocean of love outside.

And the ocean rejoiced, embracing our little space capsule, and gently began pulling us in with the drawing tide.

Where Zen Meets Passion

"**D**o you have any preference where you would like to live and open a practice once we have our degrees?" I asked Carmela one day while we were stuck in traffic on our way home.

"Definitely not here," she said without hesitation. "I've lived in Southern California all my life, and I think I've had enough," she added with a sweeping gesture at the surrounding traffic jam.

"Fine with me," I laughed, "but where would you want to go?

Carmela was quiet for a moment.

"How about Australia or New Zealand?" She looked at me, curious how I would react. Her eyes were excited.

"Hm," I thought for a second, "I don't know about their immigration and licensing laws, but we can do some research. Australia or New Zealand, interesting, I wouldn't have thought of it, but I like the idea. Let's just toss it up and see what comes down."

This was our standard procedure when it came to a new idea. Once formulated, we would simply broadcast it into the ether with a big question mark. I literally visualized throwing the idea up into space, and then I switched into receptive mode to see if anything would "rain" down over time that made it a viable option. In this case nothing remarkable happened. Licensing turned out not to be a problem and immigration obstacles seemed surmountable. We received no particular indications, so there was no point in actively pursuing the idea for now. In any case, there was still plenty of time until we had to make a decision.

Most of our intent in those days was directed towards cultivating our relationship. From the beginning we had kept a maximum of awareness on every aspect of our interactions, determined to use our love affair as a tool for awakening. It felt somewhat counterintuitive to apply a strategy and so much scrutiny to our young romance while everything was utterly harmonious. But we found that it is exactly during these early and seemingly perfect stages that the seeds of disharmony and future problems will sprout and take root. It often starts with a harmless tease, a careless word, or even just a gesture of impatience. A joking "oh you know how women are" or "boys will be boys" while in the company of friends can be a first sign of a subconscious power play, setting the stage for a life of misery.

We found it worthwhile to bring awareness into everything that transpired between us and were determined to go a different route. Together we wrote out and frequently reviewed our statements of intent, creating a powerful dynamic to stay aware and eliminate the smallest signs of competitiveness or self-righteousness as they arose. Our respective experience made us believe that simple but relentless mindfulness while communicating as a couple is one of the most powerful spiritual avenues available.

After several months of cocooning, while Carmela and I were growing together as a unit, I began to notice the reappearance of occasional synchronicities. It was sporadic at first, nothing yet compared to the dreamlike level that I experienced while the energy bubble of the Nagual's myth was still intact, but I couldn't help noticing it. These were only faint perceptions, barely discernible, but conspicuously superimposed on the more arbitrary background of everyday reality. And once alerted I quite naturally shifted into something like a "Find Waldo" mode, eagerly scanning for anything that stood out or seemed to speak to me.

Examples don't adequately communicate the compelling nature of these perceptions. It may just be a loud bird call that highlights a thought, a surprise phone call from someone that I had just spoken about, a bumper sticker or billboard relating to a problem I was just pondering, the digital clock showing 4:44 at the moment the door bell rings giving the visitor special significance. Particularly nice are unprecedented waves of green lights on the way to an important appointment, or an unexpected financial windfall after a series of expenses. Even though these events still happened rarely, every instance was a little spark, re-awakening my curiosity and enthusiasm for life. And before long we were in the game again and embarked on our first major navigational maneuver. We moved back to Los Angeles.

Our quaint little Spanish colonial style house in one of the oldest neighborhoods in Long Beach had served as our cocoon for over six months, when a series of events suggested that we move on. The decisive momentum came from Carmela's former partner who insisted on taking care of Orion and Juno, the German Shepherd and Doberman they had reared together. He had moved into a new house with extended grounds where the dogs would be much happier than in our tiny backyard. It was a painful step for Carmela to let them go, but it was prudent and also in the dogs' best interest.

As they were gone, the urge to move increased and we started to open our eyes for some input from the universe. A few days later we drove by the Marina City Club, whose distinctive curved towers overlook the Marina del Rey yacht harbor not far from our Acupuncture College. Having a knack for numbers we couldn't help but noticing the address, 4333 Admiralty Way, in large golden letters next to the main gate.

"That sounds like a good address," Carmela laughed. Three was her favorite number, and four was mine.

"You are right," I said, slowing down. "Let's take a look."

"It's probably way too expensive," Carmela cautioned.

"Well, let's see." I was already turning around and heading for the leasing office.

After a short conversation and a long tour with the leasing agent we were hooked. Unit 704 in the central tower was available, surprisingly affordable, and not a bad number either after we had adopted seven as our common favorite. The condominium had spectacular views over the yacht harbor and Santa Monica Bay, where we would be able to watch the sun go down as it rose over Australia. The towers felt incredibly powerful and assertive, just what we needed to fire up our intent. Definitely a good place to re-emerge into the world. We moved in on New Years Eve, and after getting set up, we watched one of the most spectacular fireworks displays of our life. From our bed we could see the glittering skyline of greater Los Angeles, from the Hollywood sign on the far right all the way to the Sydney opera house far to the left—in our dreams.

Yes, we had somehow thought that the energy of the yacht harbor and the view over the Pacific Ocean would perhaps stimulate the idea of us sailing beyond that westerly horizon to the great "down under," but it did not happen. The universe had other plans for us, as we would soon find out. Meanwhile, life in the fortress of the three towers was amazingly energizing. Before long we were engaged in a flurry of activities. We recruited many new clients, became partners in a health-related import business, flew to tradeshows in Hong Kong, and studied Oriental Medicine full time. If there was any time left, we spent it in the fitness center or practiced Tensegrity.

The change that our new environment affected in us was nearly dizzying. This was an aspect of intent that I had never experienced so strongly. So far I had only focused on the effects of individual and universal intent and the intent of family and friends and society at large. But here, within the clearly defined and gated Marina City Club, I found yet another intent at work. It was characterized by the massive architecture, an aura of affluence, rigidity, and self-importance on one side, and health and fitness consciousness combined with the relative care-freeness of financial independence on the other side. The tug on our assemblage points was strong, and we became part of the pack for a while.

On a practical level, this experience gave us a third variable when it came to understanding and calibrating our intent. While universal intent and the general intent of our species are unalterable, we can definitely work with our individual intent, the intent of friends and family, and that of our living environment.

With increasing energy levels, our navigational perceptions intensified, and we felt better and better connected. To my surprise I even began to have spontaneous episodes of lucid dreams again. During one of my last meetings with the Nagual, we discussed my dreaming practice. It usually had taken me a great effort to become conscious in my dreams. I had to get up in the middle of the night, lie down at a designated place, go through a lengthy auto-suggestive process, and then I only became lucid about twenty percent of the time. When I asked the Nagual how I could do better, he just laughed and said:

"Forget about it. Just focus all your energy on stopping your internal dialogue. Once you are silent, you can step in and out of dreams at will. Just like that." And he snapped his fingers, putting me in a daze for a moment.

I followed his recommendations and never set myself up again for lucid dreaming. But now, to my delight, lucid dreaming had come back without any effort on my part. The first few incidences were short and uneventful, but on one occasion I had a fairly good grasp of my dreaming awareness. As I was outside my body, I moved through the wall into the next room and tried to figure out how to make the best use of my state. Suddenly I found myself walking down a street, arm in arm with Florinda. I was no longer in conscious control of my dream, but I remember asking her where she lived now and that we were all missing her very much.

"We are living in Santa Fe now," she said happily. "But this is only for you, you understand?" she squeezed my arm for emphasis.

"Of course," I said matter-of-factly. In my dream, her revelation did not have much importance. Then we continued walking down the road, gossiping about some of the other apprentices. I kept wondering about her outfit, which was untypical for Florinda, who had always been impeccably dressed. She was wearing a wrinkled white gown with a noticeable stain in the front, which I found quite odd. Suddenly she was gone and I woke up.

I could not sleep another moment that night and had to force myself not to wake up Carmela. I assumed Florinda had meant Santa Fe, New Mexico, but the more I thought about it, the less certain I was. There probably were Santa Fe's all over Spain and South America. I had driven through Santa Fe, New Mexico once and was fairly unimpressed, after all I had heard about it. It was quaint and refreshingly different from the average American city, but I did not like the surrounding high desert much. It had been arid and windy.

"What do you think?" I asked Carmela after I had related my dream to her.

"I'm afraid we'll have to go to Santa Fe one of these days and look up Florinda," Carmela said only half jokingly.

"I guess so," I agreed. "We just have to find an independent movie theater and go there on an opening night. If she's in Santa Fe, she'll be there."

We both laughed, warmly remembering one of her few predictable idiosyncrasies.

"I actually always wanted to see Santa Fe," Carmela added.

The next day we attended a lecture about acupuncture laws and licensing differences across the US. In some states it was still illegal to practice acupuncture and the requirements for licensing varied considerably from state to state. The highlight of the lecture, especially for us, was the fact that, at the time, New Mexico was the only state where acupuncturists were automatically licensed as Doctors of Oriental Medicine. The lecturer explained that the educational standards in New Mexico were quite high, and he particularly praised the Southwest Acupuncture College in Santa Fe.

The lecture was on a Friday afternoon, and on Saturday morning I went to see Claude, one of my Shiatsu clients, for her weekly therapy session. While I was setting up the treatment table, Claude asked me what our plans were once Carmela and I had finished our education. I told her that our dream was actually to open a holistic medical spa, rather than just an acupuncture practice. And as I proceeded to go more into detail, she suddenly stopped me:

"Wait, I've got to show you something."

She disappeared into another room for a moment and brought back the current weekend edition of the *Los Angeles Times*. On the front of the travel section was a full-page article about "Ten Thousand Waves," a Japanese style spa resort in Santa Fe, New Mexico. I had to laugh out loud.

"Have you been there?" Claude asked, puzzled about my reaction.

"No, no, it's just that we talked about Santa Fe the other day —"

"You would love it," she cut me off excitedly. "John and I got married there. Actually we lived there for a while. Oh, it's my favorite place . . . and Ten Thousand Waves, it is so beautiful and unique, all made of wood, Japanese style . . . " And the she went into great detail about her favorite spa in the world, her wedding, and wonderful, one-of-a-kind Santa Fe. She was overflowing and could hardly contain herself.

"Maybe it is not the kind of spa you have in mind, but you should definitely check it out some time," Claude concluded emphatically.

I was pretty much helpless against this kind of navigational onslaught. Yes, I had entertained the idea of visiting Santa Fe sometime to look for Florinda, but I had felt no urgency. Instead, Carmela and I had been planning to fly to British Columbia during our summer break to spend a week canoeing near Tofino on Vancouver Island. But after telling her my experience with Claude, who had made sure I took the whole newspaper home with me, we realized we had better change our travel plans.

                              ⩔ ⩔ ⩔

By chance, we arrived in Santa Fe just before the first weekend in August, which traditionally hosts Indian Market, the biggest local event of the year. It showcases over twelve hundred Native American artists from about one hundred different tribes. It is a huge event, and I have no idea how we even got hotel accommodations on such short notice. Actually, we found a gorgeous patio-style suite with a real fireplace, the most tasteful interior design, and a great energy. The weather was fantastic, with the deep blue sky of the high desert at seven thousand feet elevation and near perfect temperatures. We even were awarded the special bonus of a brief but spectacular lightning storm, complete with rainbows, on our first afternoon. Friday night we went to stalk out Florinda at the opening of a European film at Santa Fe's independent movie theater. We actually hid behind some cars and carefully scanned everybody, prepared that she might be disguised. I am not sure if we really believed we could find her there, but it made for an exciting experience. Unfortunately, but not surprisingly, she did not show up.

The town was abuzz with exotic culture and arts, interesting people, and good food. The weekend was unreal, everything we experienced turned out to be exceptional, including and particularly—our sexual chemistry. Having exceptionally good sexual energy is always a good navigational indicator, at least so we decided. We felt supercharged during our entire visit. This was an unparalleled experience, but we were still not giving it too much thought as we visited Southwest Acupuncture College on Monday morning, just out of curiosity. We liked very much what we saw, and everybody was extremely friendly and welcoming. After a short conversation with the director of admissions, it looked like we could easily transfer all our credits from California if we so desired. Our academic education was basically completed and all we still needed for graduation was a year of clinical internship.

Once back in Los Angeles we sent our transcripts to Santa Fe, and as we had been told, everything was accepted. Our minds still didn't quite

225

understand what had happened, but in our hearts we had already moved. We felt so strongly about this that we were convinced that we would spend the rest of our lives in Santa Fe. Australia and New Zealand were forgotten.

Late in the afternoon on New Years Eve of 1999 we arrived at our new home in Santa Fe. During a second exploratory visit we had found a perfect little house. It was completely quiet and private, with magnificent mountain views and ideally located between the college and downtown. To our surprise and delight, three good friends and former fellow apprentices of Carlos Castaneda had independently moved to Santa Fe in the meantime. They were already waiting as we arrived and helped us unload before we went to their house to celebrate the new millennium together. It all made for a perfect start, and we never doubted for a second that our move had been magically ordained.

Two of our friends were also health care professionals and we immediately began cooperating on a common project. Angelica, an MD, had actually been Carlos Castaneda's personal physician, and it had fallen upon her to sign his death certificate. Brigitte was a gifted massage therapist, and Francois a fabulous chef. Together with the two of us, who would soon be Doctors of Oriental Medicine, we imagined having a great team for our envisioned medical spa.

We were enthusiastic, and I immediately began to work on a business plan. Every morning we spent four hours treating patients at our college clinic, and in the afternoon we did research in the library and online in preparation for our business venture. As always, the most fun was scouting for a location. As time progressed, our friends had to follow some overriding dynamics of their own and pulled out of our project. Their initial participation had given us valuable momentum though, and we decided to go ahead on our own with a scaled down version at first. The core and foundation for our future medical spa was to be an herbal teahouse, serving medicinal grade herbal teas, tonics, and elixirs as well as health-promoting food and merchandise. The "Longevity Café and Emporium," as we called our creation, was to be a meeting place "where food is the medicine," as our initial slogan proclaimed.

We were careful that every aspect of our venture was navigationally supported. There were a multitude of big and small decisions to make, and we uncompromisingly tried to go with the flow of things. Sometimes this does not leave much of a choice, and the location that Intent selected for us had some challenges. But it was downtown, next to the Plaza, affordable, and easily expandable to integrate our future vision.

While Carmela did product research and secured suppliers, I allowed myself to be absorbed by the interior design and build-out of our venue. This involved a lot of micro-navigation in the choice of colors, decors, building materials, sub-contractors, all the way to lighting and sound. Incidentally, the color we chose for most of the walls was called Pandora Red, which we found out only after we had picked it. Pandora, of course, was also the name of the street where the Nagual had lived in Los Angeles. It goes without saying that little synchronicities like that only fueled my enthusiasm.

We were determined to use all our knowledge of feng shui and geomancy to make the Longevity Café and Emporium a precise expression of our intent. And as it grew, we became aware that doing our impeccable best with this project also meant that it would indeed reflect our intent precisely and ultimately become a window into our soul. This was a fascinating realization, and we were increasingly curious how it would turn out. I even integrated my lucid dreaming practice into the design process. Whenever I succeeded in slipping out of my body, I visited the dream representation of our building site and dreamt up improvements or changes. The most notable of which was a "burning bush" I had dreamt for a corner that had a particularly low energy. In my dream visit to the site I literally saw a burning bush in that corner, and while shopping for an accent that would resemble my vision, I found a high vase with a bundle of reeds, which, once lit up from the back with an amber colored spotlight, resembled what I had seen during my astral projection.

227

I did not go along any more with the Nagual's recommendation to exclusively focus on internal silence instead of lucid dreaming. While it is true that we play out our conditioned follies in dreams, just as in the so-called waking state, we can also use our dream states for spiritual practice as recommended in the teachings of Tibetan Dream Yoga, for example. In my experience, cultivating awareness while dreaming is the best blueprint for cultivating awareness during waking hours.

As our creation slowly took shape, and especially after it blossomed into full life once we were open and operating, we became aware of an interesting synergy that had manifested itself within its walls. Everything that represented an element of "Longevity," as our meeting place was soon known, was wrought of two distinct moods. Overall design, colors, soundtrack, merchandise, furniture, dishes, menu, and even our staff were woven together from the seemingly incompatible elements of Zen and Passion. Unintentionally we had simultaneously done everything possible to create the minimalist, pragmatic, and mindful ambience of a Zen style Japanese teahouse, and then we had rounded, colored, and enriched this ambience with as many elements of life-affirming passion as we were capable of.

As we realized how our intent had manifested, the words "Where Zen Meets Passion" became our slogan. It headlined our advertising campaign as well as our website, and the more we recited it, the more it defined where we wanted to be in life: wherever Zen meets passion.

▿ ▿ ▿

Zen classically describes the process of waking up to the present moment through practical and experiential means, through action rather than theoretical knowledge or spiritual studies. The Japanese tea ceremony is a good example for the Zen approach to awakening. Matcha or powdered green tea is prepared and served in a highly refined ritual with great emphasis on detail. The intent is to engage all participants in utmost mindfulness, thus bringing everyone's full attention into something as simple as having a cup of tea and staying present with the experience. The ritual has its own aesthetic, characterized by quiet attention, precision, simplicity, humility, restraint, and profundity.

In common usage, the meaning of Zen has been stretched considerably, but usually it includes elements of austerity, serenity, and mindfulness. Passion on the other hand is more descriptive of emotional absorption, excitement, and of not being overly mindful. Zen as a direct and experiential path to enlightenment has a positive connotation for most people. And so has passion, which is a natural ingredient of a path with heart. How can they be compatible? How can they meet?

Well, aesthetically or as a design concept it is not difficult. Creating the

Longevity Café we used plenty of bamboo, small fountains, Japanese art, calligraphy, and authentic tea ware. We allowed for spaciousness and a sense of minimalism, sold Zen-related art, books, and other merchandise, held tea ceremonies, and even had a Japanese chef.

Passion was represented by painting most of the walls red, and using warm amber lighting and sensual music. Many of our tonics and elixirs were aphrodisiacs and we sold a variety of books on Taoist and Tantric sexual practices. Most of our staff proved to be quite sensual and passionate as well. The events, lectures, and art shows we hosted regularly represented both elements equally.

It was no coincidence that we intended and materialized a place where Zen met passion. Most of my life I had harbored a strong and intuitive defiance towards the dualism that was inherent in my Christian upbringing and in most other spiritual traditions I had encountered. The path of good always seemed to imply sacrifice and suffering. Spiritual advancement was synonymous with some form of asceticism. Zen and the path of awakening had no tolerance for passion. I never could settle for this either/or scenario, initially because I simply did not want to give up one or the other. But as I moved through life, I gradually realized that I did not have to. I stubbornly kept my intent on living a life where I could have my cake and eat it too, so to speak. I found that awareness and presence can grow well while we are passionately in love with life; that we can experience intense emotions without having to hold on to them; that Taoist and Tantric sexual practices can be dynamic meditations and tools for realization; and that enthusiasm, compassion, and love grow beautifully in the space where Zen meets passion.

229

Things went well for us in the "City Different," as Santa Fe calls itself, but our engagement was total. We worked around the clock, treating patients in the clinic every morning until noon, just to rush to the Longevity Café where we stayed until closing time at 11 PM. Soon the place where food was the medicine and where Zen met passion became the favorite hangout for Santa Fe's sizable healing-arts community and many of its other eclectic citizens. For us, it turned more and more into our living room, and we found ourselves hosting a never-ending party.

Even Starbucks employees came regularly during their breaks to get their fix of Emerald Dragon, Tahitian Magic, Black Thunder, Kava Colada, or Andean Delight, to name just a few of our numerous magic potions that were laced with potent ingredients and herbs from all around the world. Even our pies were super-charged. Ginseng Chai Pumpkin Pie, Ginger Ginkgo Apple Pie, Wolfberry Cherry Pie, Magic Blueberry Blaster, etc., everything was organic and loaded with herbs and other health promoting supplements. Batteries of herbal tinctures behind the counter allowed us to address any conceivable health or lifestyle concern. The concept proved to be a resounding success, and soon we began preparing our intended extension towards a medical spa. But just as we were getting settled in, life threw us an unexpected curve ball.

"Hi, my name is Joao Santoro; I would love to talk with you if you are not too busy." The well mannered gentleman with the slight Portuguese accent had been sitting in a corner of the Café for most of the afternoon, sampling a few of our alchemical creations and seemingly enjoying himself. He was soft spoken and had warm eyes. I followed him to his table and we sat down.

"I am just visiting Santa Fe and will be leaving tomorrow, but I have been in your Café every day, and I want to make you a proposition," he began. "I absolutely love your concept and I am wondering if you would be interested to open another location in Maui, Hawaii."

"Maui?! Well, I don't know what to say, we just opened and . . . "

"I would be interested in financing it," he injected, correctly assessing my hesitation. "I have been looking a long time for something that I could be passionate about," he continued, "and what you are doing here is exactly it. Just think about it, and if you are interested, I would love to invite you to Maui so we can discuss everything in detail."

Carmela joined us and we talked for a while longer, and when Joao left we hugged like old friends. We liked him tremendously, as we did his proposal. He was a wealthy Brazilian businessman living in early retirement on Maui, and his idea was to open a few "Longevity" locations first, before trying to expand our concept into a franchise operation. A few months later he flew us to Hawaii and generously put us up in a house right on the beach near Paia on Maui where he lived with his wife and three children. We got along fabulously and agreed to proceed with the project. After two more visits we had found a location and everything was ready to go. We had trained a young acupuncturist couple to take over our operation in Santa Fe; we terminated the lease on our house, ordered the moving truck, and bought the airline tickets. Everything was lined up and we were ready to jump into our next adventure when, only weeks before our scheduled departure, on the morning of September 11, two airplanes crashed into the World Trade Center in New York, changing everyone's fate.

Hawaii's tourist-based economy collapsed temporarily, and nobody knew what was going to happen, prompting us to put our project on hold. Then the Brazilian currency suddenly devaluated dramatically, affecting Joao's liquidity so much that he had to return home to attend to his business interests. In the blink of an eye a year of preparations evaporated, and we woke up back in Santa Fe, which unfortunately would never be the same for us. Our roots, which had just begun to take hold beautifully before we met Joao, were now irreparably severed. Instead, we had hopelessly fallen for the charm of the tropics. I have always had a love affair with coconut palms, which had brought me to Sri Lanka in the first place.

It was not all bad though. The Longevity Café actually benefited from the national trauma after September 11. People seemed to need each other's company, and we were busier than ever. A month later, an adjacent art gallery closed and we expanded, more than doubling our space. The excitement of designing and building the expansion and all the subsequent action drowned out our background longing. But we had lost our original vision of the medical spa in Santa Fe. We could not see it any more. Our antennas were focused on Hawaii, but there was no reception whatsoever. I regularly talked with my friend Joe who lived in Honolulu, trying to engage his intent to pull us there, but there never was the slightest opening. Joe was energetically cyclic with me and had been a fellow student of Carlos Castaneda as well. He would have loved for us to come, and I could not imagine a better navigational beacon. But we could not generate the energy, at least for now.

Santa Fe had been good to us. Not in the usual sense though. It had never indulged us. People say that it sits on top of a massive quartz formation, and for us it energetically resembled something like a stovetop, forcing us to keep moving all the time while still cooking us in the end. We tirelessly worked around the clock to make our concept work and to keep Zen and passion alive and together. We had no financial safety net. It had to really work, and this alone accounted for a lot of intensity. There actually was no end to intensity during our time in the City Different. Exposed as we were, we interacted with the most interesting people, hosted hundreds of events, lectures, art shows, and workshops. Santa Fe is a nexus of the New Age movement and at Longevity we were plugged into a high voltage outlet, for better or for worse.

Looking back I can still feel the strain. But when I close my eyes and let the images arise slowly, tears well up and a deep shiver runs through my heart and soul. Santa Fe had been good to us indeed. In the end it all came together, we were released transformed, and love and passion had everything to do with it. Our huge and beautiful communal living room with its "Pandora Red" walls, bathed as it was in the rich warm glow of its many amber colored lights, had been an oasis of the heart. And I can never express enough gratitude for all the affection we received there—and still do to this day.

And thank you, Florinda, even if we never found you.

Infinity and the Path of the Heart

T he art of navigation is not just a strategy to move forward in alignment with Intent. It is also the exhilarating experience of being in a state of flow and of feeling connected. Once I had learned to pay attention, I not only received constant guidance with my decisions, but I also received regular reminders that there is a much larger—and apparently scripted—dimension to life that I am normally not aware of. Often, synchronicities felt much like a friendly wake-up call or even a supportive pat on my back by an unfathomably present and caring universe.

An example was my encounter with Pola Lopez, a gifted Santa Fe artist who had rented the adjacent space to use as a studio/gallery while I was finishing the build-out of the Longevity Café. When she introduced herself on the day she moved in, I expressed my concerns that she might be disturbed by our music, once we were open and running. I suggested we perform a sound check and asked her to go back into her studio while I put on some music. As she walked over, I simply pushed the play button on our stereo system, which was a fully loaded two hundred CD changer, set on random. Incidentally, the piece of music that started playing was one of three rare Tangos that Carlos Castaneda had once played for us during a workshop to set a specific mood. The title was "Esperanza Inutil" (Useless Hope) by Puerto Rican singer Daniel Santos. As the first notes started playing over our speaker system, Pola came running back excitedly:

"This is amazing," she proclaimed. "Have you ever heard of Carlos Castaneda? This was one of his favorite songs." She looked at me, seemingly incredulous.

"Yes, I know," I laughed, "I knew him well, but how do you know?

"Oh, I went to some of his workshops in Los Angeles a few years ago; that's where I heard it; and then I got the CD myself." Pola replied.

There were nearly two thousand music titles in our CD changer, and the chances for one of these three Tangos to come on had been extremely small. It instantly formed a bond between Pola and us, and of course, she did not mind our music in the least. We became good friends, and a year and a half later, when Pola realized that she preferred painting at her studio at home, we integrated her gallery space into Longevity.

Santa Fe is one of the largest art markets in the United States with an artist community to match. This enabled us to stay specialized and hold an art opening every six weeks, exclusively showing art with a healing or spiritual intent. For our first show that coincided with the opening of our extension, we found an exceptional artist. Robert Schrei had been a Zen priest for seventeen years before he left the monastery to work as an energy healer and painter. All his artwork was carefully conceived and calibrated to assist his healing work, which made him the ideal artist to set the intent for our gallery addition. What I didn't know until we had interacted for a while and become friends was that his energy happened to be cyclic with mine. In my entire life I have met only three men that were undoubtedly cyclic with me, and it had always been and continues to be meaningful.

The expansion and art opening was a great success and Longevity began to thrive. Even so, our long-term intent regarding Santa Fe had been broken, and additionally, I began to develop respiratory problems due to the dry high desert air. As much as we loved our ever-growing family of employees, customers, and friends, we couldn't help but perceive a slowly increasing sense of restlessness. So when we met Abhay Vishwakarma a few months later, we made sure to rearrange our line-up of artists to make room for his work right away. Abhay is a sixth-generation sculptor of sacred Hindu art and specializes in sculptures of the elephant-headed deity Ganesha, the bestower of luck, and the remover of obstacles. This sounded exactly like the energy we could use, and before long we had a well publicized art opening, and Ganesha's intent was flooding our world. Ganesha reliefs and statues were everywhere we looked. My favorite piece was an exquisite white marble sculpture of a big bellied, absolutely adorable depiction of the elephant god, nearly two feet high. I couldn't help but touch him every time I went by.

Then Carmela's thirty-third birthday was approaching and since three was her favorite number, I wanted to surprise her with something special. We were not really given to celebrating our birthdays, but I decided to make an exception. I knew she loved the performances of the Cirque de Soleil, and a new show had just recently opened in Las Vegas. As I tried to book this little surprise vacation, however, nothing went smoothly. There was apparently a big convention in Vegas around that time, and I could get neither a reasonable flight, nor affordable hotel accommodation. Worst of all, the good tickets to the Cirque de Soleil show on her birthday were already sold out. At this point it became obvious that my initial idea was not supported at all. While researching online, though, I noticed a Southwest Airlines special promotion, two for the price of one to Tampa, Florida. We had never been in Florida, and as I was having visions of coconut palms and white beaches, I spontaneously booked the flight. It happened to cost exactly $ 333 for the both of us, which made me chuckle. To make up for the Cirque de Soleil, I chose a room at the famous Biltmore Hotel in Coral Gables.

Carmela was excited and happy when I told her about the surprise a few days before our departure to allow for the necessary preparations. In Tampa we picked up our rental car and drove leisurely south along Florida's West Coast. In the early evening we arrived at the Biltmore, and as I parked the car and turned off the ignition, I noticed the trip odometer reading. From Tampa airport to the Biltmore parking lot we had driven exactly 333 miles.

"Wow, look at this," I laughed; turning the ignition back on, so Carmela could see the numbers.

"It looks like we are in the right place then," she laughed.

We stepped out of the car.

"Definitely the right place," Carmela mused, after taking in the scenery.

"It's beautiful, just perfect, thank you."

The dinner, the hotel, the room, the bed, the weather, everything indeed turned out to be perfect. We realized how starved we were for the lushness of the vegetation and for the soft, sweet, nourishing humidity. As we had dinner on the hotel terrace and afterwards, while sitting on the balcony of our room, our skin and lungs happily soaked up the rich, thick air like a soothing balm. Later that evening we went for a drive without any purpose other than feeling more of this fragrant softness that was everywhere. As uniquely beautiful as Santa Fe was, it also was high and dry in every sense of the expression. The contrast was overwhelming. After driving for a while through the parks and past the mansions of Coral Gables, the energy changed. The vegetation became even thicker and more tropical, and at times we drove through tunnels of trees with lushness all around us. There were no streetlights and we couldn't see much detail.

"I wonder where we are," I mused. "This is incredible, I would like to come back in the daytime and see what kind of neighborhood this is."

"Let's write down some street names, so we find it again," Carmela suggested.

After checking with a map the next day, we learned that we had been driving through an area of Miami called Coconut Grove. It is the oldest residential area in South Florida, and therefore it has the lushest and most mature vegetation. We also found out that the zip code of Coconut Grove was 33133. We could only laugh again, but this was getting increasingly intriguing. Playfully following our trail of threes, we left the Biltmore the following day and moved to a hotel in Coconut Grove instead. In the afternoon we went to explore South Beach, Miami's famous playground. As we were meandering down Ocean Drive, a sudden thunderstorm made us run for cover in a place called Mango's Tropical Café, and since it looked like it was going to rain a while, we sat down and ordered some food.

Mango's turned out to be an entertaining venue. It was oozing sensuality. Male and female staff alike, all obviously selected for their sex appeal, were dancing scantily clad on top of the bar when they weren't busy serving customers. The decoration, menu, and music were Caribbean and South American at its most colorful. Romero, our server, a young man from Puerto Rico, was exuberantly friendly and talkative, and because it was still early and not too busy, he frequently sat down at our table, entertaining us with his life story and the background of every one of his colleagues. He was obviously proud of being on the Mango's team.

"See that girl over there? The one that just got up on the counter? That's Maria. She's from Cuba. She used to be a ballet dancer. And the guy that is joining her now? He is from Venezuela. A bodybuilder. They are dancing really well together. Look!"

We enjoyed ourselves tremendously. With Romero filling us in, even on the juicy details of who was sleeping with whom, soon the whole big place came to life in an unexpectedly familiar way.

"Oh, you have to watch him, this is Carlos," Romero pointed to a particularly well built young man who had just taken off his shirt and begun dancing with two girls on top of the main bar. "He was a runner-up at last year's Mister Columbia contest," Romero proclaimed proudly. "He is the star of the show, and we are both born on the same day," he added excitedly.

"Really? When is your birthday?" I asked

"It was yesterday!" he beamed, "May 16, we celebrated together last night."

"What?" Carmela and I burst out simultaneously. "May 16 is Carmela's birthday too, that's why we came to Miami. This is unbelievable." We were stunned.

While driving back to our hotel that night I kept shaking my head.

"I think Intent is trying to tell us something. What do you say?" I turned to Carmela.

"It sure looks like it," she smiled.

Our hotel room was on the eighth floor, and the next morning I was standing at the window for a long time, looking down onto the tree-covered streets of Coconut Grove.

"I guess this probably means that we should seriously consider moving here. What do you think about Coconut Grove?" I asked Carmela without turning around.

"The name certainly has a good ring to it," I added, laughing.

But before Carmela could answer, my cell phone rang. It was Frank, our landlord from Santa Fe. He wasn't aware that we were out of town.

"Felix," he began, "I am so sorry for having to do this to you guys, but my son is moving back to town, and we will need the house for him. Do you think you could move out by August 15? This would give you nearly three months. If you need more time to find something, we can talk about it . . . " Frank was seemingly uncomfortable.

"No, no, it's okay Frank, we understand. We'll be out on August 15," I said in a daze.

"Well, I guess that was loud and clear," I pronounced after relating the content of the phone conversation to Carmela. I wasn't sure if I was happy or terrified by that much guidance. Florida was not Hawaii, after all, but there didn't seem to be much of a choice.

"Coconut Grove it is." Carmela exclaimed cheerfully, offering me a "high five," which I forcefully returned.

"Deal!"

❦ ❦ ❦

Synchronicities continued to abound, never leaving us in the slightest doubt about our decision to leave Santa Fe for Miami. We sent out an email to our patrons and friends announcing our intentions to sell Longevity, and before long we came to an agreement with a young couple from Santa Fe's healing arts community, Yukiko and Jordan. We had known them for quite a while. Besides their passion for the healing arts, they both had been students of Miguel Ruiz, an initiate of the Toltec wisdom tradition and the author of *The Four Agreements* and *Beyond Fear*. So we regarded them as "energetic cousins" and were confident they would be a perfect fit to carry the Longevity concept to the next level. Entirely by coincidence, but hardly surprising, after all that had happened, the escrow closed and Longevity legally changed hands exactly on August 15, the day we had to move out of our home. We moved in with Jordan and Yukiko into their spacious house to help them through the transition for another month. And after a grand and unforgettable farewell party on their grounds we hugged every one of our huge and beloved extended family good-bye and left Santa Fe in the middle of the night. During a large part of the hour-long drive to Albuquerque we were both in tears.

238

❦ ❦ ❦

We had decided to go traveling for a few months before immersing ourselves in our next business venture, and the next day we flew out of

Albuquerque to Bali, an island in Indonesia we had been curious to visit for a long time. Unlike the vast majority of Indonesians who are Muslims, Balinese people adhere to an ancient form of Hinduism that is strongly influenced by animism and naturalism. In practice this means that the Balinese essentially perceive all elements of their environment as conscious or possessing a spirit that should be kept happy and benevolent at all times. This sense of seeking harmony with every element of nature is ultimately what drives Balinese culture and can be seen in all aspects of life. The employees of our hotel in Ubud, for example, started each day by collecting baskets of flower petals and adorning a myriad of shrines and other objects on the property. This process lasted up to an hour every morning. Every taxi cab, every room in every house, every coconut tree in the garden has a spirit that is revered and appeased on a daily basis. As primeval as this may seem, it makes for a conscious and integrated life experience, and as an ethnic group, I found the Balinese to be the most peaceful and enchanting people I had ever met.

After a few weeks of explorations, we decided to stay in Bali for a while to recharge in this ambience of peace and practical spirituality. We found and rented a beautiful house that was owned and designed by an Italian fashion designer. It had a spectacular open architecture and was located in the middle of rice paddies just outside of Kuta, Bali's main tourist district. On the following Saturday, on October 12, 2002, we had dinner in town. Over dessert we discussed if we still wanted to go somewhere else or return home early.

"How are you feeling?" I asked Carmela. "Do you want to go dancing a little bit to work off some calories?"

"Sure," Carmela answered. "Where would we go though?"

"Well, there is Sari's just down the street and a few more clubs along the beach," I suggested without too much enthusiasm.

"How do *you* feel? You don't sound too excited." Carmela smiled.

"Honestly, I am a little tired tonight. Maybe next weekend," I replied.

"Ok, let's go home then," Carmela agreed.

Less than an hour later, a massive car bomb turned the Sari Night Club into rubble around a crater several feet deep. In the explosion, one of three near simultaneous attacks that became known as the Bali bombings, over two hundred people died and hundreds more were severely burned and

239

injured. We had just sat down to read on our patio as our entire house shook under the impact of the blasts, even though we lived several miles away from the site of the attack. We thought it had been a sonic boom or an exploding gas pipeline and were only informed about the bombing the next morning by a friend who called us from Jakarta.

Our near-fatal proximity to this event affected us even more profoundly than the terrorist attack on the World Trade Center a year earlier. The magical island paradise with its beautifully innocent and peace-loving people had instantaneously disappeared from the radar screen and re-emerged as part of an ever more desperate, violent, and deeply unconscious international community.

From an energetic perspective, these two events had been incredibly precise and far from arbitrary. The World Trade Center had probably been the most prominent representation of the unconstrained materialism that is at the core of our current world order, just as Bali had been the epitome of authentic spirituality and earthly paradise. Like two opposing archetypes they had defined the dualistic modality of our time like no other pair of symbols. For both of them to disintegrate so close together in time had a mythological quality and suggested that this modality may have outlived its usefulness. The modality of our time is the modality of our collective consciousness, which apparently has to change. I strongly perceived these two disasters as a dramatic wake-up call that far transcended the motivations of the perpetrators who caused them. From a navigational perspective these paired events suggested an urgent need to awaken and move towards the non-dualistic essence of awareness, or possibly face an evolutionary re-booting event, which most likely would turn out to be catastrophic.

240

The bombings represented a tremendous shift in energy, and our feelings of contentment and peace were replaced by a sense of urgency. We felt that we needed to do more than just relax and recharge. Guided by the resulting intent to be more actively constructive, our navigation brought us to Beijing, China, where we entered into an internship at the world's largest hospital for Traditional Chinese Medicine. Our work there was immensely enriching and grounding, and as we returned to the United States several months later, we felt stronger and more confident to play a constructive and healing part in these turbulent times.

∨ ∨ ∨

Before we finally arrived in Coconut Grove, however, the universe had another remarkable event up its sleeves, one that was filled to the brim with opportunities to grow, learn, and navigate. As we traveled across the country with our belongings, we woke up one morning near New Orleans to discover that our moving truck had been stolen overnight from the hotel parking lot. Except for the clothes we were wearing, a bag with toiletries, and the laptop computer we had taken into the room, everything was gone. Documents, valuables, our entire household—everything!

I don't know how or why, but we were surprisingly calm. We did the obvious, like informing police and banks, and then just tackled the issue one moment at a time. There was a puzzling dual perception of disaster on one side and liberation on the other. We actually laughed a great deal as we attempted to go in pursuit of the stolen truck. With all our credit cards now compromised and canceled, we could barely rent a car. One of my first thoughts had been that, from a navigational point of view, this event could only suggest starting our new life without any baggage from the past, to intend a clean and fresh beginning—once again.

Nevertheless, we tried everything conceivable to recover our loss. I called all my "cyclic brothers" to engage their intent, and a psychic friend of ours to enlist his talents as well. At Longevity we had allowed a number of psychics and medical intuitives to offer their services to our patrons, and James had been the most talented of them all. We had become good friends. As I told James over the phone what had happened, he immediately reported that he was *seeing* a small airfield. "Not a large commercial airport," he continued, "I only see small airplanes. Is there such an airport close to where you are?" he asked.

"I don't know," I said, "we'll find out. Thank you very much James. We'll keep you in the loop. If you *see* anything else, give us a call."

There were two small community airports in the area and after thoroughly searching the vicinity of the one closest to our hotel, we drove to New Orleans to investigate the other one. It was already the second day since the theft, and we were not too optimistic. At the moment we pulled up at Lakefront Airport in northwest New Orleans, we received a call from the rental company, informing us that our moving truck had been recovered. It was found abandoned, the tailgate suspiciously open, in a neighborhood less than a mile from this airport.

"Congratulations James!"

To our utter surprise most of the contents were still there; only flashy items and most electronics were gone. Since the door lock and the ignition had been broken, we loaded everything into another truck and were on our way again. We vowed, however, to heed the hint and intended a completely open-minded and unencumbered beginning at our destination.

Our initial vision had been to create a holistic medical spa where becoming, being, and staying healthy would be a pleasurable experience, where pleasure meets health, so to speak. After this experience, however, we thought it was appropriate to revisit our intent.

We had certain qualifications and professional experience, as well as passions that clearly supported this vision, but we also loved traveling and living in many different places, which conflicted with the intent to create a stationary wellness center. Following this realization, we began playing with the idea to get one of the large international hotel chains interested in our wellness concept, to eventually spend our life moving from hotel to hotel, implementing it. We wrote a detailed business proposal to that extent and decided to pursue both alternatives as impeccably as possible and then see which one was more supported.

Upon arrival in Coconut Grove we had rented a small house in the oldest and most lush area of town and thoroughly enjoyed our life in the "jungle." Our street was a tunnel of trees, covered with moss, lichen, and bromeliads, just as we had seen it on our first exploratory drive. Wild peacocks were roosting everywhere, their characteristic calls piercing the soft air at all hours.

Nearly two months had passed without any significant leads in either direction, when the energy suddenly shifted, and we received two different proposals, both unexpected and unsolicited. One came from a fellow acupuncturist who had also graduated at the acupuncture college in Santa Fe and who was now practicing in Coconut Grove. We had been loosely in touch, and he made us an interesting proposal. One of his patients was an executive of a major cruise line headquartered in Miami, and both of them had been talking about the idea of offering acupuncture services on cruise ships. The talks had been informal, and our colleague did not know how to go about it. But knowing that we were still uncommitted, he thought we might be interested in a partnership.

The other proposal came during a chance encounter with the director of a specialty boarding school for troubled teenagers in Montana. He felt that the modalities of Oriental Medicine could be an interesting adjunct program, helping his students in their rehabilitation. He invited us to visit the school and even offered to pay for the flights.

Committed to keep an open mind, we decided to follow both leads. First, we met with cruise line officials, entering into a long series of meetings, gradually developing a concept for "Acupuncture at Sea," as we called it. There was general enthusiasm, but many small hurdles, particularly in regards to liability and other legal issues. There was no precedence; acupuncture had never been offered on cruise ships. Between meetings, we flew to Montana to visit the boarding school.

The contrast between the two worlds was fascinating from the start. Here was the glittering headquarter of a major cruise line, catering to leisure, luxury, pampering, and indulgence. And there, hidden from public view in the forests of northern Montana, we found the other side of the coin and a sad monument to a dysfunctional society. Over five hundred adolescents were held there, mostly against their will, dropped off by parents unable to cope with them any longer. We didn't even know of the existence of such places and eventually learned that there are hundreds of them all over the nation. There was no question at all. If we could make a difference in helping these young people to feel better and regain some degree of control over their lives, we wanted to do it.

"So what do you think?" Cameron, the school's director asked us after we had spent a few days on campus and had met a variety of students and faculty.

243

"We would love to offer a program for the students, but we feel that we should do a controlled study first to see if we can get measurable results."

He promised us all the support we needed, and as soon as we were back in Miami, we went to work on the study design. There were only two weeks out of every month when we could schedule treatment sessions. The rest of the time the students attended developmental seminars. So we proposed to offer four sessions per participating student per month for four months. The two-hour group sessions consisted of Qigong and acupuncture, and the participants were to be put on herbal protocols as well. At the beginning and end of the study we would make a thorough emotional and cognitive assessment, based on questionnaires to be filled out by students and faculty. Participation was to be voluntary and needed a parent's consent. A control group that did not receive treatments was to be equally assessed at the beginning and end of the four-month period, and results were then compared to see if there would be a significant difference between treatment group and control group.

Meanwhile our negotiations with the cruise line met with success and all hurdles were cleared much faster than anticipated. We signed an agreement for a series of trial cruises, during which we committed to offer lectures and acupuncture services on one cruise ship. We would be converting a conference room into a makeshift clinic with four treatment rooms, and the program was to launch in September, exactly when we had scheduled our first round of sessions with the troubled teens. Fortunately the cruise line was understanding, and we were cleared to conduct both trials simultaneously. In practice it meant that we flew to Montana to work two weeks with our teenage clients and then flew to Vancouver, British Columbia to join the ship on its two-week cruise to Hawaii. From Hawaii we flew back again to Montana for another round with our students, to re-join the ship two weeks later in San Diego for its cruise through the Panama Canal to Miami, etc. It was an incredible experience. The contrast between our alternating lifestyles could not have been stronger.

Our intention to let go of our preconceptions and ideas after the New Orleans experience had obviously produced exciting results. Most amazing for us was the unexpected emergence of "Acupuncture at Sea." We would never have thought of it, but it embodied exactly the intent we had pursued by offering our wellness concept to luxury hotels. Instead of moving from hotel to hotel, as we had envisioned, now the entire hotel was moving.

It was a picture book example of the mysterious workings of the spirit that is inherent in life. Following the navigational input that we extracted from the New Orleans event, we had revisited our innermost desires and re-formulated our intent. Then we did our impeccable best to follow every lead that presented itself; and as a result the universe promptly rewarded us with its own version of our vision. We just needed to be fluid enough to adapt. Incidentally, and in retrospect, it would soon become clear that "Acupuncture at Sea," which was a much more concise version of our idea than the hotel project, would actually fit a lot better into our journey.

From living a life where we had to make countless decisions, we had gradually moved to the point where we were left with only one single decision, which we had to continuously renew: to simply do our impeccable best in every situation. Everything else seemed to just fall into place. With this in mind, we could only be curious how our dual engagement would play itself out.

⌄   ⌄   ⌄

Working with our wayward teens in Montana was the most heartwarming experience we had ever had. They absolutely loved our sessions, and the trial was an unprecedented success. The group of about forty students that were enrolled in our program dramatically improved their emotional wellbeing and academic performance over the four months trial. As measured subjectively and objectively with the help of fifteen parameters from anger to depression and from motivation to the ability to concentrate, their quality of life at the end of the trial was nearly fifty percent better than that of the control group.

"Acupuncture at Sea" was in no way less exciting. The cruise liner we boarded in Vancouver to open a new frontier for Oriental Medicine was a magnificent ship, carrying three thousand passengers and crew. Her name, just for good measure, turned out to be "Infinity." How could we not feel in complete alignment with life as we went onboard?

On our first work-day on the "Infinity," however, our alignment was slightly off, which was not the best omen. We both woke up seasick and could hardly stand upright. A large swell, remnants of an early season storm off Alaska, had been hitting the ship from the side all night long, as soon as we had passed Vancouver Island. Thanks to a vigorous advertising campaign the onboard theater was already filling with guests to hear our lecture on Oriental Medicine, and most available clinic appointments had been booked. Our alternative remedies were not working fast enough, and we had to use some good old-fashioned motion sickness pills. This took care of it, but we were in a fog most of the day.

Other than that, we were off to a great start. We lectured on Oriental Medicine, Five Elements Theory, Feng Shui, nutrition, and herbal medicine throughout the cruise, and after each lecture the guests usually lined up at the clinic for available treatment slots. It was nothing short of sensational, and our only problem was that we hardly found time to eat and rarely had a break during clinic hours. Some days, each of us treated up to twenty patients. The setting was perfect. The passengers had plenty of time during the days at sea, and tales of successful treatments and vanishing symptoms made the rounds quickly. Most of our patients had never tried acupuncture before.

Fortunately, due to licensing laws, we were not allowed to offer treatments when we were in a harbor, so we could go on land and enjoy some recreation. But even during busy treatment hours we had amazing experiences. Our makeshift clinic had large windows, and I recall some rather unique moments of us propping up our patient's heads, so they could see the jungle floating by while we were cruising through the Panama Canal. Or, even more surreal, was the scene of a patient watching Cape Horn during one of our later cruises around South America, his body nearly immobilized by two dozen acupuncture needles. He definitely had a story to tell.

And then, within a day, we were back in the snowy forests of Montana, trying to avoid hitting wildlife as we navigated dirt roads towards Spring Creek Lodge Academy—definitely a euphemism—where our students were already waiting for us. Two different planets, one more intriguing than the other. The last day of our controlled study was just before Christmas and most of our troubled teens were *not* going home for the holidays.

"When are you coming back?" Many of them were crying as we hugged good-bye.

"We don't know yet; hopefully soon," we replied, fighting back our own tears.

We really didn't know. The students, the parents, and the school naturally wanted us to continue after the trial had been such a success, but for the moment, we just had to put it on hold. The cruise line wanted more trials on different routes before making a decision on a fleet-wide roll out.

The "Infinity" was scheduled to sail twice around South America with "Acupuncture at Sea," including a three-day stop in Rio for the Carnival. This second trial phase was quite a gift for us, and even financially it was very lucrative. The clinic continued to be booked solid, and after we successfully treated a few VIPs that were on this inaugural South American cruise, things suddenly got serious. Our VIP patients had enthusiastically urged the cruise line to roll out our program to the rest of the fleet, and while we were peacefully cruising through the Chilean Fjords, we received an email to that effect. For some reason, everything had to happen fast, and we were asked to start the fleet-wide expansion immediately.

Instead of jumping up and down in celebration, however, we felt rather paralyzed. We had not thought much about the conflicting dynamics of the two projects that we had been advancing simultaneously. We were not consciously aware which way we wanted to go and had hoped the universe would take care of it, as always.

The cruise line was waiting for an answer, but no matter how keenly attentive we were, this time universal Intent did not speak to us in the usual manner. There were no obvious signs, omens, or synchronicities. Nothing stood out enough to point the way, at least not on the outside. This situation required some serious soul-searching. Which path was the path of the heart?

Rolling out "Acupuncture at Sea" as a revenue partner of the cruise line was a tremendous business opportunity with potentially huge financial rewards. But it would also remove us from actually treating patients. We would be sitting in an office in Miami, organizing logistics, hiring and firing personnel, performing crisis management, living the corporate life.

Or we could pass this opportunity on to our colleague in Miami, now that everything was already set up and running. He would probably be thrilled. The future of "Acupuncture at Sea" would be assured; and we could resume our work with our teens in Montana—with those endearing little troublemakers who badly needed to be protected from themselves.

It was a memorable moment in our lives. What a privilege, to even have a choice between two such attractive avenues—if there ever was a choice, that is. Could we really have decided against our hearts? Wasn't our whole Infinity adventure just a gracious way of the spirit to show us that the world of luxury hotels and cruise ships was not to be our playground for now—or ever for that matter?

We thought so, at least. We felt so. Once our mental chatter subsided, our hearts became the most powerful navigational beacons there are, and we knew that our place for now and the foreseeable future was indeed with a bunch of endearing little troublemakers in a faraway forest.

Once we were aligned with our hearts and at peace, everything fell into place. We contacted our colleague in Miami, who had put us in touch with this opportunity in the first place, and we offered to help him take over the project. We already had pre-screened a number of acupuncturists, which greatly facilitated the roll-out. As anticipated, he was delighted, and now acupuncture is offered on virtually every cruise ship. And we were delighted that even four months of cruising Infinity could not distract us from following the path of the heart.

The Audacity of Surrender

I t had become quite apparent that our navigation was leading us along the path of the heart, a path that was getting wider and wider. With Castaneda's death, the external constraints of the warrior's way disappeared. The fierceness and discipline that had been imposed by the dynamics and dogma of our sorcerer's myth fell away, and I abandoned my quest of becoming a man of knowledge, or anything else for that matter. In a strangely paradoxical way I had been liberated from my quest for liberation. But even as I let go, my behavior did not change. I did not fall back into the cynicism, hedonism, and aimlessness of old, and I did not feel attracted to the materialistic value system of the social order around me, either. Even though the race I had been engaged in had lost its finish line, I stayed on course just for the hell of it. I kept practicing the Magical Passes, aimed for internal silence and tried to be as impeccable as possible. Anything else just seemed wrong. My overriding purpose had disappeared, however, leaving an enormous void. Consequently I found purpose in my daily pursuits and particularly in my love for Carmela, which grew to become the guiding force in my new life.

The void had been vast though, and my heart could not fill it without some serious prodding. We consciously and tirelessly set our intent for our hearts to open wide and our love to keep growing. To support this intent, we drew from several different traditions. There was a Tensegrity movement, called the "Pass of Affection," which we practiced daily. We also integrated various forms of Heart Qigong and heart chakra exercises, and we continued to cultivate our unrelenting awareness in this regard. Once, while visiting the ancient temple city of Machu Picchu in Peru, we spontaneously decided to renew our intent of affection with a private little ceremony in the temple of the moon. A powerful thunderstorm had cleared out the entire site, and we suddenly found ourselves alone in this breathtakingly beautiful place. We climbed up to the temple, which occupies the highest and most auspicious spot of Machu Picchu, and kneeled down on either side of the altar. Then we drew a few drops of blood from our wrists and joined them in a sacred moment.

The results of our efforts on our personal relationship were nearly uncanny. We grew accustomed to live in total absence of friction or disharmony, and we wondered again if a marriage could not generally serve as a complete and all-inclusive path towards personal transcendence and spiritual awakening, if it would only be seen as such.

Navigating to Santa Fe afforded us a unique opportunity to expand our cultivation of the heart to include our relationships with patients, staff, customers, and friends. Where Zen meets passion is probably a good place for love to emerge. We had never been surrounded by so much genuine affection as during the years we operated the Longevity Café and Emporium in the City Different.

Until we began working with our troubled teens in Montana, that is. Within weeks, the only way we referred to them was as "our kids." And we meant it. Even the most troublesome ones quickly found their way into our hearts. We had an unfair advantage though. Most of the students at Spring Creek Lodge were emotionally between a rock and a hard place. They neither felt good towards their parents who had brought them there, nor towards the school staff that kept them put. We were the outsiders who were determined to make them feel better for a few hours at a time. They trusted us, they loved us, and we loved them back and adopted them all. And they quickly became the center of our life.

But all this affection and purpose came with a price. Once we resumed our sessions at Spring Creek Lodge, we felt a tremendous pressure to succeed in making a difference in these young lives. A majority of our students had traumatic histories. Many had been sexually or physically abused, nearly all had been heavy drug or alcohol users. One of our girls had been prostituting herself from age twelve to support her heroin addiction. Some were self-mutilating, others on constant suicide or runaway watch. A few were just unruly, unmotivated, or depressed. And all of them were extraordinarily defiant.

But every time we watched their peacefully sleeping faces during the acupuncture part of our sessions, none of this seemed to matter. As those confused and tortured young minds were dormant, it became obvious that every one of them still had all the chances in the world to lead a happy, constructive, and inspiring life. And we wanted to make sure we did everything we could to help tip the scales. We constantly fine-tuned our treatment modalities to maximize the effect on their individual problems. We combined various movement forms, breathing exercises, music therapy, and meditation with all the modalities of Oriental Medicine. We began each of the two-hour group sessions with questions and answers that helped us to gauge the energy and group dynamic. These exchanges were completely open and honest, and we were put on the spot like never before in our life to find out what we truly believed, and what we thought really mattered. The answers, solutions, and life skills we had to produce needed to be true, concise, practical, and above all, effective in bringing about happiness. Because happiness, of course, was ultimately all they were looking for.

We talked a great deal about the relationship between awareness and happiness, about the benefits of bringing awareness into everything we do, instead of dividing the world into things that are good or bad. We saw the futility in simply denouncing the use of mind-altering substances, so we tried to educate and differentiate, bringing awareness into their respective choices, and we urged them to always observe carefully how their choices affected their awareness. We shared our fascination with the power and intricacies of intent and with the compelling beauty of impeccability. We labored hard to introduce an energetic perspective on perception, how to look at things energetically, and how to manipulate and cultivate one's own energy. Most of all, we talked about the compulsive nature of the thinking mind, how we are completely at the mercy of our incessant internal dialogue, and how we can change that. And naturally we talked about our passion for the art of navigation, about establishing an ongoing communication with the universe and about turning life into a magical treasure hunt.

Of course, we tried to illustrate all the above concepts to the best of our abilities. They are the core elements that make navigation a learnable skill. But it was mostly our navigational tales that caught the attention of our young audience. They seemed enthralled with the magical nature of navigation, and everybody had had some first-hand experiences with synchronicities, hunches, signs, omens, and other such phenomena. We shared why we had moved from Los Angeles to Santa Fe, how the trail of three's had brought us to Miami and taught us about the priority of the heart. We told the story of how two mating owls had talked me into buying a house in the desert, how a firework of shooting stars had told me something about Tucson, how a rainbow had ended my vision quest in Alamos, Sonora, and how a magical series of synchronicities had led me into a silent meditation retreat in Thailand.

But we also gave everyday examples of how shopping for food can be turned into a navigational experience by simply letting intuition and energetic perception pick the groceries. If we are standing in front of the produce rack with a still mind, some vegetables or fruits that we had no intention of buying might call out to us. It just means that we will perceive them as more vibrant and appealing than others, perhaps because they are more alive, clean, and fresh, or because our body is communicating a specific need at that moment. We made the case that nutrition is linked to our overall wellbeing to such a high degree that it should warrant a maximum of awareness, and that we should be receptive to intuitive guidance.

While illustrating such everyday applications of navigation to our students, we ourselves became for the first time fully aware to what extent this receptive and interactive way of life had shaped our reality. With more and more synchronicities and other inexplicable input informing our life, we felt naturally compelled to keep our attention turned outward, away from our thoughts. As a result, our sensory environment increasingly began to resemble a three-dimensional movie that we kept scanning for cues that would prompt us to act in accordance with an apparent script. Our sensory environment, of course, included our internal, bodily, and emotional perceptions, which are all part of the movie. With a growing number of elements of this movie appearing to make sense, we eventually had to open to the possibility that everything might indeed be scripted in some incomprehensible way. And what once had been challenges, obstacles, or other forms of antagonism in our daily lives, gradually transformed to become nothing but navigational elements of this interactive movie as well.

If inclement weather, traffic jams, car troubles, illness, and other unexpected events seemed to interfere with the flow of things, we learned to accept and integrate these "interferences" as part of the storyline. And the more we surrendered to life as it unfolded, instead of insisting it should be otherwise, the more sense everything began to make, and the more benevolent life became. However, all these observations were difficult to share with an audience of adolescents whose minds were on overdrive most of the time and who perceived nearly everything as antagonistic. So we stuck with the most obvious and practical stories to illustrate the dynamics of navigation.

There was, for example, the rather mundane story of how I found "Tolteca," a beautiful, blue Harley Davidson motorcycle. During the first year of our engagement at Spring Creek Lodge, we had still kept our residence in Miami, and every month we flew to Montana for two weeks to conduct our treatment sessions. We thought that by living in two places at once, we could perhaps cultivate some consistency. It was actually a fortunate constraint that we could only work with our students half of the month. In this way we did not burn out on each other. We always would bring new energy with us from our travels.

The first signs of spring in rural Montana are neither birds nor flowers, but the roar of countless Harleys, thundering down the country roads on the first snow-free weekend of the year. I had never been particularly attracted to the Harley mystique, but the sound still made my biker heart beat faster every time. The previous year we had bought a used Honda Goldwing touring motorcycle and driven it across the country from Montana to Miami, where it provided our only means of transportation. As the days got longer, the roaring grew louder, and my heart began to beat precariously fast. Most likely I began intending another motorcycle to materialize in Montana. I did not actively pursue it though. We did not have much free time in the two weeks we worked with our kids, and there was so much wildlife in the area where we worked that it made biking particularly dangerous. I was careful with everything that had to do with motorcycling, since I had already suffered a serious accident in Santa Fe that sent me to the hospital. Even more sobering was the fact that my father and my grandfather had each died on a bike eight years apart. My father's death had been particularly momentous. His fatal accident occurred on the way home from visiting his father's grave on the Day of the Dead, which is celebrated in Germany on November 1, a little over a month before I was born.

But as it were, without being prompted by me in the slightest, our landlord surprised me one day, just before Memorial Day weekend:

"Felix, don't you miss your motorcycle? My friend Gary just bought a Harley, and now he wants to get rid of his Goldwing. I am sure you could get it for a good price."

"Hm, we don't really need a bike here," I said. "What year is it? Oh well; actually, don't bother, but thanks anyway."

An hour later he called: "The Goldwing is a '94, great shape, and Gary wants only $1,800 for it; just thought I let you know."

"Thanks Don, I'll think about it."

Carmela was unexpectedly excited: "Maybe we should have a look at it. We could actually use it around here to drive out to the school and the Ranch whenever the weather is nice."

By now our program had grown and we worked with our students in three different locations. The main campus was about half an hour's drive from the small town of Thompson Falls, where we lived while in Montana. The "Girl's Park," which housed girls eighteen and older, was about twenty minutes in another direction, and the drive to the "Ranch" where the eighteen to twenty-four year old boys lived was nearly an hour away. The older students were mostly on drug rehabilitation, court-ordered, or just needed to finish high school in a controlled environment. The roads to all three locations led through spectacular Rocky Mountains scenery and were perfect for motorcycling.

When we went to see Gary the next day, I only had eyes for his brand new Harley. The Goldwing was all right, but far from exciting. All we talked about was his new bike, and he even let me take it on the road for a quick spin. There was no thought, however, for us to make an investment like that, and we would only have use for a touring bike anyway. We needed plenty of luggage room so we could haul around our equipment. In the end we unemotionally agreed to buy the Goldwing as soon as the banks opened after the long weekend. On the way back home we stopped for gas at the local pump. A large group of Harleys had just rolled in as well, and as I filled up our car's tank, I caught sight of a magnificent motorcycle that was being refueled right next to me.

"Wow, that's a really nice bike," I said with my mouth slightly open. "I didn't know Harley made touring bikes like this, with the hard bags and the large box in the back. Nice indeed!"

"Thanks," the young man who stood next to it shrugged, "It's a '99 Electra Glide Ultra Classic. It actually belongs to a friend of mine, and as far as I know, he wants to sell it," he added.

"Really?"

Yes really, and that's how Tolteca came into our life. With so many bikes from all over the Northwest rumbling through town on Memorial Day weekend, it was quite auspicious that Tolteca's owner actually lived just outside Thompson Falls. The bike couldn't have been more perfect for us if it had been custom-designed, and we were able to buy it for several thousand dollars below its Bluebook value. As if in a dream, Tolteca appeared out of nowhere without any solicitation on our part. She was an exact composite of the utility of the Goldwing and the emotional appeal that Gary's Harley had presented. The word "Ghostrider" was engraved on the engine block, which made me decide that my father, who had been a passionate motorcycle lover, must have somehow facilitated this event. This way I didn't have to feel so bad about spending all that money on something that may not have been absolutely necessary, to say the least. But strangely, there were no doubts at all. Everything had been perfectly serendipitous and compelling.

And not surprisingly, Tolteca turned out to be quite a catalyst, affecting our life profoundly from day one. Miami became instant history. All we wanted now in our spare time was to ride through the Great Northwest. Consequently we gave up our residence in the Sunshine State and brought tales of the Big Country to our young friends instead, of our adventures in the Canadian Rockies, of spectacular mountain roads, waterfalls, and hidden hot springs.

The threat of colliding with the ubiquitous wildlife proved to be extreme indeed, and we had many close encounters early on. Adjusting to this reality brought a unique opportunity though. We always had to be one hundred percent present and alert in a way I had never known before. Applying impeccability while motorbiking in these areas meant

255

that we could not allow for one second of daydreaming, no driving on autopilot, no lapse of consciousness, ever. Mountain sheep, elk, moose, wild turkeys, and especially deer would unexpectedly cross the road at any time of the day, leaping out of the forest or materializing otherwise just behind a bend. I made it a conscious task to turn bike riding into a moving meditation, and Carmela, always looking over my shoulder, joined in, giving us two sets of eyes and twice the foresight.

Sitting behind me didn't do Carmela's spirit justice though, and it was only natural that she began dreaming of riding a Harley by herself, graduating from the "bitch" to the "boss," as biker lingo would have it. And this intent to graduate led to another mundane story of everyday navigation.

Whenever we were at a Harley dealership for maintenance or just for fun, Carmela sat on all kinds of different models and allowed her dream to take form.

"So which one do you like best? What's your favorite model?" I asked one day while observing her climb down from one of the larger bikes.

"Not one of these big ones," she said. "They are too heavy for me. I like the Sportster, the 1200 Custom model. But I would want it to have hard bags, just like Tolteca."

"What color?" I was curious.

"Silver, definitely," Carmela answered smiling. "Lots of chrome and custom pipes." She laughed, feigning a tough biker face. "I want it to sound really good."

But then she shrugged. "I have never seen one like that, and anyway, I don't have a license, and I am not sure if I could even ride such a big motorcycle."

As I saw a sales person approaching, I asked if Harley made hard bags for Sportster models.

He thought for a moment, and then his eyes lit up and he said, "Actually, I think we even have a used Sportster with hard bags in the basement. It just came in as a trade. The first one I've ever seen. If you want we can go down and have a look."

We followed along. The Missoula dealership was one of the largest in the nation with nearly a hundred bikes on display and, as we found out, a few dozen more in the basement. And before we knew it, we stood in front of the exact same model Carmela had just described, all in silver and chrome, with all the custom features to the tee. We had never seen one like it, and we would never see a second one. We were speechless.

There were a few deep scratches on one of the bags, and the salesman let us know that the bike would not be going on the floor for a few days until it was repaired.

"What are we going to do now?" I asked, as we were alone again.

Carmela shook her head. She was still in awe about this bizarre synchronicity.

"Well, if you are serious, you need a license, and the best way to do that is to sign up for one of the weekend safety rider courses."

"I know," Carmela answered, "but someone told me that they are always booked for months in advance."

And as it happened, they were indeed all booked up for the rest of the year even, all throughout the state. But Carmela asked to be put on a waiting list, which suited her just fine.

"If I get into a course within the next few weeks and the bike is still available, I'll take it as a sign to go ahead, if not, then not," she said matter-of-factly, preferring to leave it up to the universe to decide. Although excited about this new development, she was not entirely comfortable with the speed of it all, and she definitely had second thoughts.

I was actually quite ambiguous myself. I wanted her to have the experience, but I was also concerned she could get hurt.

Only one day after she had been put on the waiting list, Carmela received a phone call that a slot had opened up for a course on the following weekend, incidentally in Missoula itself, which was very convenient. While she spent two full days learning to ride a motorcycle and earning her license, I bargained to get a good price for her dream bike, bought it, and had it all ready for her as she finished the course. That same evening she rode it flawlessly over a hundred miles back to Thompson Falls, graduating "summa cum laude" from "bitch" to "boss."

Again, there was not even the shadow of a doubt that we had acted in accordance with the universe. The whole affair had felt so pre-ordained that we thought it nearly ominous. We were aware of the perils of motorcycling. Nearly every weekend bikers died in our region, and everybody had a story or two about someone hitting a deer. But the exhilaration and bliss of the experience itself—of becoming one with the machine and nature simultaneously, of the synchrony while roaring along, stacked side-by-side, leaning into wide curved mountain passes, of having the wind blow every bit of thought out of our minds while flying along the freeway, facing oncoming time, keenly and utterly present and aware, of being so close to death at times, so one with life, so filled with living air—oh yes, it is worth it. It made perfect sense.

Even before we arrived at home that first night, as Carmela bonded with her machine during that brave maiden voyage, she had dreamt his name: "Zazen"—sitting meditation. We both had a habit of infusing our vehicles with a living spirit by giving them names. The Nagual had always felt that machines could become permeated with our energy, just like prosthetics, and turn into a veritable extension of our energetic totality. It made intuitive sense to me, and as we rode our beloved machines for nearly thirty thousand miles over the next two summers, Tolteca and Zazen grew very alive. And so did we.

▽ ▽ ▽

The more navigational tales we shared, the more interested our students became in this way of living. But being basically locked away and most decisions being made for them, there was not much room for navigational experimentation on their part.

"How can we remember all this when we leave Spring Creek?" "Are there any books about navigation?" These and similar questions prompted us to create a small handout where we summarized the concept and listed the main parameters that we found necessary to successfully engage in this interactive lifestyle we called the art of navigation. It was a concise and most definitely incomplete summary, but we hoped it could serve as a rough guideline for our students:

NAVIGATION: *An alternative way of living life, being guided every step of the way, always following cues, signs, hints, pointers, hunches, or even an entire universal script that leads us along. Cues can be anything, often synchronicities (improbable yet meaningful coincidences), or anything else that stands out. These navigational pointers, hints, signs, hunches, or omens become obvious, compelling, and all-encompassing by developing awareness* *as outlined below.* **Navigation is dancing with reality,** *listening and moving to the music of the universe. Skilled navigation provides the perfect momentum, speed, and direction towards attaining one's full potential, awakening, liberation, or enlightenment.*

Navigation is living magic and experiencing flow, belonging, and happiness. Ultimately, **Navigation is living the life of life itself.**

To develop navigational skills and to program our navigation system, we must understand, clarify, develop, and nourish INTENT.

INTENT: *The universal and individual force that shapes our life in all its complexity. It is based on our innermost beliefs and convictions. We can only intend successfully what we truly believe. In order to influence our intent it is not enough to simply want something. We have to affect and energize our core beliefs, our visions, and ambitions. This can be done by programming our totality with the intended state; much like a good actor acquires and impersonates a new role. We have to pretend that the intended state has already manifested and inundate our subconscious mind with all the respective perceptions. Action, gestures, posture, mannerisms, and detailed visualizations are key to successful intending. The more often they are repeated, the stronger they are affecting our core beliefs and are thus turning into intent and reality. Wishful thinking and psychological games have little effect.* **Action rules!**

To energize our intent and to unleash its creative powers most effectively, we need to charge it with ENTHUSIASM.

ENTHUSIASM: *The most inspired emotional energy we are able to generate; a free-flowing stream of joyful exhilaration, springing from the heart itself; at once liberated and energized by the fact that we are finally taking charge of our intent, and at the same time instrumental in powerfully and directly turning this intent into reality.*

259

"Nothing great was ever achieved without enthusiasm," *wrote transcendentalist philosopher and poet Ralph Waldo Emerson.*

Enthusiasm has to be facilitated, allowed, and nourished, rather than forced. It arises naturally out of the alignment of heart, spirit, and mind once our innermost beliefs are in harmony with our intrinsic and acquired wisdom, and once we engage in something that is not only utterly enjoyable, but also feels deeply right and wholesome.

Taking great care while formulating our intent so it is in alignment with our wisdom and what we perceive to be universal intent will facilitate enthusiasm. Action, movement, a healthy lifestyle, visualizations of joyful high energy states, heart Qi Gong, and anything else that increases our vibrational rate will facilitate and nourish enthusiasm.

To hold, support, and sustain enthusiasm, and all the other elements of navigation for that matter, it is absolutely essential to cultivate PERSEVERANCE.

PERSEVERANCE: *The indispensable element of dedication, constancy, patience, persistent stability, and level-headedness that sustains, nourishes and ultimately balances all the other elements of navigation. These elements can only evolve synergistically in the purposeful stability of unrelenting perseverance.*

Transforming our life with the art of navigation, from the subjective experience of being usually at odds with a large part of our reality, to the continuous experience of complete harmony and flow, requires all the perseverance we can cultivate. **Cultivating perseverance is like providing and tending the ground from which all the other elements of navigation grow.** *Perseverance should not have a straining quality. It is ultimately very earthy, nourishing, supportive, and natural.*

Spending time in nature and connecting to the ground and earth itself in any conceivable way greatly helps to develop steadiness and perseverance. Abdominal breathing and certain grounding yoga postures or Qi Gong exercises are also helpful to nourish this precious trait. Aiming for balance in every aspect of our life naturally produces patience, stability, and stamina, which are all aspects of perseverance.

"If we are facing the right direction, all we have to do is keep going," *says an old Buddhist proverb.*

Once our navigational system is programmed with intent, charged with enthusiasm, and sustained with perseverance, we have to calibrate it with IMPECCABILITY.

IMPECCABILITY: *The rather self-explanatory practice of doing one's best in any given situation.*

Impeccability is wisdom in action. *The degree of our impeccability and precision determines the reliability of our navigation. Impeccability* *and integrity prevent us from interpreting our navigational input based on wishful thinking. Without the commitment to be impeccably observant and honest with ourselves we might just make up navigational support for a counter-intuitive and counter-productive trait or idea. Or we might feel that a certain situation that came into our life is the result of navigation when in reality we were just not supporting possible alternative outcomes with equal impeccability.*

Impeccability and integrity imbue our life with beauty and elegance. It nourishes healthy self-confidence, self-reliance, and self-respect. Continuous impeccability and integrity move our individual intent closer and closer to the universal intent, unifying them eventually, resulting in total liberation, and unlimited experience.

Impeccability is incredibly powerful! *To gain the wisdom of impeccability, to understand and affect our intent, and to perceive as much navigational input as possible, we have to practice, accrue, and maintain PRESENCE.*

PRESENCE: *The silent awareness that becomes apparent after the reduction and eventual cessation of our compulsive internal dialogue, the mostly useless chatter going on in our head at all times. Our internal dialogue keeps our world and intent as it is. It causes endless suffering and prevents us from being present and alert enough to perceive the sensory input that enables us to navigate. It thwarts any significant spiritual development and causes separation from everyone and everything around us.* **Our internal dialogue has to be reduced and brought under control at all cost.**

Meditation techniques that focus on attaining inner silence seem to work best. Flooding the mind with perceptual data, like walking while maintaining a peripheral vision, and similar techniques can be helpful. Long forms of martial arts, Tai Chi, Yoga, etc., also build silence due to the concentration needed for the execution of the movements; so can elaborate dance forms. Listening to all ambient sounds simultaneously instead of just focusing on a single one leads to presence.

Silencing our internal chatter and reaching a state of alert awareness takes patience and perseverance, but it is absolutely essential for navigation and liberation.

261

▽   ▽   ▽

While all these parameters belong together and work in synergy, in our work with the students we always emphasized internal silence the most. Not only was it our own highest priority, but we were also guided in this regard by a significant navigational event that happened towards the end of our first year at Spring Creek Lodge while we still commuted from Florida.

In November 2004 we had been strongly affected by the outcome of a presidential election in the United States. As a result we surprisingly lost our equilibrium and had great difficulties in quieting our internal dialogue. This interfered significantly with our wellbeing.

"Maybe we should go to one of those silent retreats you told me about," sighed Carmela, who generally had a balanced nature. She was unusually affected.

I did not answer immediately. As much as I treasured the outcome of the retreat that I had attended in Thailand many years ago, I was still equally aware of the rigors of the experience. It had been quite an ordeal, after all, and we would be separated for the duration of the retreat.

"Well, let's just throw it up in the air and see what comes down," I said, following my usual approach. "This is not something I feel comfortable deciding on the spur of the moment." And we left it at that.

Only two days later, as Carmela was talking on the phone with the mother of one of our students, she received the following feedback:

"I can't believe that my son actually enjoys Yoga and meditation now." She was appreciative and excited. "A few months ago, all he was interested in was rap music, drugs, and alcohol. Thank you so much for all you are doing for these kids," she continued. "Have you ever heard of Vipassana? These are ten-day silent meditation retreats that have been successfully conducted in correctional facilities, and I wonder if that would be something you could get them to do at Spring Creek Lodge. I will send you a video that I have about these programs and some other material. Please look into it. It would be fantastic if these kids could experience that."

A few days later we received her package with the promotional material detailing Vipassana meditation retreats within the prison system. But we had already done extensive research immediately following the phone conversation. I had not quite expected this to come down on us so powerfully and inescapably just two days after we had tossed it up, but here it was. We had not talked about silent retreats for years and nobody around us had either. The school was not open for such an experiment at this time, but incidentally there was a ten-day retreat scheduled in our region, exactly during our break over Christmas and New Year, less than a month away. And we were not at all surprised that there were still two spots available for us. Well, we had asked, and the universe had answered. Even after so many years of engaging in this dialogue with life, it still felt uncanny at times.

❧   ❧   ❧

Vipassana means to see things as they really are. It is one of India's most ancient meditation techniques. Ten-day residential retreats are continuously offered in numerous centers all over the world. There is no charge for these retreats, not even to cover the cost of food and accommodation. All expenses are met by donations. Vipassana is a serious, no frills, non-denominational, totally pragmatic head-on assault on the compulsive nature of our internal dialogue. For ten consecutive days, retreat participants keep complete silence, avoid any eye contact, and meditate approximately ten hours per day, interspersed with breaks. The first three days, concentration is trained by keeping the mind focused on the area below the nostrils where the movement of the breath can be felt. Beginning on the fourth day, the sharpened attention is directed to systematically scan the entire body for any perceivable sensation. It is an exercise of perception only, and thoughts are merely noticed as they continually try to distract. The main effort for the beginning meditator lies in the continuous re-direction of his or her attention, away from the distracting thoughts, back to the body.

Our retreat location was on Whidbey Island near Seattle, Washington. About eighty people, from age eighteen to eighty-two had gathered to spend the holidays, tackling the compulsive nature of their minds in order to see things as they really are. With a heavy heart and some apprehension, Carmela and I hugged good-bye and surrendered to that innermost of all desires—our longing for freedom, freedom from the dominion of the thinking mind. Prying open this suffocating chokehold is a brutal endeavor, no doubt, but these ten-day Vipassana retreats are probably the single best and most concise crash courses available for anybody who is defiant enough to attempt it.

The meditation technique that is utilized during Vipassana uses our attention to re-kindle the awareness of our entire body, which normally has been relegated to virtual unconsciousness by the dominance of the thinking mind. As our totality gradually awakens, our perception of reality changes so profoundly that we are no longer able to put it into words or even thoughts. Our understanding of the world is replaced by silent knowledge, an undifferentiated, boundless knowing that transcends all concepts.

The thinking mind, however, is the center of our universe. It has created and upholds everything we know, and naturally it feels obligated and determined to defend a lifetime of its creations. Consequently, during the course of the retreat, it will go to any conceivable creative extreme to maintain the status quo.

But we are also permeated by a universal intent that keeps us restless and longing to awaken to our boundless nature. Many of us are intuiting on a deep level that we are on the verge of a truly enlightening discovery, the discovery of how all the pieces of the puzzle come together just perfectly. Following this intuition, we will want to fight the mind as it obscures our vision with its endless stream of thoughts. The struggle can be intense, and I have had sweat dripping down on my meditation cushion many times while sitting motionless, solely as a result of my internal battles and mental convulsions.

Yet fighting is the domain of the mind, and before we know it, we are lost in a futile travesty. I realized that if we find ourselves fighting for internal silence and peace, we may be falling prey to a ruse of the mind, as it is pretending to fight itself, creating a perpetual problem. And since the mind is in essence a problem-solving machine, problems are its lifeblood and serve only to prolong the status quo.

Our fighting spirit has a definite place in the pursuit of happiness and liberation, however. Without persistence, discipline, and other virtues of the warrior's way, we would never advance on this journey. But for our essential nature to prevail, an eventual somersault is necessary. Instead of fighting what holds us back, we have to align ourselves with the universal intent that beckons us on.

In order to win, we have to surrender—not to anything or anyone in particular, just to *what is*. And as we do so, we find that surrender is the ultimate audacity.

Into the Blue Yonder

"How was your retreat?" "Oh, yes, tell us everything." "Did you guys really go?"

Our students were obviously curious if we indeed spent ten days in silent meditation over the holidays as we had announced. Getting up voluntarily every morning at four o'clock and sitting motionless for ten hours was too much for most of them to imagine. And, since they knew that we were generally given to enjoying life to the fullest, they were genuinely puzzled and intrigued.

"Of course we went," I answered. "It was absolutely awesome."

"Incredible," Carmela added. "You should all do it, first thing after you graduate."

"I could never sit still that long," one of the students said, "My back would kill me."

"Vipassana usually takes care of things like that," I said. "On the first day, I felt like a knife was being twisted between my shoulder blades after only twenty minutes of meditating. The muscle pain was excruciating. But all I had to do was keep my awareness with the sensation, and eventually it just dissolved. On the fourth day I was able to sit for two hours without moving an inch, and there was no pain at all, anywhere. I felt completely weightless."

Nobody looked very convinced.

"What did you guys do when it was over? How did you feel?"

"We took a ferry and went on a tour of the San Juan Islands for a few days before we came back here," Carmela answered.

"Quite frankly," I added, "when we left the retreat, we felt like we were on 'acid' for three days straight. That is the best and shortest way I can describe it."

Now I had their attention.

"It was absolutely unreal," I continued. "Everything was magical, unfamiliar, and beautiful. There was no sense of time, and we felt like part of a fairy tale, completely in harmony with the world around us. Actually, we are still only slowly coming down from this sensation."

"I never took acid," someone said.

"Well, it is really hard to describe. It was actually much better than being on acid. In terms of navigation, it was as good as it gets. Our experience of timing after the retreat was absolutely perfect. Whatever we did, felt smooth and meaningful. Everybody we met was friendly. We were simply part of everything, feeling happy, light, and playful, like two children, but without taking anything for granted. I wish all of you could have that experience just once."

"I did a yoga session in the afternoon after we left the retreat," Carmela went on. "It was the best yoga experience I ever had. I was able to observe where I was holding tension and simply release it and go further than I ever did before. Basically, my whole body was aware and I was just flowing with it. It was truly incredible!"

"As we were having lunch the next day," I continued, "someone at another table ordered a Cappuccino, and when it arrived, I had an instant reflex that was about to grow into a craving. But before I could even think about it, my attention went automatically straight to the physical sensation that had been triggered in my body, the moment I saw the cup. It felt like a slight pressure just below my throat. And as I kept my attention on this sensation for a moment, just as I had done it so many times with any other bodily sensation during Vipassana, the pressure, and with it the craving, simply dissolved. It was gone before I even became fully conscious of it."

As we enthusiastically shared the many empowering and liberating experiences we had during and following the Vipassana retreat, most of our students seemed genuinely interested. They all wanted to know the contact information and the location of these courses, so we made another handout. We also integrated Vipassana into our treatment sessions, ten minutes at a time. Much encouraged by this interest, we focused even more strongly on techniques that helped our students to become aware of their internal dialogue and to experience moments of stillness. Based on Eckhart Tolle's work, which we found to be the most accessible set of teachings in this regard, we developed a series of practices, we called "mind-yoga." These were simple but effective exercises, like listening to the fading sound of a bell or a singing bowl, allowing it to carry one's attention all the way into silence while staying keenly alert. Another practice dealt with listening to all ambient sounds simultaneously, without focusing on any one in particular. We even coaxed our students to become aware of the silence out of which all these sounds emerge and back into which they eventually fade again—or the silence that surrounds the sounds and stretches between them. We compared sounds to letters on a white piece of paper and suggested to think of the white paper as the silence that makes the sounds stand out like the letters on the whiteness.

In the same way, we attempted to train the students' awareness on the space between the objects in our visual world. Normally we only take note of the objects themselves. Unless we are trying to gauge the size of a room, to see, for example, how many people it could hold for a function, space has no information for us, so we filter it out of our perception. But just as the white paper allows the letters to stand out and silence the sounds, so does space enable objects to exist. During our respective mind-yoga exercises, we guided the students to become aware of the space and distance between things and of the volume that objects occupy. When we all went outdoors, these spaces and distances greatly expanded. And as we directed everyone's attention to the spaces that became apparent in the night sky, between celestial objects and particularly beyond, all our minds necessarily had to stretch into this unlimited vastness, challenging our concept of space altogether. If we allow our attention to stay with this unlimited vastness, we realize that infinity is ultimately the *absence* of space, in the same way as eternity is the *absence* of time. The thinking mind cannot wrap itself around these concepts, of course; it cannot grasp or understand such boundless and indefinable realities. Therefore, if we force the mind to face infinity that is undoubtedly apparent in the night sky, it will stall temporarily, resulting in precious moments of silent awareness: Stillness!

269

⌄   ⌄   ⌄

Our kids never ceased to surprise us. Mostly puzzled, but also obviously intrigued by all these exercises, they asked us to recommend books about this strange new world of perception we imposed on them. We felt that Eckhart Tolle's *The Power of Now* would capture the essence of what we were trying to impart most appropriately and accessibly. Following the respective school policy, we asked the parents of interested students to send them a copy. These requests produced some of the most amazing and unexpected results of our entire time at Spring Creek Lodge. As the first few books arrived, they acquired something of a cult status within weeks. It was suddenly the coolest thing to have read *The Power of Now.*

"When are you finally done with it? I'd like to read it too. My parents didn't send me a copy yet."

The books went around and students proudly proclaimed when they had read it, or they asked specific questions relating to the content. Further encouraged by this development we offered to play recordings of Eckhart Tolle's talks on Sunday afternoons during the students' free time and more than half of them showed up. We could not believe it. Here we were, dealing with troubled teens, a wayward generation of supposed misfits, troublemakers, drug addicts, and runaways. They were perfectly capable of drinking hand sanitizer for its alcohol content or snorting kitchen herbs to see if they could get a high out of them. They huffed Clorox or gasoline from the lawn mower for the same reason, and once even hit a staff member over the head with a metal bar from a vacuum cleaner.

But those same kids were also perfectly capable of following the sound of a bell into stillness, of listening to silence and of taking note of the space between things. They became aware of their compulsive internal dialogues, practiced lucid dreaming techniques, attempted to understand energetic perception and intent, and even considered the power and beauty of impeccability. Those same kids were looking forward to navigating their way into college after graduation. And to top it off, they had made *The Power of Now* into a cult book among them. Even if not *all* of them showed the same kind of enthusiasm or even interest, how could we not be thrilled?

❧ ❧ ❧

Providing our young friends with bodily memories of stillness and peace became our highest priority. We felt that these memories strengthened and nourished a center of gravity away from their raging world of thoughts and desires. We could not do much to lastingly reduce their feverish internal dialogues, but we could reassure their silent souls with moments of peace and pure being. This seemed to be our best chance to create and nurture the intent necessary to attract circumstances into their lives that would help them eventually break the dominance of the thinking mind.

The majority of our movement, acupuncture, and herbal protocols were aimed at providing first-hand experiences of balanced, centered, silent, and peaceful states, providing the mind-body with respective points of reference. Most of us know only two states of mind—sleeping and thinking. We have completely forgotten how to be fully awake and keenly aware without engaging in endless mental chatter. The peace and bliss that is inherent in those moments of stillness is the seed of liberation. The intent of any seed, of course, is to sprout and grow. And we feel that the best way to connect this intent with the beckoning sunrays of the universe at large is to open ourselves to the interactive way of life that we call the art of navigation.

v   v   v

Living life in the exciting spirit of a treasure hunt is actually quite satisfying and entertaining for the thinking mind, and therefore less antagonism is created between our innermost desire for liberation and the mind's obsession with thinking. The only requirement is an open and curious mind that is awake and alert to all its sense perceptions. All we have to do is turn our attention outward, facing oncoming time, instead of getting caught up in endless processing. When we eat a delicious meal, we have a much more fulfilling experience if we focus on the dish in front of us, on the colors and fragrance of the food, on the taste as it makes contact with our tongue and palate, than if we would allow our attention to get absorbed by the digestive process or by the movement of the bowels for that matter. If there is a problem with the bowels, we can take note and action if needed, but there would be not much benefit in keeping our attention there. Essentially, however, that is what we do with most of our sense perceptions. Our attention is nearly always absorbed by our thoughts as they are processing reality. As a result, our experience is completely internalized, condemning us to live in a virtual reality, forever hungry for the real thing.

When we are navigating wholeheartedly, we are letting the real thing directly connect with our soul, simply by being perceptive and present, triggering whatever action is most appropriate. To ensure that indeed the most appropriate action is triggered, we rely on our commitment to impeccability. The thinking mind has to be kept at standby as much as possible, allowing it to observe everything with curiosity and a sense of wonder, ready to unleash its power whenever needed, just to retreat again into wonder, once the task is completed. But until we are living the life of life itself, all we have is our unbending intent.

▾ ▾ ▾

Our students certainly gave us a momentous opportunity to nourish our own unbending intent. In over one thousand group sessions we had to walk our talk and keep our enthusiasm alive. And as our program at Spring Creek Lodge Academy came to an end, we realized that we had undoubtedly been its biggest beneficiaries. Towards the end of 2006, the organization to which Spring Creek and another dozen of such specialty schools belonged went through a major restructuring process, creating a series of new schools while downsizing existing ones. Our student population went down to about a third of its original size, effectively eliminating the economic basis for our program. Additionally, the director who had brought us in left the school, prompting us to discontinue our sessions by May 2007.

As we learned that our time in Montana would soon be over, we were obviously curious where our journey would lead us next. Naturally we intended a warm and pleasant climate and a location where we could continue our work. Without any apparent navigational directives to guide us yet, we considered three different places that all seemed attractive in their own way. First, there was Hawaii, of course. Our friend Joe was urging us to finally make the leap and join him in his beloved island paradise. He never tired of singing its praises. We were open, and as far as our intuition went, the energy seemed favorable this time. However, there always had been a slight challenge in terms of my astrological alignment with the island state.

Originally we had not thought much about astrology, but after getting to know several internationally renowned astrologers who regularly lectured at our event space in Santa Fe, we came to the conclusion that it can actually be a fascinating and valid art, as well as an asset in navigating life. We even included it into the large group of cultural phenomena we referred to as "spiritual software." On a deeper level, astrology seems to contain the same essential blueprint as divination systems like the I Qing or the Tarot, and like mythologies, perennial philosophies, and religions. On the most basic level, all appear to have the same common denominator, pointing towards the evolutionary necessity of transcending our personal self so we can awaken to our essential or divine nature, and all attempt to guide us in a myriad of different ways to accomplish this feat.

As we were contemplating our first move to Hawaii in 2001, Arielle Guttman, one of our astrologer friends, had cautioned me about a strong Saturn influence that I would encounter there. She said that Saturn is the most dominant aspect of my relocation chart for Hawaii. Saturn generally symbolizes challenging energies. In the words of our friend Alan Oken, another member of Santa Fe's "astrologer elite":

"Saturn forces the individual to give up illusions and misconceptions that hold him back from the liberation and freedom that come through a depersonalization of the Self. Saturn requires the death of the personality so that the Spirit can emerge from the density of one's being."

On a practical level this apparently meant that I would most likely encounter restrictions, limitations, and karmic lessons, unless I rise to the occasion and conform to Saturn's influence. While a strong Saturn aspect does not deny or diminish imagination, inspiration, spirituality, or even good fortune, it does demand that these things be given structure and meaning. Arielle summarized that the astrological energy in Hawaii would not support me much in any expansive and materialistic endeavor, like creating a business, for example, but it would be a good place for introspection, transformation, or to write a book. With all this in mind, we decided to embark on an exploratory mission.

The second place we were drawn to was Barcelona in Spain. Another dear friend of ours, Ferran and his wife Brooke, both also acupuncturists, had just recently moved there. They were in the process of opening a clinic, and upon learning that we would soon be on the move, they immediately urged us to join them. Carmela and I both loved Barcelona, and we were already talking about motorcycle tours all across Europe. There were no astrological concerns and no licensing problems, as far as we knew. Again we decided to schedule a visit to test the energy.

The third place we considered was Tucson, Arizona. We had just recently spent a week in Southern Arizona and found it as welcoming and friendly as ever. Nothing particularly exciting happened, and I was not overly enthusiastic about moving to a place where I had lived already. But it felt like a good option, in case both of the other projects were not supported. Tucson had been good to me and, incidentally, it has Jupiter in the mid-heaven of my relocation chart, which generally stands for joy, luck, wellbeing, expansion, and success.

▽   ▽   ▽

Even though we were both leaning slightly towards Barcelona, it soon became apparent that we would have to deal with the intricacies of Saturn instead. The universal script clearly and unmistakably sent us to Hawaii. As usual with big changes in our lives, there was no ambiguity. Shortly after we had broadcast our request to Intent, the Spanish government decided to regulate acupuncture to the extent that we would have to sit for a comprehensive medical exam in order to practice there. Of course, the exam would be in Spanish, which did not make it any easier. I also learned that I would face significant hurdles in re-establishing my European work privileges, after having recently assumed American citizenship.

The state of Hawaii, on the other hand, accepted our application for licensure without the slightest ripple or additional requests, which is quite rare. Our license was granted in record time and incidentally issued on December 4, my birthday. Many smaller but no less compelling signs of the universe's support, related to housing and work, amplified the navigational input. And just for good measure, Intent threw in another major synchronicity, in case our desire for motorcycle trips through Europe should cloud our perception. On the final day of our scouting mission to

Hawaii, we drove by the Honolulu harbor on our way to the airport. Instead of taking the freeway, we wanted to soak in a few last impressions of the beaches and the downtown area. As we turned a corner on Ala Moana Boulevard, which runs along the coast, a massive cruise ship suddenly appeared right in front of us, ten stories high. It was the Infinity in all her glory. This was a truly magnificent synchronicity. A shiver went down my spine. The Infinity docks in Honolulu on only two days out of the year during her seasonal journey from Alaska to the Caribbean and back.

"What can I say?"

❖ ❖ ❖

Obviously, Hawaii had finally yielded to our intent and opened its doors to us. But as Saturn's energetic shadow would imply, paradise did not come unconditionally. Intent actually went out of its way to make this point abundantly clear. Our scouting mission did not just supply us with a green light for our relocation to Hawaii, it evolved into a full fledged instructional movie of mythical proportions, of which the meaningful images of Infinity against the backdrop of downtown Honolulu were just the rolling credits.

❖ ❖ ❖

We already had received discouraging news from Spain, but did not yet know about the birthday surprise of Hawaii's Acupuncture Licensing Board when we embarked on our exploratory trip to the islands. Following several recent suggestions by friends to include the Big Island in our considerations, we arranged to spend a week there, before visiting Oahu. Two of these friends had been Rosie and Misha, whom we knew from our Santa Fe days. Both were also working in the healing arts. Rosie practiced psychology and Misha acupuncture, and we were looking forward to hearing about their professional experiences. Unfortunately they had not been able to take root on the island and were planning to move back to the mainland soon after our planned visit.

275

On the morning of October 15, 2006, we left Thompson Falls for our trip to Kona, Hawaii. I had just started the car engine when Rene, our friend and neighbor, came running towards us, her eyes wide, and her arms waving.

"Did you hear? Did you hear? They just had a huge earthquake on the Big Island, 6.7 magnitude. It's all over the news."

Carmela and I looked at each other.

"I like earthquakes," I said after a moment's pause, smiling. But seeing the frown on Rene's face, I changed to a more concerned expression and asked, "Did anybody get hurt?"

"I don't think so; they didn't say anything," Rene answered.

"Well, I guess we are off then," I smiled again.

"There could be aftershocks," Rene added while our car started rolling. "Please take care of yourselves." She waved good-bye.

"No worries, thanks for letting us know," we waved back

"Wow, what strange timing." Carmela shook her head in disbelief.

"I have no idea what to make of this," I said, quite puzzled myself, "but I can't help it, I really like earthquakes."

"Me too, I always did, even as a child," Carmela said. Her eyes sparkled adventurously.

As we arrived in Kona on the Big Island the next day after an overnight stop in Seattle, the after-effects of the quake were still noticeable. Some roads were cracked and strewn with boulders, and a few hotels were shut down for damage assessment. Nobody seemed too worried though. Earthquakes are fairly common on a volcanic island, even if not of this magnitude. From our navigational perspective it felt neither good nor bad, more like a big exclamation mark, heightening our awareness.

The next thing we noticed was that Kona, with its roughly ten thousand inhabitants, was inundated with triathletes. Nearly two thousand competitors were warming up for the Ironman World Championship that was to take place on the upcoming weekend. Wherever we went, we were surrounded by fiercely determined extreme athletes and the super-charged energy field they generated. In their midst I continuously oscillated between feeling weak and soft, and fiercely determined as well to get into top physical shape so I could do the Ironman one day myself. Overall it was a refreshing influence, but eventually we had to get out of town to calm down. The theme for our visit to the Big Island seemed to be intensity, for all I could tell. This was not surprising, considering that it sits right on top of a hole in the earth's mantle out of which lava is continuously deposited onto a tectonic plate. The island's highest mountain is one of the world's most active volcanoes, rising to a height of over 33,000 feet from the ocean floor. The sheer weight of this gigantic heap of lava sometimes causes the earth's crust to buckle, triggering an earthquake like the one that had just occurred. At only a few hundred thousand years of age, the Big Island is also one of the earth's youngest formations.

On our way over to Hilo, where our friends Rosie and Misha lived, we decided to pay our respects to Pele, the Hawaiian fire goddess, generally believed to be in charge of the islands. Supposedly she lives inside Kilauea Volcano, but we were told that the best way to make a connection with her was close to the area where the lava was flowing into the ocean, continuously birthing new land. Some of the lava tubes had burst open, exposing the flowing magma, and as we stood there in awe, just a few arms lengths away from the red-hot liquid stream of molten rocks that flowed below our feet to meet the sea, the level of intensity moved up yet another notch.

The best time to catch a glimpse of Pele's splendor is at night, when her glowing spirit emanates through countless fiery eyes, and when she unleashes those gigantic, dancing red clouds of steam as she fervently mates with the ocean. The arduous two-hour hike over lava fields to the open tubes and the sulfurous red clouds made our experience even more otherworldly and unforgettable—especially once the batteries of our flashlight failed on the way back, forcing us to develop senses we didn't even know we had, so we wouldn't fall into cracks and cut ourselves to shreds on the razor-sharp edges of the lava. That night we slept at the Volcano House, just steps away from Pele's home in Kilauea Crater, nurturing fiery lucid dreams—passionately in love with the earth.

Filled to the brim with respect and appreciation for this magical and powerful island, we arrived at Rosie and Misha's house around noon on Sunday. It was a small and friendly wood structure, perched on the eastern slopes of fourteen-thousand-foot Mauna Kea Volcano, overlooking the ocean. The area receives a lot of rain, and consequently the vegetation around the house was lush and green. Rosie came out to greet us; her beautifully freckled face with the big smile was as radiant as ever. We hugged warmly after not having seen each other for several years.

"Where is Misha?" I asked, looking around.

"He should be here any minute," Rosie answered, "he is looking forward so much to seeing you guys. But . . . you know how he loves the outdoors. Because we are leaving the island at the end of the week, he wanted to go camping one last time. He left on Friday, and I am not even sure exactly where he went; he's out of cell phone range."

Misha was Russian-born and an extreme outdoors enthusiast. He even used to take part in wilderness survival competitions. We had known Rosie for quite a while before we met him the first time. Misha was an ardent follower of Carlos Castaneda's writings and the warrior's path, and of course he was curious to hear about my experiences when he learned that I had apprenticed with the man himself. On one occasion we were hosting an art exhibit by our friend Pola Lopez who had created a series of oil paintings, depicting elements from Castaneda's world. The paintings showed her rendition of such elusive concepts as "The Sea of Awareness," "Double Beings," "The Energy Body," "Flyers," and "The Dance of Navigation." Pola, who was more visual than verbal, as she put it, asked me to give a talk during the art opening to connect the audience with her work and the world it portrayed. At this event I met Misha for the first time. He had accompanied Rosie to the art opening and asked if he could film my presentation. I had no objections, and a few weeks later, while we were attending a dinner at their Santa Fe house, he handed me a copy of the recording. The video turned out to be a precious gift. It was impeccably done and gave me the unique opportunity to observe myself while I defined the world of the Nagual and how I related to it.

❧ ❧ ❧

"Are you guys hungry? Or would you like a tea?" Rosie asked us as we sat down inside the house.

"A tea would be nice, thank you," we both answered.

After about two hours of animated talking and sharing, Rosie became increasingly restless. She had tried to call Misha's cell phone several times, but there was still no reply.

"There are many areas on the Big Island where there is no reception," she said, trying to calm herself. "Maybe his truck broke down. He talked about driving up a dirt road behind Mauna Kea, and it would take a long time to walk back down," Rosie pondered.

We tried to put her at ease, but did not really know what to say, without even knowing where Misha had gone. After a while, we all went for a walk to a spectacular waterfall nearby, but when we came back at nightfall, there was still no sign of Misha.

"This is not at all like him," Rosie said. "He knew you were coming, and he is really looking forward to talking with you," she repeated nervously.

After an uneasy dinner we went to our hotel for the night. Rosie had warned us beforehand that her house was already packed up for the move to the mainland, so we had checked into a hotel in Hilo. As we left for the night, we agreed to go to the police for help if Misha had not returned by morning.

At eight o'clock in the morning, Rosie met us at the hotel, and we jumped into action. We filed a missing person report, and with a tremendous combined effort we talked the police officer into sending a helicopter on a search mission.

There were four areas that Misha had mentioned before he took off: the back road on Mauna Kea, the Volcanoes National Park around Kilauea, Green Sands Beach at the end of South Point Road, and a small unnamed bay at the end of the Road to the Sea. We had the same guidebook that Misha used to research his camping trip, and upon careful comparison, I had a hunch that he had chosen the Road to the Sea. The description was intriguing. It involved traversing a nearly un-drivable six mile lava road, and the bay at the end was described as "the perfect place if you want to get away from it all." This was the place I would have wanted to see, and I was sure Misha did too. It was about a two-hour drive from Hilo, and we took off without delay.

The helicopter crew had been directed to search in all four locations. After about an hour of driving we received a call that they had already searched both beach places, South Point Road and the Road to the Sea, without finding a trace of Misha's truck. We stayed with my hunch, nevertheless, and decided to see for ourselves. The helicopter went on to search the larger areas around the volcanoes.

The Road to the Sea is not from this world. It took us about forty-five minutes with a Jeep in four-wheel drive to negotiate the six miles from the main road to the ocean. We had to battle through a sea of broken lava that stretched all the way to the horizon on both sides. Even the deep blue Pacific, far ahead and below, seemed menacing in its vastness, as it wrapped around the southern tip of the island. No life for miles. Fast moving clouds kept changing the shimmering shades of black and silver of the hardened lava streams, creating a most ominous atmosphere. I began to doubt that Misha, or anyone for that matter, would have persisted on this gloomy road to nowhere in search of a camping spot.

It felt so bizarre that we actually ended up laughing a lot on the way down. Rosie's mind was distracted by all the action, and she had to focus on not getting ejected out of the Jeep. Of course, we also had been primed by the helicopter crew that we were not going to find anything down there.

▼ ▼ ▼

But unfortunately they had been wrong.

As we finally reached the beach after turning around one last bend, we saw Misha's truck. The blow to our hearts was nearly audible. The doors and the camper shell were locked, but after breaking in and examining Misha's supplies, we were able to determine that he had left two days ago, on Saturday morning, with only his snorkeling gear—and he never returned.

Rosie was clinging to the slim chance that Misha could have fallen into one of the many cracks in the lava surface on his way to find a suitable entry point for snorkeling. He could have broken a leg, leaving him unable to move. So we fanned out and desperately searched the area, soon joined by the helicopter, which we had called back immediately. The coastline was extremely rugged, and it was not too farfetched that someone could break a leg trying to access a good diving spot. But all our efforts were in vain, and by nightfall we drove back out through the lava field to stay in a nearby motel so we could resume the search with the first light the next morning.

But Misha's body was never found.

▼ ▼ ▼

If we had perceived an earthquake, two thousand Ironman competitors, and the flowing and exploding lava as expressions of intensity, sharing this abysmal nightmare with Rosie gave the term "intensity" a whole new meaning. From the moment we found the abandoned truck to the moment we had to leave Rosie with her friends and parents who flew in the next day, the world was not as we knew it. Instinctively the three of us held on to the present moment, trying to give the past and future as little reality as possible. This seemed to be the only way to cushion such a devastating blow to the heart. Rosie proved to be immensely strong and full of instinctive wisdom. Whenever her mind brought in the perspective of time, it was to soothe and heal her bleeding heart.

"You know," she told us during the long hours of that fateful evening, "when Misha left for this trip, he stopped at the door, turned around, and looked at me with his beautiful blue eyes for a moment. Then he shook his head just a little, as if he was at a loss for words, and said: "You know, I love you sooo much!" Then he left."

∨　∨　∨

As terrifying and tragic as it was, Misha's death was also magical. Every detail surrounding it had an element of a rare and otherworldly beauty. This had not been a freak accident. Misha had spent his life challenging nature, inching his way closer and closer to that point of no return. Free diving had been his latest obsession, and he had loved the ocean more than anything. Now he had only been days away from moving to the desert, to Tucson of all places, where Rosie's family lived. One last time he wanted to merge with his beloved element, so he drove down the Road to the Sea through this veritable purgatory of lava. As he arrived at the end of the road, he set up camp and explored the coastline. A few hundred yards down a westerly path he found the magical bay that was "the perfect place to get away from it all," as the book had said.

The setting was truly amazing. The cove was perhaps two hundred yards across, where a uniquely beautiful beach of the finest black and green lava sands formed a nearly perfect half circle. On the opposite side, the black sand was marbled with thick strands of bright green creeper plants. The center of the beach was sheltered by an overhanging rock face, formed by a broken lava stream that had oxidized into a bright array of colors. On both ends of the beach, where the bay joined the open sea, was a set of rugged cliffs, guarding it from the waves. The path ended, quite conveniently, on a smooth rocky ledge from which a few natural steps allowed easy access into the crystal clear water that was perhaps twenty feet deep.

"Absolutely perfect," Misha must have thought, and he went back to his camp to prepare dinner, filled with excited anticipation for an early morning dive.

▽　▽　▽

And here we were, three days later now, separated from him by an un-fathomable abyss. Yet the magical beauty that permeated his disappearance was reaching across universes—expressed in the timeless space of presence we upheld, in Rosie's serenity and poise, and in the magnificent tree of Angel Trumpets that was in full bloom right in front of our motel room that night, its huge white flowers spectacularly lit by the moon.

The next morning, while Rosie, Carmela, and the helicopter crew still tirelessly searched the coastline, I sat down on the smooth steps at the edge of the bay. The water was calm and translucent, nearly without color when I looked straight down. I could feel Misha's excitement and anticipation. Floating and diving in water like this feels like flying—twenty feet above the ground, thirty, fifty, one hundred, one thousand feet and falling away fast as the ocean floor dropped into a void just outside the bay.

I could see a red starfish at the bottom, right in front of me. There were a few corals and colorful small fish swimming around playfully. The gentle waves, lapping against the rocks, released a pure, fresh, salty scent that was intoxicating. Mesmerized, I imagined myself floating in the water, weightless and happy, my back warmed by the tropical morning sun. What a glorious place!

What a fascination we have with getting away from it all, I wondered. Away from what?

Slowly my gaze went across the translucent surface towards the opening of the bay. There was a definite line between the rugged cliffs. The ocean turned deep blue, and big rolling waves were moving by fast, driven by strong currents. Only a short distance out and stretching thousands of miles in all directions was an unimaginable vastness of ocean, ten thousand feet deep.

I found it hard to breathe now as I strained to follow Misha where he had dived, probing ever further and deeper into the blue yonder.

Yet as I dared to press on, my terror unexpectedly dissolved. Misha had left, but the door was still open, and what I saw took all the pressure off my chest. Suddenly I felt tremendous peace and weightlessness, as if gravity had been turned off in the midst of falling. Looking through that door I saw the end of fear. For a timeless moment I awoke from the dream of life and death and everything was plain and clear. The pieces of the puzzle had come together once again.

Rosie silently sat down beside me, following my gaze. There was no need to talk.

Later that day we left for Oahu. Rosie's parents had arrived, and together with the many loving friends she had on the island, they offered their embrace to ease her pain.

⌄ ⌄ ⌄

The preceding two days had been among the most intense and meaningful of our life as well. Only gradually would we allow ourselves to take the events of our exploratory mission at face value; and only after the dust of our emotional strain had settled, did all the navigational elements stand out, clearly and unmistakably.

There was no way we could treat Hawaii as just another stop on our journey. It was obvious that our move to Oahu, where we eventually ended up, was very much supported and encouraged. But the earthquake, which happened at the precise moment as we left on our exploratory venture, undoubtedly carried extraordinary implications. We did not perceive it as threatening at all, but it had significantly raised the stakes. It registered as a huge exclamation mark, imbuing everything we encountered with an uncanny importance. Equally remarkable was our immediate and unexpected immersion in the energy of the Ironman competition. Generally this had struck us as a rather positive and powerful omen, but as an indication for the new mood that would greet us on the islands, it only added to my apprehension. Known as the holy grail of endurance sport, this event is all about pushing one's limits to the extreme, which has nothing to do with the easygoing and somewhat indulgent lifestyle that had been my lifelong preference. And how far I would have to push my limits became clear soon enough as my dance with impermanence grew exceedingly intimate.

Every aspect surrounding Misha's death had been utterly meaningful and metaphorical. Spending these fateful forty-eight hours with Rosie had given me an unforgettable taste of the true meaning of impermanence and the chilling realization that there is no refuge whatsoever—not even in the deepest and most intimate human relationships. But it was especially the stunning and otherworldly setting in which this beautiful tragedy had unfolded that made everything stand out so deliberately—elevating it to near mythical dimensions.

Wanting to get away from it all—the urge to experience weightlessness—holding the breath longer and longer while trying to venture ever deeper into the unknown—the unbending intent to overcome all physical constraints—to stretch and ultimately transcend what is human—to vanish in the end without a trace—to dissolve into the blue yonder . . .

"How much more metaphorical can it get?"

▿ ▿ ▿

Apparently Pele was in complete agreement with Saturn about the transformational and definitive energy that was awaiting me in Hawaii.

"Saturn requires the death of the personality so that the Spirit can emerge from the density of one's being."

There was no ambiguity in Alan Oken's words, and together with the way all the events had unfolded during our scouting mission, there could be no doubt:

My *personal* journey had come to an end. The treasure hunt was over.

Everything was going to be treasure now, as that last bit of density would give way to the incredible lightness of being.

Epilogue

Obviously, my navigation guided me into writing this book, and I am happy to report that, once I had found a beginning, the story began telling itself. I simply recounted the events as they surfaced from memory. There was no initial structure, and I did not know how it would end. Immersing myself in this process for the better part of a year had a most peculiar effect.

In a manner of speaking, I wrote myself out of the story. While looking at the last thirty years of my life through the particular lens that is evident in this book, I eventually had to completely surrender to the realization that, all along, everything had felt ordained; that every little detail has, and had always had, this scripted quality that only occasionally manifests as an obvious synchronicity or a major navigational event. The more I became aware of this unfathomable cohesiveness, the more I felt myself reduced from the protagonist of my story to a simple witness, and my predominant emotions became curiosity and a sense of wonder.

This I could only indirectly convey through the story, and therefore I am giving it special expression in this epilogue. Navigation is only initially about the discovery of synchronicities and the validation of hunches, signs, omens, etc., but once we wholeheartedly open all our communication channels with the universe at large, it becomes increasingly impossible to maintain our insistence on being an independent and separate entity. The mental operation necessary to project and uphold this separateness consumes a tremendous amount of energy, which we will find much better invested in heightening our awareness to experience the infinite splendor and complexity of life as it presents itself in every moment.

Sometimes I was interrupted in the writing process or I lost a few paragraphs due to a computer glitch, but I found it practically impossible to allow myself to get frustrated. After all, I was writing about navigating reality as it presented itself and not as it *should* present itself. Initially only grudgingly, but gradually with less and less resistance, I was guided into accepting absolutely everything that happened as an integral and meaningful part of my life experience. And it was then that I noticed that the more willingly and curiously I accepted a perceived antagonism, the more benevolent was the turn of events—and the entire concept of antagonism disappeared. This I found to be quite revolutionary!

v   v   v

For the most part during the last year—while beckoning inspiration—I have been feasting my eyes on the magnificent array of tropical plants that completely encloses the lanai of our little home at the foot of Diamond Head Volcano in Honolulu. I am watching green Geckos move up and down the bamboo palms and the acrobatics of the birds as they are performing mating dances or search for food on the tender young palm leaves right in front of me. Several times a day a bird with an elaborate and beautiful call comes to visit, and we whistle back and forth for a while.

If I am not writing or whistling, I am practicing Oriental Medicine, indoctrinating my unwitting and trusting patients with the intricacies of navigation. Not long ago I was working with Jim who had come to see me because he wanted to quit smoking. Before the acupuncture treatment we were going over a few mental strategies that help with addictions. I suggested that he keep a watchful eye on his internal dialogue, as it would undoubtedly become an instrument of his addiction and undermine his resolve. We talked about the bliss of inner silence and the experience of pure being.

"Do you know what I mean?" I asked

"Oh yes," Jim answered, nodding his head emphatically. "I know exactly what you mean. I play the guitar," he continued, "and sometimes when I am playing, it is just me and the guitar, you know . . . one on one . . . no thoughts at all."

"One on one," I repeated, "Oh, I love the sound of this. *One on one!*

That's exactly what I meant. Beautiful! Thank you, Jim. I'll have to put this into my book."

∨　∨　∨

And if I am neither writing, nor whistling, nor practicing medicine, I might be out surfing, which strikes me as a perfect analogy for the one-on-one of navigation. Surfing, as I experience it, entails first of all a love of the elements, in this case the ocean. While intimately immersed in this most ancient of environments I simply float on my surfboard in a spot of my choice, enjoying the scenery with all my senses. Part of my attention is always directed at the open ocean from which, inevitably, the next set of waves is going to come, and one of the waves will call out to me. With a few strokes I align myself, and then the wave takes me along. There always seems to be a perfect line, a perfect alignment and harmony—and sometimes I find it, and the wave may carry me all the way to the shore.

But even if the ride is less than perfect, or even if I fall and tumble and feel the full force of the wave crushing down on me—even then there is still only exhilaration and the blissful experience of one on one.

ABOUT THE AUTHOR

German-born Felix Wolf is an author, teacher, and transformational healer with academic degrees in Cognitive Psychology and Oriental Medicine.

While on a two-year writing retreat in Sri Lanka, Felix found himself unexpectedly initiated into the mythological world of anthropologist and shaman Carlos Castaneda. This initiation led to a magical and extended odyssey around the globe and culminated in a three-year apprenticeship, during which he was inducted into the art of navigation. Felix also translated some of Castaneda's writings into his native German and served as his simultaneous translator.

Felix practices shamanic and energy medicine, teaches workshops on the art of navigation, and lectures internationally to a variety of audiences. He lives in Honolulu, Hawaii, with his wife, Carmela, and is currently writing a workbook on the "Five Elements of Navigation."

www.theartofnavigation.com